Peer Counseling
Skills, Ethics, and Perspectives

Second Edition

Edited by

VINCENT J. D'ANDREA
and
PETER SALOVEY

 Science and Behavior Books, Inc.
Palo Alto, California

Printed in the United States of America.
Library of Congress Card Number 94-073999
ISBN 0-8314-0084-6

By permission of The Haworth Press, this book includes material that was originally
published in the *Journal of College Student Psychotherapy* as: "The RA and the Fine Art
of Referral for Psychotherapy" by Jan P. Boswinkel [vol. 1(1): 53-62, Fall 1986] and
"Peer Counseling in Colleges and Universities: A Developmental Viewpoint" by
Vincent J. D'Andrea [vol. 1(3): 39-55, Spring 1987].

By permission of the Helen Dwight Reid Educational Foundation, this book includes
material that was originally published in the *Journal of American College Health* as "A
Survey of Peer Counseling Activities" by Peter Salovey and Vincent J. D'Andrea
(1984), 32: 262-265. Published by Heldref Publications, 1319 18th St. N.W.,
Washington, DC 20036-1802. Copyright 1984.

Editing by Rain Blockley
Book design by Gary LaRochelle/Flea Ranch Graphics
Printing by Haddon Craftsmen

Contents

FOREWORD

by James W. Lyons

*Dean Emeritus of Student Affairs
and Lecturer in Education,
Stanford University*

Really good ideas last. Peer counseling has stood the test of time; it is no longer a new idea—just a well tested and refined good idea. Most good campuses and communities would not be without an extensive program of peer counseling, and for good reason.

A good program of peer counseling offers:

- An opportunity for members of the community to reach out and help each other

- Opportunities to serve in ways that really count

- Involvement and investment in the community (a known cause of personal growth and enriched education)

- A concrete way to help students take responsibility for their own affairs, one of the most powerful of educational ideas

- A potent way to help individuals move from dependence on professionals to independence and interdependence with lay people

- A cost-effective way to provide for personal and community help

Peer counseling is relevant to each of these developments; it is a process that goes beyond thinking of just helping a "client"; it also benefits the peer counselors and their community. The skills of peer counseling do not cost much to teach, are practical, and are transferable. Those skills include listening attentively, understanding others, recognizing and dealing with feelings, suspending judgment, using nonverbal communication, paraphrasing, and recognizing the important and relevant in personal dialogue. There are also some less easily defined skills. How can one locate, for example, that elusive boundary beyond which individuals must be responsible for helping themselves—the boundary beyond which the helper ought not go?

Many roles and jobs in our society depend on people with such skills—skills that are not often learned well in the classroom setting. This is why I am pleased that the authors have not limited the scope of application of the concepts and information to students and campuses. Much of their training can easily be incorporated into community programs that use volunteers to provide needed services not available in more formal and funded programs.

While cost-effective, peer counseling programs are not a panacea for all economic ills. Nor should such a program be used as a basic building block for an effective student affairs organization. It cannot be a substitute for a clinically solid counseling service or a responsive and competent community clinic or center. Community self-help groups, drop-in centers, and hotlines provide important adjuncts to more traditional clinics.

Let me turn to my area of expertise: the college student community. I cannot imagine a good student-affairs program without peer counselors integrated into its fabric of counseling and social programs. Peer counselors have much to offer and deserve a presence in our medical programs, personal counseling, academic advising, special-interest organizations (such as ethnic and gender groups), residential advising, and career planning programs.

The campus with a good peer counseling program benefits significantly. It is important that students know they are assuming responsibility for their own affairs. Most students learn they can be independent of home, family, and adolescent structures. On the other hand, those things would probably happen even if they were not in college. But independence is not enough. The real challenge is to develop interdependence—those webs of social and personal relationships that develop mutual support and helping among friends. Peer counseling provides the opportunity to learn, practice, and appreciate interdependence.

A related benefit is the sense of community that often flows from a strong tradition of students helping students, and students taking responsibility collectively for their own affairs. Students on campuses that include peer counseling feel like full members; it is *their* campus and community. Students in such programs also learn about making referrals and providing helpful information. To do this, they learn about the texture and missions of the campus's academic and support services.

The personal benefits to the student peer counselor are real. For many, these benefits add up to an effective way of testing their own vocational interests and skills. Further, they can transfer what they learn as peer counselors into life after college. The experience of being part of a helping group may well lead to an increased awareness of needs in the communities where those graduates live and work.

Finally, good peer counseling programs possess another important yet often understated or overlooked virtue. They offer constructive means for students to serve and do good. That alone is reason enough to pay close attention to the theories and practices of Vincent D'Andrea, Peter Salovey, and their colleagues. Their work, aptly described in this book, has resulted in enormous benefits to Stanford University and its students for over two decades.

PREFACE

This book provides specific, practical, and easily grasped materials for training peer counselors in a variety of applications (including crisis counseling, academic and residential advising, career planning, family planning, and general psychological support). It can be used as a core handbook, supplemented with videotaped materials, or in conjunction with existing counseling texts.

In the thirteen years since the first edition, important evolutions have shaped a new set of challenges for peer counselors. This edition addresses such changes:

- The increased awareness of and need for attention to specific ethnic perspectives and concerns

- The increased visibility of gay and lesbian people

- The complex ethical issues facing peer counselors

- The Acquired Immuno-Deficiency Syndrome epidemic (which currently affects approximately one in five hundred college students and has brought about radical changes in dating and sexual practices)

- The increasing concern regarding sexual assault, rape, and the rape trauma syndrome

New and updated chapters address these issues, with new information and suggestions for training peer counselors and developing programs. Our hope is that this edition will, like its predecessor, serve as a starting place for counselors in many settings. May they continue to discover new ways of enabling people to help other people.

—*Vincent J. D'Andrea*
Peter Salovey

ACKNOWLEDGMENTS

To Allen Ivey and Norma Gluckstern, whose pioneering work in developing microcounseling skills attracted our attention, and who have graciously and generously encouraged us to "develop our own style."

To Martha Martin and Bill Leland, who were instrumental in working to develop The Bridge in 1971, and who gave of their time and talents to establish peer counseling at Stanford University.

To Andrew Gottlieb, Matt Wolf, Steve Hibschman, Don Gallagher, Lee Rowen, and Sue Crissman, student teachers who contributed much to the form and content of the training programs at The Bridge and other peer counseling efforts.

To Joan Evans, Mike Boyd, and the Riverside California Suicide Hotline for the suicide checklist and I.Q. test.

To Jim Lyons, Jim McClenahan, Dave Dorosin, Thom Massey, Patricia Brandt, and Michael Jackson, whose administrative support and continued encouragement have been of invaluable help in developing peer counseling at Stanford.

To Peggy Smith and Barbara Binkley, whose teaching expertise in communication skills helped refine and develop our training materials—in particular, our videotape modules.

To Fritz Bottjer, whose skill and technical expertise enabled us to produce high-quality videotape modules, and who gave generously of his time in other ways.

To Herant Katchadourian, Mike McHargue, Cary Walker, and Ewart Thomas, whose efforts put peer counselor training courses in the catalog, and gave impetus to peer counseling programs to increase the academic merit of their offerings while substantively adding to the quality of services offered to students.

To Jonathan Zittrain for his helpful and systematic review of the first edition. Many of his constructive criticisms were incorporated into this new edition.

To Rain Blockley for editorial comments and considerable help in pulling together the book.

To Mary Cunha and Win Vetter, whose cheerful and competent translation of our atrocious handwriting into beautiful typescript has earned our thanks and respect.

To all the hundreds of peer counselors and student coordinators whose many contributions over the years have refined our training and service programs to their present form.

To all, many many thanks.

CONTRIBUTING AUTHORS

Sally Baird, M.A., is the sexual assault prevention program manager, Cowell Health Promotion Services, Stanford University. She is former program director of the Rape Crisis Center, Mid-Peninsula YWCA, Palo Alto, California.

Jan P. Boswinkel is a graduate of Swarthmore College, where she served as a peer counselor.

Fritz Bottjer, Ph.D., was a media specialist at Counseling and Psychological Services, Cowell Student Health Center, Stanford University. He is now in private practice in Palo Alto, California, and is a media consultant.

Thom Cleland served as a peer counselor at Whitman College and is a graduate student at the University of California at San Diego.

Vincent J. D'Andrea, M.D., is at Stanford University as staff psychiatrist, Student Health Services; clinical professor of psychiatry; adjunct staff in psychology; and former director of Counseling and Psychological Services, Cowell Student Health Center. From 1964 to 1967, he was Chief Psychiatrist with the U.S. Peace Corps. He now teaches peer counseling, and teaches and consults at the School of Medicine and the Student Health Services.

David Dorosin, M.D. (deceased), was director of Counseling and Psychological Services, Cowell Student Health Center, Stanford; and clinical professor of psychiatry, Department of Psychiatry and Behavioral Sciences, Stanford University School of Medicine.

Sam Edwards, M.S.W., is on the staff of Counseling and Psychological Services, Cowell Student Health Center, Stanford University.

Andrew Gottlieb was a peer counselor at Stanford University, earned a Ph.D. in Clinical Psychology at the University of Washington, and now practices in Palo Alto.

Nadja B. Gould, L.C.S.W., is a clinical social worker at Harvard University Health Services and consultant and trainer to peer counseling programs, including services for gay/lesbian student and students with Acquired Immuno-Deficiency Syndrome.

Karen Huang, Ph.D., is a clinical psychologist at Counseling and Psychological Services, Cowell Student Health Center, Stanford University. She teaches peer counseling and consults to Asian/Pacific-American students at Stanford.

Jean O'Gorman Hughes is a former research associate, Project on the Status of Women, Association of American Colleges (Washington, DC).

Richard N. Jacks, Ph.D., is director of the Counseling Center, Whitman College, Walla Walla, Washington.

Alejandro Martinez, Ph.D., is clinical psychologist and the director of Counseling and Psychological Services, Cowell Student Health Center, Stanford University.

Franklin Matsumoto, M.D., is a clinical professor of psychiatry at Stanford University School of Medicine and also practices in Menlo Park, California. Formerly, he was a consultant to Cowell Student Health Center and to the Job Corps programs in the western United States.

Jane Pao, Ph.D., was a staff counselor at Counseling and Psychological Services, Cowell Student Health Center, Stanford University.

Sharlene C Pereira was a peer counselor and co-director of the Anonymous HIV Antibody Test Peer Counseling Program at Stanford University and is currently in medical school at the American University of the Carribean (Montserrat).

Peter Salovey, Ph.D., is a professor in the Department of Psychology, Yale University, where he also serves as the Director of Graduate Studies. He did his undergraduate work at Stanford University, where he was a live-in peer counselor at The Bridge.

Bernice Resnick Sandler is a Senior Scholar in Residence at the National Association for Women in Education (Washington, DC) and editor of *About Women on Campus*.

Peggy Smith, Ph.D., is an assistant professor of Counseling Psychology, San Francisco State University.

Alice Supton is a former associate dean of students and director of Residential Education, Stanford University.

Matthew Wolf, Ph.D., is a clinical psychologist practicing and teaching in San Rafael and San Francisco, California.

Joann M. Wong was a peer counselor and co-director of the Anonymous HIV Antibody Test Peer Counseling Program at Stanford University. She is now in the master's program at Boston University Medical Center's School of Public Health.

Laraine Zappert, Ph.D., is staff psychologist, Counseling and Psychological Services, Cowell Student Health Center; and the Sexual Harassment Coordinator, Office of the Ombudsperson, Stanford University.

Part I

Peer Counseling Skills

1

WHAT IS PEER COUNSELING?

by Peter Salovey

Peer counseling is the use of active listening and problem-solving skills, along with knowledge about human growth and mental health, to counsel people who are our equals—peers in age, status, and knowledge. Peer counseling, then, is both a method and a philosophy. Its basic premise is that people are capable of solving most of their own problems if given the chance. The role of the peer counselor is not to solve people's problems for them but rather to assist them in finding their own solutions. Peer counselors don't tell people what they "should" do, nor do they give advice; peer counselors generally do not interpret or diagnose. As *peer* counselors, we are not professionals, and we cannot assume that we know what a person is thinking or feeling any better than that person does. Rather, by using the active listening and counseling skills presented in this book, the peer counselor helps people clarify their thoughts and feelings and explore various options and solutions.

Peer counseling is practiced actively in many settings. A component of peer counseling, education, or training exists in virtually every effort in education (at all levels), self-help groups, preventive medicine and wellness programs, and helping programs generally. Most colleges and universities have drop-in peer counseling and crisis intervention centers; many cities have telephone crisis and suicide hotlines run by nonprofessional counselors; self-help group activities may include large amounts of peer counseling among participants; and many businesses are training supervisors in peer-counseling skills to increase their ability to understand and help solve the work-related problems of their colleagues. Since the late 1960s, peer counseling (as opposed to professional counseling) has been used with increasing acceptance and success in various situations. In fact, a review by Durlak (1979) showed that nonprofessional (peer) counselors were as effective as professionals in helping people cope with many of the hassles of daily living. Thus, as listeners, clarifiers, and information providers, peer counselors can play an important role in assisting others with significant problems.

THE EIGHT COMMANDMENTS

Whether you are simply listening to another person's problems, actively helping someone make a critical decision, or counseling someone during a crisis, there are eight important rules to keep in mind.

1. Be nonjudgmental.
2. Be empathic (not a brick wall).
3. Don't give personal advice.
4. Don't ask questions that begin with "Why."
5. Don't take responsibility for the other person's problem.
6. Don't interpret (when a paraphrase will do).
7. Stick with the here and now.
8. Deal with feelings first.

We call these rules "commandments" not because they cannot be broken, but because they apply so consistently across many of the counseling situations in which you will find yourself.

Be Nonjudgmental

Being nonjudgmental is essential to effective peer counseling. As a peer counselor, you will undoubtedly be exposed to problems and situations quite foreign to your own experience and style of life. You may even find yourself thinking, "This person is really strange" or "If I were this person, I would do X." It is important, however, to remember that you are *not* that person, and that what you would do if you were that person is not particularly relevant. Stick with the listening and counseling skills, helping your peer client to clarify and perhaps solve his or her problem. Don't try to "size up the person," diagnose him or her, or compare the person's problem or background to your own. Let's look at some examples:

Client: *I have this problem. Every time I'm on a date, I get very nervous and say stupid things.*

Judgmental response: *It sounds to me like you are not particularly experienced in sexual partners.*

Nonjudgmental response: *How does it feel to be nervous?*
or
So you tend to feel nervous in dating situations.

•

Male client: *I find that I'm attracted to other men.*
Judgmental response: *So you have latent homosexual tendencies. I'd imagine they are quite common.*

Nonjudgmental response: *Tell me more about your feelings toward other men.*

(Note: *Don't use words such as "gay" or "homosexual" unless the other person uses them first.*)

If you are uncomfortable as a counselor in this situation, an alternative is:

Nonjudgmental response: *This is a situation that I'm not entirely comfortable talking about. Could I find a different counselor for you?*

This last response brings up an important question: Are there any situations that you would feel uncomfortable talking about? That is, are there any topics about which you would find it very difficult to remain nonjudgmental? If so, it is important to identify these situations and decide what you want to do when they come up. Most likely, you'll want to refer some people to another peer counselor. But perhaps—through role playing, discussion, etc.—you could learn to be nonjudgmental even in such situations. Just because you are personally opposed to abortion, for example, does not mean you couldn't counsel someone nonjudgmentally who is considering having one. The peer client is not you, and it is important not to let your own values and experiences interfere with your effectiveness as a peer counselor. If you think that they will, however, you would do well to help the person find a different counselor.

Be Empathetic (Not a Brick Wall)
Empathetic counselors—no matter what their training, orientation, or level of experience—are much more effective than counselors who are not empathetic. By *empathy*, we mean the ability to see a problem from the other person's point of view and, accordingly, to be warm and supportive. Or, as Barbara Okun (1976, 1990) puts it, empathy is the understanding of another person from that person's frame of reference. Empathy, she says, underlies the entire counseling relationship.

Just what do we mean by being empathetic? In the counseling situation, you need to do more than see the world through the other person's eyes. You need to show him or her that you are doing this. Empathy is demonstrated every time you accurately paraphrase something the person has said, every time you use a *minimal encourager* (smile, nod, say "uh huh," etc.), and every time you make or maintain eye contact.

Being empathetic also means adopting a counseling style that suits the client. Animated people should be counseled in an "upbeat" way; depressed, quiet, or shy people should be treated in a softer, more gentle manner. An effective peer counselor must learn to adjust his or her behavior so that it accurately reflects the mood and style of the client.

The worst approach to peer counseling is to be a brick wall—to let your client express all kinds of feelings and thoughts without your showing any kind of response at all. Unfortunately, old Hollywood films depicting therapists as ancient, bearded Viennese men who do little more than sit behind their clients' heads and grunt once in a while have perpetuated the brick-wall-is-good-therapeutic-style myth. Unless you're a highly skilled traditional psychoanalyst (and even if you are), providing little empathy is not a productive way to deal with the thoughts and feelings that people bring to a peer counseling session.

Don't Give Personal Advice

When speaking with a friend about a problem he or she might be experiencing, we often offer our opinions—in the form of advice—about what our friend could do to solve the problem. Likewise, we are often tempted to give advice to a client; but in this case, it is important to refrain from doing so. No matter how empathetic we may feel, we do not have the same thoughts, feelings, and experiences as our clients. As a result, advice coming from our own experience is generally inappropriate.

Trying to give advice during a counseling session usually leads to the unproductive exchange that Eric Berne (1964) called the "Yes-But Game." For example,

Client: *My roommate disturbs my studying by playing the stereo too loud.*

Counselor: *Well, have you tried talking to him?*

Client: *Yeah, but it doesn't seem to work.*

Counselor: *How about telling his girlfriend?*

Client: *Yeah, but she would be on his side.*

Counselor: *Hey, have you tried putting a sign on the stereo that says "No loud music after 10 p.m."?*

Client: *Yeah, but . . .*

We have found that when counselors structure the session so that clients generate their own alternative solutions, these clients are much more likely to act on any decision made during the session. They feel they have the ability to solve their own problems. On the other hand, recommendations made by the counselor are frequently not followed—or, when a client does follow suggestions, it is often with a sense of resignation or helplessness.

Giving advice should not be confused with providing information. Often per counselors have access to vast stores of information about community resources, mental health services and agencies, support groups, classes, and the like, and an important function of the peer counselor is to dispense such information. Information should be passed along in a tentative but straightforward way, not cloaked in advice. For example:

Good:
We've received some information about self-help groups for weight control. Would you like a brochure?
Bad:
Have you thought about joining Weight Watchers? I could give you their brochure.

Sometimes counselors feel that if a client takes their advice and it "works," then they were justified in giving it. Such Machiavellian thinking about ends and means, however, does not lead to effective counseling in the long term. When people receive advice, they are deprived of the opportunity to develop their own brain-storming and decision-making skills. Furthermore, giving advice fosters unproductive, dependent relationships— which can be problematic even with professional counselors. When such a dependent relationship exists, we can no longer say that we are helping a *peer* to solve his or her own problems.

Don't Ask Questions that Begin with "Why"

Why shouldn't peer counselors ask questions that begin with "why"? Generally, we have found that "why" questions put people on the defensive, making them feel as if they are being interrogated. "Why" implies that you are demanding an explanation rather than simply desiring more elaboration. It is easy to rephrase "why" questions into less threatening language, and we encourage you to do so whenever possible. For example, compare the tones of the two dialogues that follow.

DIALOGUE 1

Counselor: *How are you feeling?*

Client: *Sort of depressed.*

Counselor: *Why are you feeling depressed?*

Client: *Well, my wife left me six months ago, and I just lost my job.*

Counselor: *Why did your wife leave you?*

Client: *How the hell should I know? She's a bitch, I guess.*

Counselor: *Why do you think your wife's a bitch?*

Client: *Look, stop playing Perry Mason with me. . . . You're the doctor, why don't you answer the questions?*

DIALOGUE 2

Counselor: *How are you feeling?*

Client: *Sort of depressed.*

Counselor: *What do you mean by "depressed"?*

Client: *Well, ever since my wife left me, I feel down in the dumps. I can't eat . . . can't sleep . . .*

Counselor: *Tell me more about that.*

Client: *Well, six months ago, my wife and I had a big fight about . . .*

In the first example, the client seems unsettled and angry, put off by the barrage of "why" questions. On the other hand, in the second dialogue, he appears relaxed and is having little difficulty responding to the counselor's questions. "Why" questions are not particularly productive in counseling; it would serve us well to drop the word from our vocabulary when someone comes to talk. Why not?

Don't Take Responsibility for the Other Person's Problem
As a peer counselor, you need to ask yourself frequently, "How can I be most helpful in this situation?" Unfortunately, counselors often make the mistake of equating helpfulness with assuming personal responsibility for the client's welfare. It is important to remember that clients come to you with their

problems, looking for help in solving those problems. By using the skills presented in this book, you can try very hard to help them. But ultimately, the problem is not yours; it is the client's, and the client must come to the final decision about what to do.

Your responsibility as a peer counselor is to provide as empathetic and supportive a counseling environment as possible and to help clients deal with the thoughts and feelings they might be having regarding the problem at hand. Your responsibility is not to solve the problem(s). If problems get solved, fine. If not, you will have been very helpful simply by allowing clients to express their thoughts and feelings. In fact, often people simply want someone with whom they can talk; they are not expecting to get their problems *solved* at all!

If you are using this book as part of a counselor training course for a particular agency or counseling center, we encourage you to discuss as part of your course exactly how much responsibility you are expected to take as a peer counselor. Are there any situations in which you might make a decision for your client's "own good" without consulting him or her? What do you tell people who insist on your solving their problems for them?

Don't Interpret (When a Paraphrase Will Do)

Interpretation occurs when you go beyond the information given and infer something about the other person—his or her unconscious motivations, personality characteristics, or social situations, for example. Although the section on interpretation in chapter 3 discusses some of the legitimate uses of carefully worded, tentative, nonaccusative interpretations, we also stress that you usually do not need to make interpretations at all. Paraphrasing information provided by the client is generally sufficient to encourage him or her to continue speaking. Interpretation in peer counseling is similar to advice: both tend to be gratuitous and counterproductive. Generally, people are interested in getting thoughts and feelings clarified rather than in listening to your explanations about the motives for their behavior. Compare the two dialogues that follow.

Dialogue 1

> Client: *I have this problem with my mother. I feel guilty every time I ask her to do me a favor.*

> Counselor: *Sounds like you have some unresolved feelings toward your mother.*

> Client: *Well, I don't know . . .*

> Counselor: *It seems that your guilt might be a projection of some kind. Are you jealous of your father?*

> Client: *No. What are you driving at, anyway?*

> Counselor: *Just a hunch. . . . What kinds of dreams did you have as a boy?*

Dialogue 2

> Client: *I have this problem with my mother. I feel guilty every time I ask her to do me a favor.*

> Counselor: *You have guilt feelings when dealing with your mother?*

> Client: *Yes. I can't seem to ask her for anything without feeling terrible.*

> Counselor: *Tell me more about these feelings.*

Client: *Well, I feel ashamed . . . and anxious. I get nervous and flustered. I can't even ask her to pick up a newspaper for me on her way home from work.*

Counselor: *So you're feeling guilt and also anxiety. Is that right?*

In Dialogue 1, the counselor is attempting to interpret the person's behavior in terms of some kind of underlying motive, whereas the counselor in Dialogue 2 is merely paraphrasing information that's "on the table." We believe the second approach is much more likely to help someone express and clarify his or her thoughts and feelings regarding the problem. There is less chance of distracting the person with inaccurate interpretations. Even if interpretations are correct (and determining this is typically impossible), they can still be distracting and counterproductive. Behavioral and humanistic therapists agree: work toward clarification and change rather than insight during initial counseling sessions.

Stick with the Here and Now

As the goal of peer counseling is to help clients solve their own problems by encouraging them to express and clarify their thoughts and feelings, it is not particularly useful (especially at first) to spend large amounts of time mulling over the person's early childhood experiences or discussing individuals who are not in the room. Instead, it is most productive if the counseling topics are in the present and if the client (rather than anyone else) is the focus of attention.

There may be times when you wish to leave the here and now. For example, it is often useful during problem solving to have the person fantasize about the consequences of particular alternatives. Or, when dealing with feelings, you may want to find out the "history" of these feelings: how long they've persisted, what has caused them in the past, etc. Both of these situations—and we're sure you can think of others—are perfectly legitimate ones for leaving the here and now temporarily.

But before you discuss feelings or future alternatives, it is important that you spend significant amounts of time counseling on here-and-now thoughts and feelings. Perhaps our rule could be more accurately stated as follows: Stick with the here and now; but if you decide to deviate, make sure to deal with the here and now thoroughly and first!

Deal with Feelings First

Because people have some kind of emotional reaction to virtually every situation discussed in counseling, it is probably most useful to elicit, clarify, and discuss their feelings before moving to more cognitive (i.e., problem-solving) matters. One of the first questions we find ourselves asking, after the person has explained his or her problem, is, "And how does that feel?" or "How do you feel about that?"

Often a counseling session involves little more than the expression and clarification of feelings. Problems don't always need to be solved, and peer counselors play a most important role in creating a safe context for the free expression of emotions. People may simply need someone with whom they can share their successes, commiserate about their failures, or cry over their losses.

Trying to solve problems before you clarify someone's feelings is generally not successful. The unresolved feelings often get in the way of discussing alternatives and options, and the counseling session can degenerate into a gripe session or a "yes-but" situation. So deal with feelings first. Ask feeling questions, paraphrase and reflect verbal and nonverbal emotions, place the feelings in context, ask more feelings questions—and then help the person solve the problem.

BECOMING AN EFFECTIVE COUNSELOR

To become effective as a peer counselor entails learning, practicing, and sharpening your skills.

Learning the Listening Skills

In presenting the listening skills in the next chapter, we use a *single skill* approach that has been extensively researched and tested. No one expects you to master all the skills in the beginning; they are arranged so that, as you learn each skill, you can add it to the previously learned skills. The easier skills are presented earlier in the chapter.

As is true with any skill—whether it be driving a car, playing tennis, or playing the piano—when you begin to use basic attending skills, you may feel awkward, phony, or embarrassed. Do not worry. If you persist in practicing, you will soon feel more natural. Eventually, the newly learned skills will fit unnoticed into your normal repertoire of behaviors.

As you are learning and practicing, remember to give and listen for feedback that is *specific*. To learn, it is important to find out exactly what is good and what is bad about what you are doing so that you can focus your learning in specific ways.

It cannot be stressed too much that each of you has an individual style. Each of you differs from the others in your group. Be brave, experiment, and find out what feels most comfortable for you. As you are learning each skill, give it a chance to work. Ultimately, you will find the right blend, or mix, for you. The most important things to remember are: Be yourself, and give of yourself.

Role Playing To Practice Skills

After learning about a particular listening skill, it is important to practice it by role playing. For example, you may clearly understand the difference between "open" and "closed" questions, but actually using open questions in a role-played counseling situation is difficult—at first. Role playing is the best way to become comfortable with the skills, to make counseling feel as natural as routine conversation. Not only does role playing let you practice your listening skills, it also allows others—the "client" and observers—to provide you with feedback about your style and skill use.

The purpose of role playing is to give you a chance to practice your skills, not to provide counseling for the "client"—although that may happen as well. It's very important to keep this in mind.

To help you practice your skills, the "client" must give an appropriate problem, and must give you an opportunity to counsel. An appropriate role-play problem is one that can be effectively counseled in a role-play situation. The "client" needs to:

1. Pick a problem that involves YOU—your thoughts and your feelings. "My problem is that my roommate is having a real bummer in her relationship with her father" is not appropriate; "I'd like to talk about my feelings about my roommate" is.

2. Pick a problem that is reasonably well defined; the role plays are short. Although "My life is all screwed up" is a legitimate problem, it would be difficult to address the problem in just a few minutes. Such things as "I have a problem talking to my lover" or "My roommate wakes me up at 5 a.m. every day and it infuriates me" are better.

3. Pick a problem that is not so heavy that you will get upset by talking about it. Again, role-play practice is for the benefit of the "counselor," not the "client." A problem that is likely to upset you is not appropriate for role-play situations. Of course, problems that involve no feelings are not very useful either. Often it is good to choose either a slightly troublesome existing problem or a problem that you have solved in the past.

As a "client," you also need to create an opportunity for the "counselor" to practice counseling. Give the counselor a chance to practice the skill, to ask questions, paraphrase, and explore feelings. Don't talk on and on without pause for ten minutes, thereby preventing the person from using the skills.

A good way to use role playing is in groups of three: a client, a counselor and an observer. After about ten minutes, the client and the observer give feedback to the counselor about his or her counseling style and use of the skills. Then rotate roles so that everyone experiences each of the three tasks.

Co-counseling for Sharpening Skills

Co-counseling is an excellent way to hone your counseling tools. *Co-counseling* is an exercise in which two people agree to meet for a particular time period and alternately counsel each other and give feedback to each other. For example, David and Ellen agree to meet for 90 minutes on a particular day at the coffee shop. During the 90-minute period, David first counsels Ellen (on a specific problem of hers) for 30 minutes, stops, and asks her for feedback. Then Ellen does the same for David.

In the context of your training, co-counseling is useful for practicing counseling techniques, role playing, developing friendships with fellow counselors, and confronting the possible problems of peer counseling. Your partner can be a classmate, peer counselor, friend, spouse, acquaintance, or anyone with whom you can meet regularly. We suggest that you spend one or two hours meeting with your partner each week. You can play both roles during this time or just the role of counselor or client, and then switch roles later in the week. You should feel free to discuss anything you and your partner feel comfortable talking about, and you may utilize any techniques that you think are appropriate.

Invariably, participants in our counseling classes find co-counseling to be one of the most useful aspects of their training. Here are one person's comments:

My experience with co-counseling was very positive! As the client, I gained a very warm, positive outlet for my problems. I could consistently and constructively deal with my situations in the supportive atmosphere of my counselor-peer. As a counselor, I was able to practice the various techniques which we had experimented with in class. I feel that I improved many of my counseling skills, particularly active listening. My co-counseling partner was a close friend, and through our counseling experience we added a new dimension to our relationship by establishing a very positive pattern of interaction.

Try co-counseling this week and see if you share these feelings. If you are using this book as part of a peer counseling training course, ask your instructor to set aside some time at your next class meeting to discuss everyone's co-counseling experiences.

2

LISTENING SKILLS

by Andrew Gottlieb, Peggy Smith,
Peter Salovey, and Vincent D'Andrea

Listening skills have broad applications. Many of you may find that you use them quite naturally. Good listening is about 50 percent of counseling, and it is also a useful tool with family, with friends, and at work.

This book does not teach you how to become a therapist. Listening is only part of helping, but it is a crucial part. A means of support, good listening helps people explore what they are thinking and feeling. Developing your skills may therefore help another person solve or clarify a problem.

A word of caution about what good listening is NOT: it is not doing all the talking. It is not giving advice. It is not manipulating. It is not taking the responsibility for the other person's problem and its solution.

The material in this chapter is based on the work of Alan Ivey (1978). We hope it will demystify the skills of active listening. These skills can be defined, taught, and learned. You do not have to be superhuman to grasp them. In fact, you may find you have acquired one or more of the skills quite naturally, while you need to learn a few others. What is most important is a sincere desire to understand other people accurately and to be more aware of these skills—skills that do facilitate interpersonal interactions.

MINIMAL ATTENDING SKILLS

Minimal attending skills are the foundation that supports all the other skills. Sometimes called "the art of listening with your mouth closed," this set of skills helps you be a more effective and empathetic listener.

Although we are not consciously aware of it much of the time, our body language is a critical part of how we relate and what we communicate. Of particular interest in this regard are eye contact and body posture.

Good *eye contact* is important but complex. Different cultures and subcultures, even different individuals, have different standards for good eye contact. Be sensitive to another person's comfort; good eye contact says, "I am with you" but is not invasive. With practice, you will come to know when you are engaging in appropriate eye contact.

Just as eye contact varies from person to person or culture to culture, so does *personal space*. Being the right distance from another person is part of appropriate posture. In addition, leaning forward with an open, relaxed stance and without extraneous, distracting movement is part of an ideal posture. Once again, it is important to remember to be yourself and to use a posture that is comfortable for you.

Another element of basic attending is *verbal following*. Verbal following differs from ordinary conversation, in which each person may be pursuing his or her own line of thought. With verbal following, you let the other person determine the course of conversation while you simply nod, respond, or ask questions. Keep interruptions to a minimum and avoid "topic jumping" or changing the subject. Although it may be difficult at first, also avoid giving advice or judging the other person's motives, thoughts, and behavior. Avoid sharing your personal experiences or "comparing notes."

Summary—Minimal Attending

1. Eye Contact
    a. Look at the person most of the time.
    b. Communicate caring: "I am with you, I'm listening."
2. Body Posture
    a. Be comfortable, be relaxed, lean forward slightly.
    b. Be aware of personal distance.
    c. Avoid distracting gestures or fidgeting.
3. Facial Expressions
    a. Don't be a brick wall!
    b. Display appropriate empathy.
4. Following the Person's Lead
    a. Don't interrupt, don't change the subject.
    b. Listen, don't talk.
    c. Don't share experiences ("Oh, I've been there . . . ")

ASKING OPEN QUESTIONS

This section concentrates on what we call "the open invitation to talk." In it, we speak of "open" and "closed" questions. *Open questions* are questions that encourage a person to talk without feeling defensive. *Closed questions* are the kind asked by a census taker, a doctor, a lawyer, or a parent: in most cases, both parties to the conversation understand that very specific information is requested in very short answers. Examples of closed questions are:

"Did you do that last Monday?"
"Is it true that there are three people living here?"
"How long have you been here?"

Nothing is wrong with using a closed question if you need to—and if the client is amenable. However, such questions do tend to cut down communication; and if used unadvisedly, they can lead to frustration for the client. Especially frustrating are questions that begin with "Have you tried" or "Do you think" or "What do you think," because such questions are really sneaky ways of giving advice or airing your opinion.

Open questions, on the other hand, are phrased for the purpose of exploration. An open question allows the other person to direct the flow of conversation, to bring up more data, and to deal with it in more depth. Open questions serve several functions: they can begin the interview, they may encourage the person to elaborate on a point or explore a point further; they may elicit specific examples to clarify what is being said; and they may allow the person to focus on his or her feelings.

Open questions often do something further. They lead the conversation into a more personal, here-and-now, *internal mode* in which the client assumes responsibility for feelings and behavior. This contrasts with the anecdotal, *external style* of conversation, in which the client blames others for what is happening.

As you encourage people to speak more personally, there is a greater chance they will find solutions to problems.

EXAMPLE: INTERNAL MODE

Counselor: *How are you today?*

Client: *I'm feeling kind of down, like everything is going wrong. I'm not much fun to be with . . .*

EXAMPLE: EXTERNAL MODE

Counselor: *How are you today?*

Client: *I'd be okay if it weren't for the people at my house. They get on my nerves and make me feel like climbing the walls.*

For open questions, "How," "What," and "Could you say more about" are appropriate beginnings. Examples of open questions are:

"What would you have done then?"
"How did it happen that you were there at that time?"
"What would you like to have happen?"
"If you could have things just the way you wanted, what
   would they be like?"

This type of question gives people permission to fantasize, and answering the question often triggers a new insight, a new alternative.

Be careful of using "why." As mentioned in the previous chapter, beginning a question with "why" often puts the other person on the defensive. It seems to call for an explanation or justification. Using "why" is good if one is asking how something works ("Why does the computer do this?") but it is not very effective in other cases. Many times, a "why" question can be rephrased so that it asks essentially the same thing but does not elicit the defensive response. For instance, try saying to yourself, "Why did you do that?" and then ask, "How did it happen that you did that?" and see which sounds better to you. Or compare, "Why are you here now?" with "What brings you here now?"

As a peer counselor, you need to be sensitive to the "temperature" of your interview. If the person seems anxious or if conversation is dying, open questions can stimulate the interchange. If you are feeling flooded with information from your client, use closed questions to cool down and slow the flow. But be careful: some seemingly closed questions can unleash a flood—for example, "Are you thinking about a divorce now?" On the other hand, some questions that sound like open questions are really "coolers," as in "Exactly what kinds of sexual activities *do* you engage in with your spouse?"

Minimal encouragements also move the conversation along. They may be either verbal (such as "Go on," "Uh huh," "I see," "Yes," or a repetition of the last few words the client has said—for instance, "So little time . . . ?") or nonverbal (such as nodding, smiling). The important part is that they be brief and natural to you. Again, by experimenting, you should be able to find your own best style. Many times an encouragement or the simple restatement of something already said has a powerful effect, so do not be afraid to limit yourself to the use of minimal encouragements if you want to keep the conversation going.

Although we do not often think of it in this way, *silence* is a useful minimal encouragement. Practice using silence instead of asking a question and see what occurs! Being patient and not asking questions to fill silence allows the client to think, talk, and explore.

Summary—Open Questions

An OPEN QUESTION is one that:

- Can't be answered by one or two words
- Usually starts with "how" or "what"
- Encourages the other person to talk

A CLOSED QUESTION is one that:

- Can be answered by "yes" or "no" or by one word
- Starts with "is," "do," "have you," etc.
- Discourages the person from talking and slows the flow of conversation

You can use open questions for:

1. Beginning a conversation
    "What would you like to talk about?"
    "What's going on with you?"

2. Clarifying and elaborating
    "How is this a problem for you?"
    "What do you mean by — ?"
    "What is it about the situation that
       bothers you?"

3. Working with feelings
    "How do you feel about that?" (Make sure you
       get an answer about feelings, not thoughts.)
    "What is [that feeling] like for you?"
    "How do you feel right now?" (This helps
       people bring feelings into the here and now.)
    "What would you like to say to [him/her]?"
       (This helps people get in touch with their
       feelings about other people.)

4. Solving problems
    "What options do you have?"
    "What have you thought of doing?"
    "How do you feel about each of these options?"
    "What's the best thing that could happen?"
    "What's the worst thing that could happen?"
    "What do you think will actually happen?"

DON'T:

- Ask questions to satisfy your own curiosity
- Ask "Why . . . ?"
- Ask long, complicated questions with lots of dependent clauses and other grammatical junk.
- Give advice in a question (e.g., "Have you tried talking to him?").

DO:

- Keep questions clear and simple.
- Keep questions in the here and now and with the person. (Don't counsel someone who's not in the room.)

PARAPHRASING

A *paraphrase* reflects the essence of the verbal content; it expresses briefly the facts of the situation but pares away details. For instance, newscasters often repeat in their own words what people said during interviews. Each of you has observed the use of the paraphrase and has probably used paraphrasing, perhaps without noticing it. When you take notes in a class, you probably paraphrase the instructor's lecture. When you send a telegram, you condense the message into as few words as possible—again, a form of paraphrase.

This skill is a bit sophisticated, taking more concentration and more practice than the open questions described earlier. The paraphrase has three main functions:

1. Verification of perception
2. Clarification
3. Demonstration of accurate empathy

First, a paraphrase acts as a perception check, to verify that you have understood what the other person has said. This is especially helpful if you are confused, or if you feel you may be identifying too closely with the person's situation. If you have heard correctly, the client may respond to your paraphrase by saying "Yes," "That's it," or "Right."

Second, a paraphrase may clarify what the person has said, especially if you pick up trends, set up dichotomies, or list priorities. As an active listener with some objectivity, you may see these trends and priorities more clearly than the speaker.

Third, a good paraphrase can demonstrate that you have what Carl Rogers called accurate empathy. *Accurate empathy* is a nonjudgmental reflection of another person's world view; it is "walking a mile in another's shoes."

It is important that a paraphrase be brief. It should almost always be shorter than what was originally said. Standard openings for a paraphrase are: "In other words," or "So I hear you saying . . .." You will discover other openings with which you feel comfortable.

Make the paraphrase tentative, so that if it is not right, the person feels free to correct you. It is crucial that you know when you have not heard correctly. You might end with: "Is that right?" or something similar. Watch out for endings such as "isn't it?" or "aren't you?" since these have the effect of a closed question.

What is especially tricky about paraphrasing is that if you parrot back exactly what you heard, you are not being terribly helpful and may even be irritating. (Sometimes, though, the client's wording is so apt that you may want to use some of the same words.) On the other hand, if you add too many of your own perceptions, you may be putting words into the other person's mouth. The former is called a *restatement*; the latter is an *interpretation*. Although both restatements and interpretations have their appropriate places, they are both quite advanced tools, and neither should take the place of the paraphrase. With a little practice, you will be able to tell the difference between restating, paraphrasing, and interpreting.

Summary—Paraphrasing

A PARAPHRASE is a brief, tentative statement that reflects the essence of what the person has just said. A good paraphrase:

- Captures the essence of what the person said; leaves out the details
- Conveys the same meaning but usually uses different words
- Is briefer than what the person said
- Is clear and concise
- Is tentative

Reasons for using paraphrase include:

1. *To check perceptions*
   When you paraphrase what you think people have said, they can react to your paraphrase and tell you whether it is accurate or inaccurate.

2. *To clarify*
   Hearing an accurate paraphrase helps clients clarify what they are thinking and feeling. Often a paraphrase will bring up new thoughts and feelings.

3. *To give accurate empathy*
   An accurate paraphrase demonstrates that you are listening and that you understand. In effect, a good paraphrase says, "I am with you."

DO:

- Keep it brief and keep it tentative!
- Use openings such as:
  "Let me see if I've got it right . . . "
  "Sounds like . . . "
  "I think I hear you saying . . . "
  "So, in other words . . . "

The Continuum

Restatement	Paraphrase	Interpretation
(OK)	(Best)	(Avoid, for now)

WORKING WITH FEELINGS

Working with feelings is difficult for two reasons. First, people are taught not to discuss feelings openly; feelings are too private, or too embarrassing, or too powerful to deal with directly. Second, partly as a result of such training, what people say may not match—or may not be *congruent* with—what they are communicating nonverbally. Nonverbal communication is more directly a reflection of feelings. Nevertheless, a timely reflection of feelings can be quite useful, since it gives people "permission" to own their feelings—it validates the emotional as well as the cognitive expression.

Talking about feelings is a limited experience, so our vocabulary may be equally limited. When working with someone's feelings, avoid pejorative or evaluative terms, such as: "That's ridiculous," or "Why would you feel that?" Stick to more specific, simple, expressive words. This is a sensitive area, and you will want to refrain from interpreting what you sense or putting the client on the defensive.

There is a vast difference between saying, "You feel . . ." and "You feel that . . .." The former is a genuine reflection of feeling, while the latter moves into more cognitive areas. Say to yourself, "I feel happy" and then, "I feel that today is going to be a happy day." Notice the difference?

It is of paramount importance to notice both verbal and nonverbal expressions when working with feelings. (Sometimes you may even get two dissimilar verbal or two incongruous nonverbal messages.) Although you may not always want to comment on discrepancies you notice, it is helpful to use this information as a cue for your own behavior. Be sensitive, again, as to when it would be appropriate to point out congruence or lack of it—and when it would be judgmental or threatening.

The four basic steps in working with feelings involve helping the person to:

1. Identify feelings
2. Define and clarify feelings
3. Acknowledge feelings and take responsibility for them
4. Deal with feelings

Identify Feelings

There are three ways to discover what someone is feeling. You want to be able to use all three and to learn when each is most appropriate.

Ask Feelings Questions

The main *feelings question* is "How do you feel?" Sometimes it is more effective to substitute "What emotions do you feel in relation to that?" Help your clients stick to the here and now. Talking about feelings in the past tends to turn into storytelling. Even when people's current problems involve past events, they have here-and-now feelings about what happened.

It is essential that you get feelings for answers rather than thoughts. Statements that begin with "I feel that" or "I feel like" usually express a thought. Statements that begin with "I feel" usually express feelings. If someone gives you a nonfeeling answer, paraphrase it and then ask the feeling question again.

Counselor: *How do you feel about that?*

Client: *Well, I feel like I should be angry at her.*

Counselor: *So you think you should be mad at her, but how do you actually feel? What emotion or emotions are you experiencing?*

Client: *I'm pissed off at her and frustrated that I haven't told her.*

Paraphrase Spoken Feelings

It's not always necessary to pry feeling out of people. Some people express their feelings quite openly. When someone does express feelings, it's a good idea to paraphrase them. This tends to clarify for people what they are expressing.

Client: *I get so angry when my sister comes to visit for the holidays and all she does is complain.*

Counselor: *So you're feeling angry, is that right?*

Reflect Feelings

Reflecting feelings is one of the most effective methods for bringing up feelings, but it is also one of the trickiest and most easily abused. The term *reflecting feelings* is slightly misleading, because what you actually reflect are a person's nonverbal expressions of feelings.

For example, a woman comes in for counseling and you notice that her face and body seem very tense. You could react in two ways:

1. "You seem to be angry."
2. "You seem to be very tense."

The first response reflects a feeling but is an interpretation. The woman might be nervous or scared and not angry at all. The second response is much better. It reflects the actual nonverbal message the woman is expressing, and it does not make a judgment or interpretation; it is not a conclusion in any sense. One of the most effective techniques is to reflect the person's nonverbal messages and then ask, "What are you feeling?" This opens the conversation rather than closing it.

Remember that reflection of feelings deals with emotions, while paraphrase deals with content and data. Sometimes the two may seem very similar, particularly if you are talking about an emotional situation. Discuss the differences with your trainers until you are sure you understand them. When you are role playing as the client, use a situation about which you have lots of feelings.

Define and Clarify Feelings

Once you've elicited a feeling, such as "I'm upset," it is important to find out what that means to the person. This process of definition is particularly important when the feeling expressed is a *global* one, such as "I'm depressed" or "I'm lost" or "I feel good." In other words, don't assume that you know what it's like for other people. Define and clarify what their feelings, words, or expressions actually mean in *their* world. Good questions for defining and clarifying feelings include:

> "What does [being mad] mean to you?"
> "What is being [nervous] like for you?
> "How does that feel physically?"
> "What other ways would you use to describe what you're feeling?"

What often happens as you help people define and clarify feelings is that other feelings come up. These also can then be defined and explored.

Client: *I feel depressed.*

Counselor: *How do you experience that depression?*

Client: *It's like a numbness, a not wanting to do anything.*

Counselor: *So you feel numb?*

Client: *Yes, I feel like there are all these feelings inside me and yet I can't really feel them.* [Counselor stays silent.] *You know, it just feels so numb.*

Counselor: *Could you describe the numbnes?*

Client: *It feels like there's a void within me. It's empty . . . no, it's not, it's full of feelings. . . . But they're dangerous. They need to be kept under control.*

Counselor: *What are those dangerous feelings?*

Acknowledge the Feelings

To deal effectively with their feelings, people must first acknowledge and take responsibility for those feelings. Many people tend to place their feelings outside themselves, saying things such as "It makes me feel . . ." or "He made me feel . . .." Although feelings may be associated with external events, they are *not* "out there"; they are within the person. Compare these statements:

> "You made me angry when you slept with Cleopatra."
> vs.
> "I felt angry when you slept with Cleopatra."

The first statement suggests causation; the second, correlation. Statements that begin "It makes me feel," "She makes me feel," or "One would feel" signal that the person is not owning or taking responsibility for his or her feelings.

All of this is well and good, but what can you do if the person is *not* taking responsibility?

Client: *You know, when you're working at a job you don't like, you just can't find any energy for other things. You feel bummed out and you feel disgusted, you know?*

Counselor: *So you feel bummed out and disgusted, is that right?*

Client: *Yeah, you just can't seem to break out of it you know?*

Counselor: *When you say, "You can't seem to break out of it," do you mean "I can't seem to break out of it"?*

Client: *Yes, I just can't get rid of these feelings.*

Counselor: *What make you want to get rid of those feelings?*

What this counselor does is first to paraphrase the statement in a way that puts the responsibility on the client. Like many people, this client doesn't recognize the distinction and continues to say "you" instead of "I." The counselor then asks a closed question that encourages the person to acknowledge the feelings personally.

This step is a tricky part of working with feelings. It is important not to challenge clients too directly, but sometimes people simply refuse to acknowledge their own feelings. When this happens, it may be necessary to take a different approach (such as a problem-solving or a "What if . . .?" fantasy approach). It is not useful to force your point of view on people. It is often more constructive to move past or around an issue.

Deal with the Feelings

Once you have elicited the feelings, defined and clarified them, and have gotten the person to acknowledge them, then what? The first part of dealing with feelings is to place the feelings in context ("What thoughts and events are these feeling correlated with?"). Good questions are:

> "What brings up this feeling of ___ for you?"
> "What's the situation when you experience these
>   feelings?"

People usually don't experience just one feeling at a time. The question "What other feelings are associated with ___ for you?" often brings up many related feelings.

It can also be useful to relate thoughts to feelings. A question such as "What do you say to yourself when you are feeling ___ ?" is helpful.

An important part of dealing with feelings is to get people to express feelings that they had previously found difficult to articulate. Examples of effective questions are:

"How would you like to express this feeling?"
"What would you like to say to that person?"

It may help to have clients pretend to be speaking directly to the person to whom they are expressing the feeling. So rather than "I'd say that I'm angry and that I never want him to do it again," have clients stay in the present and say, "I'm angry and I don't want you to do that again!"

If people have difficulty or are uncomfortable with this, questions such as these may help:

"What's the best [worst] thing that could happen?"
"What would you like to see happen?"
"How have you dealt with this before?"
"What could you do to feel better?"

If clients depict a situation that seems hopeless and they see no possibility for improvement, then they may be really stuck. In such cases, acknowledging this reality and their feelings about it may be more helpful than encouraging a possibly premature course of action.

Finally, the best preparation for working with feelings is to deal honestly with your own. This can be approached by role-play practice or co-counseling sessions specifically devoted to exploring your personal style of dealing with feelings.

Summary—Working with Feelings

Working with feeling is an *essential* part of counseling. It is difficult to explore alternative solutions to problems until the feelings surrounding the problem are clarified, vented, and dealt with.

1. Identify the feelings
   a. Ask feelings questions
      "How do you feel about that?"
      "How do you feel?"
      "What feelings does that bring up in you?"
   b. Paraphrase spoken feelings
      "So you are feeling ___, is that right?"
      "Sounds like you are really ___."
      "You must feel pretty ___."
2. Define and clarify feelings
   a. Elicit feelings that accompany the one that is primarily expressed
   b. Discover the individual's personal experience of a given feeling (what does the person mean when he or she says, "I feel X"?)
3. Acknowledge the feelings
   a. Assist clients in taking responsibility for their feelings
   b. Reinforce them for stating feelings in a direct, personal way (e.g., "I feel X" rather than "I feel that one should feel X in this situation, don't you?")
4. Deal with feelings
   a. Relate thoughts to feelings
   b. Further express feelings
   c. Help people express hidden feelings through best/worst fantasizing and other open questions

SUMMARIZING

A counselor's *summary* is like a combination of one or more paraphrases and often includes a reflection of feeling. In addition, it tends to cover a relatively long period of time—several statements of the client, perhaps from even more than one session. A summary attempts to capture the essence of what the person has said, to tie together content and feeling, to put things in perspective, and to identify important trends, conflicts, or possible decisions. Even so, it is a good idea to keep the summary brief. Being concise reduces confusion.

With summarization, more than with any other skill, there is the possibility of distortion or interpretation, so be especially sensitive. Constantly check with the person to verify that you are not adding to or subtracting from what he or she has said. Be tentative in your remarks.

As you sum up what you have observed as the two of you have talked, emphasize the positive aspects of the situation: what has been accomplished, what could be done, what the possibilities for the future are. Dwelling on the negative aspects rarely leads to constructive action, so while you may not be able to ignore them, do not limit yourself to enumerating them!

A good summary has several functions:

1. It acts as a perception check (and is especially helpful if you find you *strongly* identify with—or *cannot at all* identify with—the problem).
2. It directs the course of future interaction, decisions, and planning. Again, you should therefore BE POSITIVE.
3. It clarifies the situation, reflects trends, points out conflicts, and lists priorities.

When should you use a summary? A summary is useful when shifting modes (for instance, after you have explored feelings and are about to go into solving problems). Likewise, a summary is useful after main events in a counseling session—for example, after you've found out what the person considers to be the problem, it is useful to summarize and then go on, using an open question. A summary is also good at the end of a counseling session. It ties things together for the person, giving a clear image of the session.

After a good summary, there may be a pause or a sense of "what now?" This indicates that you are ready to move into new territory, and an open question is appropriate at that point. Learn to be sensitive to this forward movement; such sensitivity is one of your goals as an active listener.

Summary—Summarizing

A summary is a cumulative paraphrase. It captures the essence of what the person said. Like a paraphrase, it is brief and tentative.

Summarizing serves many of the same purposes as paraphrasing:

- It serves as a perception check.
- It demonstrates accurate empathy.
- It clarifies for you and the client.

A summary is not a sequential recounting of what the person said. A good summary organizes what has been said into a logical, usable form. It mentions both thoughts and feelings and ties them together. A summary helps people see where they've gone and where they are going.

INTEGRATING SKILLS

Integration is putting all your skills together and using each when appropriate. This is where the art and the finesse of counseling has its fullest expression.

OPEN QUESTIONS turn on the flow of conversation. They encourage people to talk. They can also direct the conversation.

PARAPHRASING tends to interrupt the flow. Because a paraphrase reflects what a person has just said, it focuses the conversation. Paraphrases fit together well with open questions: first, you paraphrase; then you ask an open question.

EXPLORING FEELINGS is useful after the initial problem has been presented. Sometimes, exploring feelings will be a very effective method of counseling. Some people and some types of problems respond less to feelings-oriented counseling, and in these situations you will want to take a different approach. Remember, use what works for the client.

REVIEW OF LISTENING SKILLS

A. Minimal Attending
  1. Making eye contact
  2. Relaxing your body posture
  3. Using a concerned facial expression and tone
  4. Using verbal following
  5. Responding with minimal verbal encouragers
  6. Using nonverbal encouragers

B. Asking Open Questions
  1. Beginning with "how" or "what"
  2. Encouraging expression rather than yes/no answers
  3. Clarifying, elaborating, working with feelings, and solving problems
  4. Staying clear and simple
  5. Avoiding "why" questions or leading questions

C. Paraphrasing
  1. Capturing the essence of what the person said
  2. Staying brief and tentative
  3. Checking perceptions

4. Clarifying for the client
5. Giving accurate empathy

D. Working with Feelings
   1. Identifying feelings
      a. Asking feelings questions and getting feelings answers
      b. Paraphrasing spoken feelings and reflecting unspoken feelings
   2. Defining and clarifying feelings
   3. Having the client acknowledge and take responsibility for feelings
   4. Dealing with feelings

E. Summarizing
   1. Capturing the essence of what has been said, cumulatively, and putting it into a logical and usable order
   2. Being brief and tentative: "Is that right?"
   3. Creating closure or shifting modes

F. Integrating Skills
   1. Using open questions to encourage talking or to direct the conversation
   2. Using paraphrase to slow down the conversational flow and focus the conversation
   3. Exploring feelings before solving problems
   4. Summarizing to help wrap things up

A FINAL WORD ON THE COUNSELING SITUATION

The guiding philosophy for peer counseling is that the peer client is in charge. You are there to help people deal with their emotions and find their own solutions. There are times, however, when something goes wrong in the counseling process itself, and it becomes necessary to talk about it—namely, when you find yourself becoming frustrated, anxious, or angry. Dealing with such a situation requires assertiveness on your part, but it is essential to deal with it in order to preserve the counseling situation. You can't be an effective counselor if you are wishing you were somewhere else.

Here are some typical situations that make some counselors uneasy:

1. You feel like you are going around in circles and not getting anywhere. The usual way of dealing with this situation is to pick one area to concentrate on and not let the client get away from it. But if it gets to be too much of a problem, it's a good idea to talk about it with the person. Expressing your feelings ("I'm getting really frustrated because I . . .") will get you farther than if you sound as though you are accusing the other person ("We're not getting anywhere because you . . .").

2. The client starts crying. This can be an essential part of dealing with strong emotions. Some counselors find that it helps to reassure the person that it's okay to cry. Sometimes touching the person, or even giving him or her a shoulder to cry on, can be appropriate, depending on your style and the situation.

3. The client becomes hysterical. Talking with people calmly can sometimes help them settle down. At times, however, clients may be too distraught to talk to you at all. In this situation, you can stay until the person set-tles down and is able to talk. Or you may want to ask whether your client prefers to be alone for a while or wishes to continue the session at a later time. In any case, try to ascertain whether the person wants you to stay. Be prepared for a rather lengthy session.

   If you are counseling on the telephone and the person cannot calm down, ask whether it would be better to talk again in a short while. Try to get the person's phone number so you can return the call in 15 or 20 minutes. Gently say that you cannot talk while the person is so overcome and that you would be willing either to stay on the line while he or she calms down or to call back at a later time.

4. You are attracted to the client, or the client is attracted you, or both; or the person is lonely and would like to have you as a friend. You may not have to deal with this situation immediately unless it is getting in the way of your counseling; but at some point, you will probably have to clarify the nature of your relationship. If the person is coming back to see you (or will call you again), and you have the feeling that it is not for counseling, you have to decide if you are willing to continue working with him or her. If so, it is a good idea to clarify the relationship and not get stuck between being the person's counselor (which is something of a position of power, even in peer counseling) and being his or her friend. It is never appropriate to maintain a dual relationship (e.g., being someone's counselor and seeing them socially at the same time).

5. A person wants to have someone to talk to, rather than to work on problems. If you want to accept this, fine. But if you don't, you can be firm about being willing to talk about problems, but not being willing just to talk. If the person starts attacking you ("I called this place because I thought you cared about people, and here you won't talk to me!"), a good rule of thumb is: DON'T DEFEND YOURSELF. It will only prolong the situation. Instead, keep repeating yourself until the person gets the message.

3

COUNSELING SKILLS

by Vincent D'Andrea and Fritz Bottjer

This chapter concerns itself with techniques usually thought of as beyond listening skills alone: contracts and the contracting process, decision-making skills, confrontation, and interpretation. Understanding these techniques helps put listening and counseling skills in perspective. These techniques give the peer counselor additional options, particularly in extended counseling situations and in working with people in crisis. The case illustrations and exercises are designed to give the beginning counselor some guidelines for the types of situations in which these advanced skills might be introduced.

OVERVIEW

Counseling is a process, usually of short duration, involving exploration and discussion of values, beliefs, and attitudes. Its goal is to promote self-rewarding behavior. Counseling is largely a cognitive process. It sometimes involves getting new information to help in solving problems, and its feasibility and outcome very much depend on the individual's intellectual, social-emotional, and maturational levels.

To the extent that counseling is a problem-solving process, it often involves: examining assumptions that clients have about themselves, their world view, their potential, ability, etc.; exploring new perspectives on a particular issue; and confronting disregarded or distorted aspects of a problem, such as neglected communication. Problems best suited to counseling include:

1. Dilemmas—situations in which there are confusing choices, value conflicts, or unclear values

2. Decisions—the need to choose among various alternatives by clarifying and exploring values, beliefs, and goals; or by verifying information and getting new information. (This process is presented in detail in the later section on making decisions.)

3. Situational problems—temporary breakdowns of coping skills, as well as challenges to values and belief systems. Examples include relationship problems, acute illness, or sudden loss.

4. Distress—disturbing feelings associated with dilemmas, impending decisions, or situational problems. These feelings usually center around anxiety or guilt, and the basic expectation is that as the situation is resolved, the negative feelings will also subside.

Advice in Counseling

Unless you can give specific, factual information that is appropriate within the context of the counseling session, giving advice is generally useless. This is true because clients usually bring counselors particular types of problems:

- Problems in living: The client's experience is more relevant to the solutions that are the counselor's opinions.

- Situational problems: The client's own knowledge of the situation is of most use for predicting the results of any course of action.

- Long-standing issues: The facts are usually to be found in the person's experience and are usually known only to him or her.

Also, because the person's autonomy is a major goal of counseling, offering advice is clearly inconsistent with that goal.

Responsibility in Counseling

Peer clients expect certain things to occur in the counseling session. They expect that you will help them:

- Explore and define problem areas

- Gain an increased understanding of their beliefs and the relationship between beliefs, feelings, and actions

- Act for themselves on the basis of that increased understanding

Professional counselors (licensed, credentialed health and mental health personnel) have a certain degree of responsibility to meet these expectations, as determined by explicit agreements (professional, societal, legal). Nonprofessional helpers must define their role and the extent to which they will agree to assume responsibility. This issue is further discussed in the following section on contracts as well as in the chapter on ethics.

CONTRACTS AND THE CONTRACTING PROCESS

This book uses the term *contract* in three different ways: self-management contracts, contracts for exploration, and contracts regarding counselor responsibility. Almost all behavioral and humanistic psychotherapies emphasize contracting as an essential part of the change process.

Self-Management Contracts

Originally developed as a tool of behavior therapists (Homme, 1970), self-management contracting is based on theories of reinforcement, which state that rewarded behavior tends to be repeated. A *self-management contract* is a specific agreement between two people that emerges from a study of target (desired) behavior. The behavior is studied from the point of view of its antecedents (A), the behavior itself (B), and its consequences (C).

You can then develop focused strategies of intervention on the basis of "A-B-C"ing such sequences (see the example in the following box). In other words, you can specify the desired behavior (B), the context in which your client wants to develop it (A), and what will happen if your client performs or omits that behavior (C). If your client does not meet the terms of a contract, the reinforcement is withheld; often, no punishment is necessary. Reinforcement is given only after the person performs the agreed-on target behavior.

Contracts may be informal (e.g., "If you do X, I'll do Y") or formal, written agreements spelling out the specifics of behavior, reward, and conditions for fulfillment of the contract. General conditions for self-management contracts include:

1. The contract is fair.
2. The terms are clear.
3. The contract is generally positive, stressing desired change rather than prohibitions.
4. The procedures are systematic and consistent.
5. Along with the client, at least one other person participates.
6. The contract has a legal objective (i.e., it should not specify illegal, immoral, or antisocial behavior).
7. All parties agree to the terms.

A SAMPLE SELF-MANAGEMENT CONTRACT

Self: Pinocchio
Other: Jiminy Cricket
Goal: To reduce my lying

AGREEMENT

Self: I agree to lie not more than once during each day.

Other: Jiminy Cricket agrees to praise me whenever he sees me telling the truth and will not play with me after I've lied more than once that day.

CONSEQUENCES

Provided by Self:
If I stick to the above agreement, at the end of each week (ending Saturday at 6 p.m.) I will reward myself with ice cream. If I do not keep the above agreement during a particular week, I will clean Gepetto's workshop that Saturday evening (no ice cream).

Provided by Other:
Jiminy Cricket will (1) praise me for telling the truth, (2) ignore me when I am lying, and (3) keep me company each week that I fulfill this contract.
 For each week that I fail to keep the contract, Jiminy is authorized to (1) insist that I go to school and (2) limit my access to ice cream and candy.

Signed: Pinocchio _____
 Jiminy Cricket _____
Witness: Gepetto _____

Review date: June 10, 2001

Adapted from Mahoney, M.J., and Thoresen, C. E. (1974). *Self-Control: Power to the Person* (p. 53). Monterey, CA: Brooks/Cole.

Self-management contracts are widely used in education. It is common for teachers and school counselors to write up contracts with students. In some school systems, parents are taught how to formulate contracts with their children and other family members. Transient behavior and habit problems lend themselves well to this approach. In general, the self-management (A-B-C) approach is best suited for working with specific behavior as opposed to diffuse thoughts and feelings. For example, undesirable habits, phobias, problems with social skills, and sexual problems lend themselves well to this kind of contracting.

Contracts for Exploration

Aside from using contracts as an end in themselves, you can also use contracting as part of a process of exploration. For purposes of this discussion, counseling as a process can be divided into various phases:

1. **Attending Phase.** "Being with" the other person, using basic attending skills (BAS) for understanding and developing a relationship.

2. **Responding/Self-Exploration Phase.** Responding with empathy and understanding through use of BAS, you establish rapport and facilitate the client's self-exploration. Contracting may come into play in this phase, if you and your client establish goals and objectives for counseling.

3. **Integrative–Interpretative Phase.** Self-understanding is enhanced by piecing together data, identifying themes and patterns (by paraphrasing, interpreting, summarizing). Insight may emerge; self-rewarding behavior may ensue.

4. **Action Phase.** The person, acting on new knowledge, begins behavior change. In a collaborative manner, you

and your client work out specific contracts for exploration or behavior change.

5. **Resolution Phase.** The person's behavior moves toward the contract goals. You may explore other resources, with appropriate referrals. Mutual agreement may emerge to terminate counseling.

Contracts in phases 2, 3, and 4 may be for awareness or for change. *Contracts for exploration* involve an agreement simply to observe behavior; they are often in the nature of experiments to discover elements about behavior that are out of awareness. This process may enable people to act for themselves on the basis of increased understanding, or it may help you and your client form reasonable, "do-able" contracts for action. Here are a few examples of contracts for exploration:

A woman reported discomfort in greeting other people. The counselor asked if she would be willing to say hello to the first ten people she saw the next day, whether or not she knew them. She did, and reported that it got easier to do, and that she became aware of a lot of "chatter in her head" about fears and embarrassment. The avoidance behavior of not greeting people was protecting her from confronting these thoughts, which were successively clarified during counseling and examined for their probability. She became more comfortable socially.

A young man reported problems with time management. The counselor helped him draw a "time pie,"* and he agreed to follow the time-blocking laid out in the pie. To his surprise, he had about four extra hours a day. This was related

---

*A circle representing an average 24-hour day. The number of hours the person wants to spend on various activities are subtracted from 24 hours (leaving an average of 8 hours for sleep). Making your own time pie is an excellent exercise.

to his general tendency to overestimate how long he needed to do things, so that he always felt pressed for time. By challenging some mild feelings of discomfort, he was able to find more relaxation time and get all his work done.

A student reported "freezing up" in small group discussions when the instructor asked her questions. The student was beginning to doubt her intelligence, memory, and competence. Among other things, her counselor asked her to track the behavior throughout the day for seven days.* A look at her reporting showed that: (1) at first, the problem diminished for four days (not unusual); (2) it was more apt to occur when she was reporting on material she had already studied some time ago; (3) the "freezing up" events themselves lasted less than a minute (a surprise to her); and (4) she saw a pattern of consistently poor preparation for her seminars. She decided she would review more completely and practice ahead of time.

It also emerged that she felt flustered in shops when approached by salespeople, or in restaurants when asked to give her order before she was ready. By rehearsing specific situations that evoked her anxiety, she greatly reduced her distress. The counselor helped her explore her more general lack of assertiveness by using role-play situations and live practice (in restaurants, shops, etc.).

A chronically unhappy but reasonably successful male graduate student sought counseling about some recent disappointments and regrets. The counselor asked him to track a specific example, and a pattern emerged: the client's indecision led to turning down invitations for social and recreational events, which led to unhappy idle hours filled with regrets that he hadn't gone somewhere.

---

*This behavior tracking is usually done in chart form, with a sheet for each day. The chart shows time of day, what was happening, what the client did or said, and what happened afterward. Briefly, the client also notes any thoughts and feelings at the time.

He contracted to say yes to the next invitation. He observed some excitement and anxiety and found he had regrets that he wasn't home working!

At this point, it seemed that the "indecisiveness" was serving to make certain that he would experience disappointment no matter what he chose to do. His counselor challenged this pattern of reporting only sadness and regrets, and instructed him to report to others only the positive aspects of his experiences. The client was also instructed to brag about his accomplishments to someone he knew.

He reported that he felt very uncomfortable bragging about himself, as though others (including the counselor) would disapprove of this. This discomfort was traced to experiences in his family, where others took his excellent grades and other accomplishments for granted. If he did brag, family members told him to be modest.

This last complex example illustrates how you can use contracting at critical points in counseling to challenge automatic patterns of behavior that are rooted in false assumptions.

To provide a framework for exploration contracts, Mary Edwards Goulding and Robert Goulding (1978) have suggested a set of questions that counselors can have clients ask themselves:

1. What do I want to change? What do I want to stop or start doing? Where? When? With whom?

2. How am I now stopping myself from doing this?

3. What am I willing to do to get what I want?

4. How will I and others know when I've done it?

5. How might I sabotage myself?

In this framework, you:

- Ask clients to be specific about what they want.

- Observe or ask how people explain away why they are not already doing what they want.

- Explore and challenge.

- Define an observable, practical end-point.

- Perhaps most importantly, ask clients to list the various ways in which they could avoid working on the contract.

Pay close attention to people's language. Expressions such as "I'll try" or "I'll make an effort to" and "I wish I could" aim at avoiding the issue or pleasing the counselor rather than being clear statements of intent. A typical avoiding statement might be: "I thought I might like to try to see how I can make some progress in exploring why I can't seem to be able to learn how to be free of my problems."

One very important underlying assumption exists about the contracting process: it is not necessary to *be* different in order to *do* things differently. Many people think that extensive personality reconstruction is necessary to change behavior patterns. This is simply not true for many of the undesirable habits or behavior patterns that trouble people.

Working on contracts often raises important issues that have to do with habits, learned helplessness, or involuntary reinforcing systems. Contracts lead to an understanding of how people "keep bad feelings going." Helping clients through increased understanding of themselves leads to further contracts for exploration and action. Much of the time, you can encourage clients to challenge old patterns, both to get information and to change behavior.

Contracts Regarding Responsibility in Counseling
A third kind of contract involves the counselor's responsibility in the counseling situation. For licensed counselors, explicit statutes and codes spell out the extent and limits of that responsibility. Licensed health-care workers learn how to

define boundaries of responsibility by clearly contracting with clients.

For peer counselors, contracting should establish a cooperative situation in which both you and your clients know what to expect. Clearly, you need to set limits on what you can do for clients and when and how often you can be available. Lack of clarity can invite clients to become excessively dependent or confused.

What, then, are your responsibilities as a nonprofessional peer counselor? Some of these responsibilities might include:

- That you have information or access to information that will be of use to peers (e.g., on learning or informational resources, career planning strategies, contraception, etc.).

- That you are available at specific times, usually in an office.

- That you maintain confidentiality unless otherwise agreed to by both parties.

- That, in the case of personal counseling, you acknowledge your competence in certain limited areas (i.e., that you can offer good listening, problem-solving techniques, help with clarifying issues that are troubling a client, and information about referral to other resources).

To protect you and your clients from possibly misunderstanding your role, you need to make every effort to delimit the boundaries of your responsibility as a counselor. If your organization publishes any brochures or descriptions of its peer counseling services, these should spell out explicitly the range of services provided.

Summary—Contracting

1. The term *contract* may be used in three different ways: self-management contracts, contracts for exploration, and contracts regarding counselor responsibility.

2. Self-management contracts are based on theories of reinforcement. A behavior is studied from the point of view of its antecedents (A), the desired behavior (B), and its consequences (C). Focused strategies of intervention are developed on this basis (known as "A-B-C"ing the behavior). Such strategies are best suited for work on behavior, as opposed to emotions and thoughts.

3. Contracting can also be part of a process of exploration, rather than being an end in itself. Within this framework, contracts may be for awareness, for change, or both.

4. An important assumption in contracting is that acting differently doesn't require someone to be different first. The "how" of behavior is more important than the "why."

5. Contracts regarding counselor responsibility specify the expectations of both parties in a counseling relationship. Some aspects of the contract are explicit, others are implicit. Implicit assumptions should be clarified as much as possible to avoid misunderstandings about the responsibility of each party. These principles apply to peer counselors as well as to professional counselors. Clear specifications of your role, as well as clear program descriptions, serve to clarify expectations about responsibility.

1. Choose a partner and review the conditions for a self-management contract. Consider with your partner how you might use the "A-B-C" approach to set up a contract regarding a habit or behavior pattern you want to change. Following the format at the beginning of this chapter, write up the contract. Arrange follow up. Report to the larger group on the process and progress.

2. With a partner, review the implicit and explicit contract you have with family, friends, institutions (e.g., your school, other groups). Are these contracts all agreeable to you? Are there any you might want to renegotiate or refine?

3. With a partner, engage in a contracting process to explore a behavior or emotional issue in your life. Use the Gouldings' questions as a guide to exploring the issue, the aim being to create a contract in which you agree to report back to your partner.

4. In class, discuss your understanding of the limits of your responsibility as a peer counselor in your program. Consider writing this down. Does your peer counseling program provide enough definition of your role and responsibilities?

DECISION-MAKING COUNSELING SKILLS*

In decision-making counseling, as in counseling in general, counselors use basic attending skills to foster precise communication. To be of help, you must thoroughly understand the

*This section is based on Fritz H. Bottjer's doctoral dissertation, on work by J. D. Krumboltz et al. (1982), as well as on the works of numerous other authors.

client's problem. This involves gaining an awareness of the content of the problem as well as the "feeling" of it from the client's point of view.

Open and closed questions focus the client's discussion on issues that require elaboration or clarification. Paraphrasing, summarizing, and reflecting feelings encourage clients to reveal their thoughts and feelings, and also act as perception checks for you. It is important that you accurately perceive how your clients view their problems.

Other valuable functions are served by your use of basic attending skills. In the process of describing a problem, clients may clarify for themselves issues that were previously less clear. Sensitive and active listening can often lead clients to see factors previously overlooked. Merely describing them to someone else can change clients' perceptions and feelings to some degree.

By using basic attending skills properly, the experienced counselor fosters rapport and demonstrates a desire to help. For many decision-making problems, active listening may be all that is required to provide the type of help desired by the client. Other problems may require additional skills in decision-making counseling.

What Are These Skills?
The decision-making counseling skills described in this section are strategies, exercises, activities, and procedures that you may suggest in certain situations. Each procedure is designed to help clients clarify an aspect of the decision-making process in an unbiased way.

The skills are NOT intended to encourage clients toward particular options or courses of action. In most situations, you should not even initiate these exercises. Instead, describe an appropriate strategy or activity for approaching the decision. If the client chooses to engage in the suggested activity, you can help him or her use it properly.

How Can These Skills Help?

Most of the important decision-making problems that clients bring to peer counselors involve many relevant factors. When a problem is highly complex, important, or overwhelming, you or your client (or both) may easily overlook valuable information. This can often lead to:

- Making rash or hasty choices

- Relying on intuition, luck, or the opinions of others

- Not being able to make a decision at all

This latter condition can cause secondary problems that can drastically disrupt people's lives and further reduce their ability to make wise choices.

Systematic procedures for making important and complex choices can provide a workable solution to many of these problems. Your use of decision-making counseling skills can help many clients to structure their decision process in an efficient way and to make appropriate, responsible choices.

Problems often include long-range planning (such as selecting an academic major or a career direction). Of course, outcomes for the distant future are harder to predict. Over time, the goals, values, or objectives that prompted someone to pick a certain option may change. These and other factors can make it *difficult to evaluate decision-making strategies*. Nonetheless, many of the principles shown to be effective in solving problems can be applied to decision-making counseling.

How Are These Skills Used?

The next section lists the skills used in many decision-making situations. It does not list all skills for all combinations of problems, counselors, and clients. Instead, it provides a beginner's guide for counselors and trainees. You need to develop and refine your skills through practice and direct application.

If you see a client for several sessions over several weeks (or longer), many of these skills may be applicable. Short-term counseling (one or two sessions) renders some of these procedures unnecessary. For most situations, it is wise to view the model as a menu of possible activities.

These elements are presented in a logical sequence, but it is not the only one. You should select appropriate elements to fit the desires of the client, the direction of the counseling, the nature of the problem, and your own counseling style.

We recommend that you obtain personal experience with the procedures described in this next section before attempting to suggest their use to clients.

The DECIDES Model

The DECIDES model applies counseling skills to the process of helping clients solve problems. Ensuing sections describe each of the acronym's seven steps:

1. Define the problem.
2. Establish an action plan.
3. Clarify values.
4. Identify alternatives.
5. Discover probable outcomes.
6. Eliminate alternatives systematically.
7. Start action.

Define the Problem

Once your client has agreed to try using this model, the first step is to help the person define the problem.

a. Provide a context of acceptance within the decision-making work by appropriate use of basic attending skills.

Use encouragements, open and closed questions, paraphrase, and reflection of feelings to establish a

---

Exercises for This Model

Each of the seven units of the DECIDES model ends with exercises. These should be practiced sequentially in groups of two or three trainees. One person assumes the role of the client and presents a decision-making problem. The second person plays the counselor and demonstrates as many of the skills for that unit as possible. The (optional) third person is the observer. After a unit is practiced, the observer leads a brief discussion of how well the "counselor" demonstrated the skills, how appropriate the skills were for that "client's" particular situation, and how the interaction could be improved. Before going on to the next unit, each member of the group should have experience in each role.

Remember, the skills presented here are the most appropriate for clients who cannot make a decision, who do not have refined personal decision-making skills, or for whom the problem is overwhelming or of great importance. The person assuming the client's role should keep this in mind when choosing and presenting a problem for practice.

---

working relationship by demonstrating a desire to understand the situation and to provide help.

b. Elicit a clear statement of the problem.

Use open and closed questions, paraphrase, and reflection of feelings to elicit the client's detailed description of the situation. Elicit discussion about the objective content as well as the emotional content of the problem as perceived by the client. Be sure to find out when the decision has to be made.

c. Recognize and summarize the problem clearly. Check for accuracy.

> When you feel that you understand the most important aspects of the problem, attempt a detailed summary of your impressions with the client. Be tentative. Express your summary as an attempt to understand rather than as a professional opinion.
>
> Be sure to include a specific statement of the goals your client hopes to achieve as a result of the decision-making work—for example, "You want to have a list of at least five possible graduate schools by the first of December so that you can get all the necessary application forms on time. Is that right?"
>
> Then, with additional or corrective input from the client, revise your summary. Continue in this fashion until the client indicates that your summary accurately reflects his or her own perception of the situation.

d. Establish the fact that responsibility for making a decision rests with the client.

> Some people may appear to want you to make a decision for them. If this is the case, clarify your role as helper. You may want to give a rationale as to why you cannot assume responsibility for someone else's decision. (All the same, be aware that you probably *will* influence the client's decision-making process, despite your efforts to remain objective and nondirective.

"DEFINE THE PROBLEM" EXERCISES

This first unit is primarily a focused application of the skills you have learned in previous chapters.

1. In groups of two or three, enact various decision making sessions, discuss the process, and switch roles.

2. Explore these questions (with your class, if possible): Can any counseling be truly nondirective? In what situations would active guidance from a counselor be most appropriate?

3. Before going to the next unit, be sure to discuss the implications of the foregoing point d (responsibility, objectivity, and directiveness in counseling) to your satisfaction.

Establish an Action Plan

After you and your client have adequately defined the problem, the second step is to come up with a plan for making decisions.

a. Describe the general strategy and introduce the various steps of the model, as appropriate.

> Your task is to encourage the client to gather, weigh, and apply all relevant information in a way that enhances his or her ability to estimate the overall consequences of a given action. As a result, the client makes a more educated choice from available alternatives. Your description may be a simple claim, such as: "An informed choice is typically a better choice"; or you may want to detail the various steps that could be taken.

b. Ask the client if this approach is acceptable and desirable.

> It is very important that the person approve of any proposed course of action. As you introduce each new element, you may need reaffirmation from the client. At other times, clients may imply consent by their

favorable reaction to such statements as, "It may be valuable to explore . . .," or "What about . . .?" or "Another way to expand your analysis may be to . . .."

c. Assess how much time and effort the person is willing to devote to the decision-making problem.

This specification can aid both you and the client in efficiently structuring the overall task.

d. Elicit specific commitments for outside decision-making work.

Clients often carry important decision-making problems outside the counseling session—sometimes to obsessive proportions. A more efficient use of time may result from your help in structuring specific decision-making activities for your client to do after the counseling session. The last part of a session is an appropriate time to discuss areas requiring additional attention.

Once an area or activity is mutually identified, elicit a specific plan (what, when, for how long, to what goal, etc.). Open-ended questioning can be an effective way to help the person define the plan—for instance:

"What can you do to find out more about . . .?"

"How much time can you devote to this exploration [task, exercise, etc.]?"

"When can you set aside time for this work this week?"

"When can we discuss your findings, or would you rather work alone from here on?"

Your goal is to facilitate the types of activities that the client actually wants to do. Be careful that your casual suggestions are not regarded as a strong message to do particular work.

"Establish an Action Plan" Exercises
For practicing the first and second points (A and B), the "client" should specifically ask for suggestions as to how to work on the problem. The fourth point is obviously a part of establishing an action plan; however, practicing the skills of describing activities and eliciting commitments for outside decision-making work is probably best done later, after you learn additional skills. Practice the fourth point as a part of each unit, beginning with the next one.

Clarify Values
The third unit in the DECIDES model is to help clients clarify any values that pertain to the decision they are trying to make.

a. Promote a discussion of the personal values that are relevant to the client in this particular decision-making situation.

A first task may be to define what is meant by values. *Values* represent personal principles, ideals, self-definitions, goals, or motivating guidelines. As such, they may underlie certain actions, feelings, and thoughts about the prob-lem at hand. Values can change over time. They may be situation-specific or be altered by various influences, such as the decision-making procedures you suggest.

Some clients may be well aware of their personal values and how these values enter into the decision at hand. Others may not have considered them at all.

Use the appropriate basic attending skills to explore the client's values.

b. Elicit and discuss any values that the client may not have considered.

Be tentative in your suggestions—for example, "What other personal values do you think may be important in this situation?" Using examples may be helpful. For a career decision, a client may profitably consider his or her feelings about prestige, security, salary, leisure time, leadership, altruism, variety, entry requirements, responsibility, and location. Other situations may require exploring the client's feelings about family ties, being loved or disliked, friendship, respect, obligations of various types, lifestyle activities, and identifications with groups or principles.

c. Prompt the client to weigh these values.

Values can be ordered, weighed, and discussed as abstract; or they may be concretely anchored to the presenting problem. Abstract weighing can be insightful and interesting. You may suggest an exercise such as: "If you had 100 units of satisfaction to distribute among those values you have identified as important, how would you distribute them?"

Many forms of comparing values may be appropriate. Allow the client to determine (and even initiate) a suitable weighing strategy.

"CLARIFY VALUES" EXERCISES

Valuable activities that clients can do outside the session to clarify their values include fantasy exercises. Clients in a career-planning situation, for instance, may profit from such activities as writing their own ideal obituaries or writing mock letters of recommendation from the perspective of significant people in their lives (boss, spouse, friends). Be creative in your practice.

If the client desires such fantasy activities, be sure to discuss the outcomes at the next session, after the client completes the exercise. You may also need to help the person reweigh values.

Identify Alternatives

Once the person has identified and weighed any relevant values, the next unit involves identifying the alternative choices.

a. Prompt the consideration of all feasible options. Whenever possible, write them on a worksheet.

> A worksheet is especially useful in situations that have many alternatives or are complex. Should you and your client desire to consider all feasible options, summarize each alternative in a few words, down the side or across the top of the paper. You may later want to illustrate values by creating a grid with alternative pairing (see the grid that follows).

b. Brainstorm new alternatives. To establish even more options, think of various information sources.

> Discussing what seem like unlikely options can sometimes generate a new feasible alternative. Be sure that any suggestion you make is viewed simply as input to the brainstorming, not as your opinion.
>
> Additional information can sometimes create new options. In the light of new information, a client may reinstate previously discarded alternatives. If you think it may be profitable, suggest that the client gather new information.

If the client agrees that additional information is desirable, commit the client to this task as specifically as possible. Feel free to make appropriate referrals; service organizations may be suitable, for instance.

"Identify Alternatives" Exercise
In practicing point b in the previous section, you need to assess your knowledge of local information sources. If you are in a class, large-group discussion and input from your instructor can help increase this knowledge.

Discover Probable Outcomes
This fifth step in the DECIDES model involves speculating about possible results or consequences of each alternative.

a. Discuss each option in terms of its expected outcome.

Expected outcomes are the client's predictions of what will result after a decision is made and acted on. Outcomes may be described as situations, or they may relate to feelings, values, or conflicts among values. Each option usually has a number of expected outcomes, both positive and negative. The person may also have both short- and long-term expectations. Some outcomes may be more probable than others; some may be much less predictable.

Discussing these expectations can help the client view the problem in greater depth. Sometimes what the client sees as probable may not seem probable to you at all. In the interest of clarification, you may want to question or challenge such statements gently.

A fantasy exercise may be a valuable strategy in some situations—for instance, "Imagine that it is five years from now. You have lived with your decision (your first alternative) for a while now. We meet on the street and I ask you how things are going—what you like about your decision and its effects on your life. What would you say?"

b. Generate other information sources for estimating outcomes more clearly.

Some expected outcomes may be better estimated with additional information. When appropriate, suggest likely sources and commit the client to gathering information.

c. Prompt a discussion of possibilities for changing course later, after the client acts on an option.

Few decisions require absolute adherence to a selected course of action if it later proves to have been a poor choice. The consequences of changing actions later can, however, vary with the options. Analyzing the potential for later change can provide meaningful input to a decision.

Open-ended questioning can facilitate this analysis—for example: "What if you later find that option A doesn't pan out? Could you change to option B? What consequences would you expect?"

d. Write down probable outcomes on a grid.

With the information gathered so far, you and your client can create a "values vs. alternatives" grid. On the left side of a piece of paper, write down each previously identified value. Across the top, write the alternatives. Ask your client about each alternative with respect to how well its probable outcome addresses each value. In the appropriate space, enter the answers (in summary form).

The following passage exemplifies this approach to decision-making counseling.

> Counselor: *There is another exercise that can sometimes help to compare alternatives and probable outcomes. You can construct a grid that shows how each alternative stacks up against the list of values you came up with. It's a way of getting an overview of the important issues all on one sheet of paper.*

> Client: *Tell me more.*

> Counselor: *Okay, first, let's use the six values you have identified as important in this decision. List them one under the other on the left side of a piece of paper, evenly spaced from the top of the sheet to the bottom. Separate each value with a horizontal line so that you have six rows.*
>
> *Now you have a grid that lets you see how each value is served by each alternative. Fill in the grid with your estimate of how well each alternative addresses each value. Are you with me so far?*

> Client: *Yes, I get the picture. So, for instance, "Desire for independence" would be well served by the alternative of taking the full-time job in Cleveland with Pressman, Inc.—at least with respect to living arrangements. But I'm less sure about independence on the job. That's a somewhat different issue.*

This client is beginning to explore the complexity of evaluating probable outcomes by alternative pairings. As the counselor, you may sometimes suggest establishing a new value category, if you think that would be helpful. To fill in each box, additional information must sometimes be gathered. In helping clients with this grid, you need to use your basic attending skills.

"Discover Probable Outcomes" Exercise
Constructing a grid is a strategy worthy of considerable practice. You may feel awkward at first. Initially, you can fill in the

grid with the client's help. Begin with a statement such as: "I'm going to write down a few of these things so I can organize all this information." Then ask questions, paraphrase, summarize, check for accuracy, enter the information, and describe what you are doing.

Later, practice ways of describing the process so that the client constructs and fills in the grid. Begin with a statement such as: "In this case, it may be helpful to organize a worksheet to enter all this information. [Describe the process further.] Would this be something you'd like to do?" If so, describe how to construct the grid.

Your training needs to include firsthand experience in organizing a complex decision-making problem in grid form. With practice, this strategy will become part of your normal repertoire.

Eliminate Alternatives Systematically

Now that you've explored possible outcomes, you and your client can talk about which alternatives are not desirable or feasible at this time.

a. Prompt the integration of all values, alternatives, and expected outcomes. Review the decision-making worksheet, if you used one.

If no single alternative seems obviously best to the client and no additional preparatory work (such as continued information gathering) is desired, suggest a review of all currently available information.

It is often the case that people's values shift somewhat during decision making, or that they view probable outcomes in a different light by the time they get to this step. You may want to tell clients to feel free to change their minds about values or expected outcomes. It is important that only the most current information is considered in this review.

Alternative \ Value Categories	Full Time Work at Pressman Inc.	Half-Time Work Half-Time Law School (C.U.)	Full-Time Work 1/4-Time Eve. Law School (S.C.U.)	Full-Time Law School (C.U.) With StudentLoans
20[1] Living Arrangement Independence (next few years)	10[2] 20 X 10 = (200)	2 20 X 2 = (40)	10 20 X 10 = (200)	5 20 X 5 =(100)
15 Personal Independence	9 15 X 9 = (135)	5 15 X 5 = (75)	4 15 X 4 = (60)	5 15 X 5 =(75)
10 Money (next few years)	8 10 X 8 = (80)	5 10 X 5 = (50)	7 10 X 7 = (70)	4 10 X 4 =(40)
25 Money (later potential)	7 25 X 7 = (175)	10 25 X 10 = (250)	10 25 X 10 = (250)	10 25 X 10 =(250)
Prestige, 15 Self-concept, Approval from others	6 15 X 6 = (90)	8 15 X 8 = (120)	7 15 X 7 = (105)	9 15 X 9 =(135)
Security 15 (peace of mind aspect more than job security)	8 15 X 8 = (120)	7 15 X 7 = (105)	9 15 X 9 = (135)	6 15 X 6 =(90)
Totals 100	800	640	810	690

1 The numbers assigned to the value categories (value weights) obtain from the exercise described on page 72. That is, 100 points are distributed among the identified values according to their relative importance to the client.

2 Each intersection of a value category and an alternative is assigned a number from 0 to 10 according to how well that particular value is likely to be fulfilled by the alternative it intersects. For instance, this client felt that full-time work at Pressman, Inc. would allow the maximum amount of "living arrangement independence" over the next few years.

3 Value weights are then multiplied by the numerical estimate of potential fulfillment, and summed up for each alternative.

It is typically most helpful to let clients provide their own unique integration of the information. As needed, you may prompt, question, or tactfully challenge a client's analysis. If it seems that closure is at hand, proceed directly to the elimination strategy (point c, which follows).

b. Prompt your client to rate projected outcomes with respect to each value, and summarize for each alternative (see the preceding grid).

This strategy can be valuable in some cases, provided that (1) two or more options remain equally desirable, and (2) the client desires a highly quantitative breakdown of the problem. Before proceeding, make sure that the client desires this approach.

Use the decision-making worksheet for displaying this analysis. Have the client assign an appropriate numerical value to each piece of data. If, for instance, three personal values are relevant to this problem, first have the client rank the relative importance on some scale (e.g., by dividing 100 points among the three values).

Then rate the probable outcome of each option with respect to how much it satisfies or conflicts with each value. For each alternative, multiply each value's number by the score for each probable outcome; then add these scores for each alternative.

You or your client should feel free to modify this scheme as needed. The objective is not to arrive at a decision by picking the alternative with the highest number, but rather to stimulate meaningful thought about the interaction of the various components involved in the decision.

We continue now with the example begun in the previous section. Assume that the grid has been completed and the client desires a quantitative breakdown of the decision-making problem.

Counselor: *Keep in mind that assigning numbers to values and matching them with alternatives is only an exer-cise to help you get an overall perspective on the problem. It is definitely not a scientific formula for making a decision.*

Client: *Yes, I understand. In fact, I think I am leaning toward an alternative already, but I want to see how this works. I've always been a numbers buff, but I've never applied math to making personal decisions before. I guess I'm just curious to see how the numbers come out. How does it work?*

Counselor: *Okay. Remember when we divided 100 points among all your values? Let's do it again. You may want to make some changes. [The client assigns points to each value so that the total is equal to 100.] Now, list each value's points on the grid in the appropriate row.*

Client: *Done. Now what?*

Counselor: *This gets a little abstract. Okay, on a scale from 0 to 10 [any scale will work], estimate how well each value will be fulfilled by each alternative. So for "living arrangements independence" [this client broke "inde-pendence" into two distinct values], how well would the Pressman job satisfy this value?*

Client: *Oh, completely, I guess. I could most likely swing a place of my own, so I'd give it a rating of 10.*

Counselor: *Half-time study at Cleveland U while living at home? How much "living arrangements independence" do you think you would have?*

Client: *Well, as I said before, it wouldn't be a total zip, but not great either. Let's say a 2.*

c. The client continues in this fashion with your help until a number is assigned to each cell. Assume that this procedure has now been completed.

Counselor: *Now we simply multiply each value's assigned points by the number you have entered in each box. [To distinguish this new number, you can use underlining or any other method that works for you. Complete this step.]*
   Now, for each alternative, add up all of these new numbers. At the bottom of each column, enter the total. Each alternative now has a single numerical estimate. You can compare the totals, but remember that this doesn't necessarily lead to the "best" alternative. It is simply a way of organizing a lot of material on one piece of paper. You may want to go over this grid and make changes where appropriate.

d. Eliminate poor alternatives one by one.

It is sometimes easier to eliminate a poor alternative than to choose the best one from among several. So have the client eliminate alternatives until only one remains. Should a client assess two or more alternatives as equal, recycle through the appropriate sections of this decision-making model (by clarifying values, gathering information, and so on) until one alternative prevails.

"Eliminate Alternatives" Exercise

To use these steps in decision-making counseling, you must be able to describe them in detail to your clients. In your practice sessions, present the elements one step at a time. Check your partner's understanding frequently.

Start Action

In the final step of this DECIDES model, the client begins implementing the best available plan or option.

a. When your client has chosen one alternative (at least tentatively), elicit commitments for specific action on the selected alternative.

> The objective is to help the person specify all the necessary actions required to put the decision into effect. Some choices require obvious, immediate action to implement the decision; others may require various preliminary steps. Elicit commitments that the situation requires and that your client desires.

b. Elicit a review of the steps in decision making.

> You can provide a great service by transmitting a general strategy for dealing with future decisions independently. Ask your client to abstract the general steps in his or her own words. Contribute as appropriate. Encourage and support statements that reflect the person's ownership of the strategies. Be sure to give your client all the credit for arriving at a decision.

"Start Action" Exercise

At first, you may find it difficult to implement point b without appearing pedantic. Therefore, keep the strategy in mind but do not attempt to use it with actual clients until you feel comfortable with it.

Most of the strategies presented in the DECIDES model may initially seem somewhat stilted or unnatural. Proper selection and use of the skills usually require considerable practice, so do not become discouraged if you are still unable to use them smoothly by the end of this chapter. Only through further practice and actual experience will you be able to integrate them into your own counseling style.

Summary—Decision Making

The preceding section describes a method for helping clients make difficult decisions. The seven units of the DECIDES model are: Define the problem, Establish an action plan, Clarify values, Identify alternatives, Discover probable outcomes, Eliminate alternatives systematically, and Start action.

CONFRONTING

In counseling, *confrontation* means "pointing out discrepancies or incongruities in what clients are saying or doing" (Ivey & Gluckstern, 1976; Ivey & Matthews, 1984). Most schools of therapy have a special technology and point of view about confrontation and give it different degrees of importance; all agree that as a technique, it works best in the context of a trusted, empathetic relationship. Unfortunately, it has also developed a bad image in counseling, probably through reports of methods in which it is overemphasized (e.g., in some kinds of encounter groups).

Within the context of a counseling relationship, confrontation can be of help in fostering insight into personal problems that result from incongruent thinking or behavior. As Ivey (1976) defines it, "a person is faced directly with the fact that he/she may be saying other than that which they mean, or doing other than that which they say."

Ivey also lists the following factors as important facets of confrontation:

1. A confrontation focuses on discrepancies between varying attitudes, thoughts, or behavior.

2. A confrontation focuses on objective data. The more factual and observable a confrontation of discrepancies is, the more helpful it will be to the client. Confrontations are most effective when they are nonevaluative.

3. A confrontation is not a blunt statement of opinion or emotion that disagrees with someone else's.

Okun (1976) presents a slightly different point of view regarding confrontation. "Confronting involves honest feedback about what the helper really thinks is going on with the helpee." This may involve a focus on genuineness, e.g., "It seems to me you're playing games here," or "I feel you really don't want to talk about this." Or, as with Ivey, it may involve a focus on discrepancy, e.g., "On the one hand, you seem upset about not getting the job, but on the other hand you seem kind of relieved."

In the beginning, you should probably focus on discrepancies between objective facts and observable behavior, rather than on what you feel is someone's genuineness. The problem with confronting someone based on your "gut reaction" (no matter how accurate that might actually be) is that it runs the risk of reflecting the counselor's personal opinion, unexamined assumption or prejudice, or overreaction.

Another point about effective confrontations concerns the use of "I" statements. As opposed to "you" statements, which clients tend to interpret as judgmental, "I" statements help keep confrontations neutral. Imagine the effect of saying, "You are sexist," vs. "I experience discomfort as you talk about your boyfriend; as a man, I'm wondering if you might feel the same way about me." This latter statement blends "I" and "you" remarks to make clear who said what, and where the responsibilities lie.

Another such example is: "You say that I seem to understand you, but I don't believe that we are communicating well."

So, then, the skills involved in constructive confrontations are:

- Accurate perception of discrepancies in observable behavior, verbal and nonverbal
- The use of "I" statements rather than "you" statements exclusively
- Responses that convey understanding, such as paraphrasing, reflecting feelings, and sharing personal reactions
- An awareness on your part that certain statements by the client may trigger responses that are evaluative or judgmental

CONFRONTATION EXERCISES

1. Divide into groups of three. One person role-plays the "counselor," who confronts a client; a second, the "client" being confronted; and a third, the observer.

   The "client" assumes four different characters: a person who is too agreeable and complains about being hurt and abused by others, a person who is extremely shy and quiet, a person who is very critical of others and complains of being misunderstood, and a person who seems to live a harried life and complains of pressure and anxiety.

   To simulate a counseling relationship, the players assume they know one another. After the confrontation, the observer evaluates and gives feedback based on the foregoing section's criteria. The "counselor" receives feedback from the "client" as well. The role-

> players then switch roles so that all three members can experience each role.
>
> When all groups have finished, the whole class reconvenes and considers the following questions: What were people's general reactions to the exercise? What did people learn about confronting others? What did people learn about being confronted? A group leader should guide this discussion.

In class, confront someone you know about the positive and negative points of your relationship. Avoid "likes" and "dislikes," and focus on actual behavior or attitudes. Take 15 minutes to do so with a partner, and then share your experiences with one another. Or, if you do this exercise in a group, members who wish to do so can share their reactions, emphasizing strengths and weaknesses about staying within the guidelines for confrontation. We also encourage you to do this exercise outside of class and then to report back about what you learned.

INTERPRETING

Interpretation is usually considered a key skill in *psychotherapy* rather than *counseling*. Wohlberg (1967) defines interpretation as a skill "by which the more unconscious elements of the psyche are brought to the patient's awareness." He states that "interpretation as a vehicle for insight is particularly valuable in reconstructive psychotherapy, since there is, in this form of treatment, an emphasis on unconscious aspects of mental activity."

Psychotherapists use interpretation to bring people's unconscious motivations into consciousness. This adds to their awareness, and people therefore have more options about their behavior and attitudes. Counseling, however, deals more with observable behavior and attitudes, so interpreting unconscious motivations and processes is less germane.

A Further Definition

Ivey (1976) views interpretation as "an act of renaming or redefining reality" (i.e., feelings, thoughts, actions, and experiences) from a new point of view. The objective is a new understanding for the client. Optimally, this new point of view is a shared one, not just that of the counselor.

We are all restricted by a particular point of view and tend to give meaning to events from that context. As counselors, we need to be careful not to substitute our own points of view for those of our clients.

The accompanying diagram may clarify the distinctions between reconstructive psychotherapy and counseling.

Distinctions between Psychotherapy and Counseling

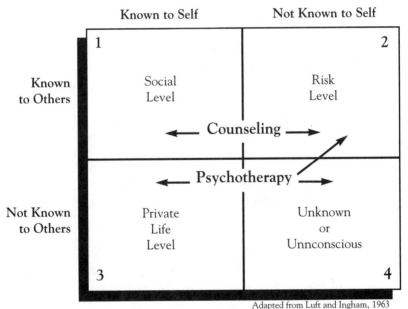

Adapted from Luft and Ingham, 1963

In this diagram, areas 1 and 2 are the province of counseling, while 2, 3, and 4 are the province of therapy. Part of the purpose of therapy is to move material from 2 and 4 into 3 and eventually into 1. Of course, to the extent that you are working in area 2, you may eventually have to do some confronting and interpreting.

Interpreting and Listening Skills

In the section on paraphrasing, we pointed out that paraphrasing stands on a continuum between simple restatements and interpretation. In counseling, interpretation involves a mix of open and closed questions, paraphrases, and reflections of feeling.

As you interpret, you must necessarily become more directive. For example, in low-level interpretation, you may wait for the client to interpret reported behavior or experiences as you have reflected them. In mid-level interpretation, you actively piece together bits of information and ask the client to reach some conclusion. And in strong-level interpretation, you may give the client a definite, authoritative interpretation.

A client has been describing conflicts with an advisor. She describes a "waiting game" in which she seems to seek advice but is prepared to resist if the advisor gives it.

Low-level interpretation: "So, it seems as though you're in a stalemate. You want direction, but you rebel against it."

Mid-level: "You know, as you talk about the situation, I'm reminded of similar episodes you've reported. They all seem to involve a tug of war with older people. What do you think?"

Strong level: "You know, it seems like you have difficulties with authority figures, and you tend to regress to very childish behaviors when you must deal with them."

Client: *Yes, and I'm torn up by it. . . .*

Counselor: *How do you feel when your advisor pays attention to you?*

Client: *I feel he will then expect more of me . . . it's always been like this with teachers. I just can't relax, but I need that recognition from them—it's like that with my father, too.*

Counselor: *How so?*

Client: *I always felt I had to jump up and down to get his attention, then I was pissed that it wasn't spontaneous with him.*

Counselor: *So what might you conclude?*

Client: [Pauses] *That I'm treating my advisor as if he were my father, or that I want him to be my father?*

Counselor: *You want him to do the right thing by you without your asking.*

Client: *You know, I've thought the same thing, in just about the same words . . .*

Counselor: *So how much longer do you want to struggle with this?*

Client: [Thoughtful] *I do act that way . . . and I do want to have a different relationship.*

Counselor: *Let's explore this a bit more.*

At this point, the counselor and client might explore the issue from a different perspective.

From these examples, it should be clear that paraphrasing and questioning are very important for interpreting. To be confident about a possible interpretation, you must stay with the material that the client puts out. In other words, you need to be tentative, just as with paraphrasing. You must learn to perceive patterns and to inquire about their meaning.

Like an incomplete or awkward paraphrase, an inelegant interpretation may still be of use; just make sure your client feels free to correct any inelegance and perhaps to elaborate on your interpretation.

Aspects of Interpretation

A useful way to frame interpretations is to look for an appropriate metaphor, such as:

> "This person is behaving as though ___."
> "This person views ___ as if ___."
> "This person generates ___ by ___"

By searching for such metaphors, you will begin to get a sense of how to frame a statement so that it will be of interest to your client. One objective of active listening is to understand the client's world view.

> A male client is describing general annoyance and resentment toward the people with whom he shares a house. He feels uncomfortable about this, but he can rationalize and justify his feelings very well. He goes on to discuss how he opted out of the "Secret Santa" plan at his house, and then felt left out, angry, and sad when others got gifts. Earlier in counseling, he has mentioned situations in which he acted in selfless, apparently generous ways, only to feel sad and angry later.
>
> The counselor sees that this man puts on an appearance of not needing anything from anyone, locks himself into a pattern of deprivation by denying his needs, and then experiences sadness and resentment.

The counselor might generate metaphors as follows:

> "This person is behaving as though he has no needs."

"This person views 'being given to' as if it's not allowed."

"This person generates sadness and anger by denying his needs."

The counselor might then begin to frame these ideas in ways that are meaningful to the client and might offer him alternative explanations for his sadness. To develop a strategy of challenging the undesirable pattern, the counselor and client could examine various patterns of behavior. They might explore the circumstances under which the client's family permitted him to express his needs. (In this particular case, this exploration brought out the fact that in his large family, the client did not have his needs met; he had learned to deny those needs while feeling sad. In his current residence, the existence of a "shadow family" had triggered his old reaction.)

Interpretations are ideally made by the *client*, on the basis of feedback from you. The interpretations are then called *insights*. Whenever possible, stimulate your clients to think through problems; you can restate, paraphrase, summarize, emphasize important connections, and explore with questions. Leading the client to the brink of an insight is the highest form of interpretation.

> *A woman in counseling comes to a session feeling depressed and sad. She describes her feelings as having come on suddenly. After some exploration, it doesn't appear that there is anything current to account for this sudden sadness. The counselor notices that she is wearing an unusual ring he hasn't seen before, and he asks about it. The client stares at her hand and says it's her mother's ring. She had put it on that morning without thinking. It is the anniversary of her mother's death. Her sadness intensifies, and they are then able to work on her grief.*

Interpretations are made within a frame of reference that may either be personal—reflecting an individual world view—or be based on the theory of a school of psychology and therapy. Interpretations that you make from your own point of view may be fairly informed, or they may be more intuitive. People who share common experiences in life may have empathy for each other's situations (an informed base of knowledge) and therefore may be able to interpret for each other accurately and intuitively. Many relationships have this kind of rapport.

In counseling, the problem with using an informed point of view is that interpretations may become projections, prejudices, or stereotypes. (To review the dangers of making assumptions about how other people feel or think, see the earlier sections on paraphrasing and reflecting feelings.) The best way to avoid advancing your own opinion is to follow what the other person is saying and to be aware that his or her world view is being examined, not yours.

Another aspect of the same problem is your own sensitivity to certain issues. A client in the midst of describing a problem may trigger uncertainties or doubts in you. Most counselors learn that they have difficulty listening objectively when it comes to certain issues or problems. Some examples:

- Romantic relationship problems

- Suicidal crises

- Death of a parent, friend, or sibling

- Reports of violence or threats to life

Interpretations are most effective when they reflect respect for the client's world view and are devoid of accusations or moral judgments. In working with clients, it can be difficult to avoid making judgments or having a strong or even negative reaction to what is said. Needless to say, you should not express these reactions. You must stay with the client, maintain an understanding attitude, and develop cues for framing interpretative interventions. In short, maintain good rapport with the person.

Schools of Thought on Interpretation

Various schools of therapy use interpretation with different emphases. As mentioned, the psychodynamic therapies deal with it most intensively. One similarity among all the schools is that they represent highly organized points of view that involve their respective belief system and technology. Each *belief system* is the body of theory in which that therapy or counseling is based, and the corresponding *technology* comprises the techniques by which proponents assist clients in self-understanding and behavior change. In order of the relative importance they attach to using interpretation, the major schools and their tenets may be summarized as follows.

Psychoanalytic–Psychodynamic (Freud, Jung, Adler, Horney, and Sullivan): Behavior is determined, choices are illusory. Behavior reflects conflict between desires and defenses. The unconscious mind is more important than consciousness, and we can only know the unconscious through interpretation of such things as symbols, dreams, fantasies, slips of the tongue, and projections from the past onto the counselor in the present (*transference*). This orientation also includes theories about past relationships and how they affect present ones (referred to as *object relations*).

Existential–Humanistic (Rogerian, Gestalt, some aspects of Rational-Emotive therapy): Behavior is not predetermined, free will exists, choices are actual, and anything that reduces the power of the past is therapeutic. The goal is to live in the present, to choose, and to act for satisfaction within ethical constraints. For example, Perls and Rogers view people as organisms striving for psychological health, reality as subjective and idiosyncratic, and psychological health as harmony between a perceived real self and an idealized internal self. They emphasize congruence between feelings and behavior, and their therapy works primarily with feelings rather than with cognitions, which they distrust.

Transactional Analysis: Freudian but not psychoanalytic. All behavior is determined by "life script" development. Increased understanding of this matrix of behavior brings about increased freedom of choice and behavior change through abandoning early decisions that led to faulty script formation. Behavior is consistent and repetitive, with understandable goals accessible to rational analysis and choice.

Cognitive-Behavioral (Meichenbaum, Bandura, Ellis, Thoresen, Beck): Specific patterns of thinking are associated with unwanted behavior. Focus is on black-or-white distinctions, overgeneralizations, "should" statements, and so forth, by which individuals become trapped in nonproductive, self-critical thinking.

Behavioral (Skinner, Wolpe): Behavior is learned. The conditions of learning appear to be more important than the behavioral outcomes. Reinforcement and contingencies seem fixed, both in and out of awareness. A study of reinforcers, contingencies, and outcomes leads to an analysis of behavior and a shaping of new behavior, based on changes in reinforcers and contingencies in the awareness of the individual.

Summary—Interpreting

- Interpreting is a skill most often used in psychodynamic, reconstructive therapies. It is also appropriate in intensive counseling (humanistic, Transactional).

- Psychodynamic therapists use interpretation to identify unconscious elements of the client's psyche.

- Ivey defines interpretation as the act of renaming or redefining reality from a new point of view, with the goal of bringing the client new understanding.

- Generating metaphors as alternative explanations is a useful way to practice making interpretations.

- Couch your interpretations in simple language and offer them in a tentative manner.

- Ideally, clients make their own interpretations, which are called insights.

- Before making an interpretation, be reasonably sure of the accuracy of your assumptions and thoughts. Offering interpretations in a haphazard manner can change the relationship with your client.

- The timing of an interpretation is important. Part of being helpful with interpretations is knowing when the person is close to understanding a particular issue.

- Try not to let personal issues intrude into interpretive comments. Focus on the client's world view and interpret that.

- In your interpretations, reflect your respect for the client's attitudes and beliefs. Avoid accusations or moral judgments.

Exercises — Interpreting

Confidentiality and discretion are absolutely essential in these exercises. It must be understood that group members will not gossip about the results.

1. Each person in a small group looks around the room for an object that catches his or her interest. Each person then tells about the object as though it were him or her—e.g., "I am an ashtray. I am round and flat and shiny. People use me to put hot things into. At the end of the day, I feel dirty."

2. After everyone has finished, a group leader asks all the members to consider how their descriptions of the objects are like them or some aspect of their lives.

3. A volunteer member of a small group reports a dream. Each group member interprets the dream silently. Next, the dreamer asks various people for their interpretations and then comments on them. Later, the leader asks group members to consider whether their interpretations reflect either some aspect of themselves or some current concern.

4. Either in class or outside, pair up with one another and take turns talking about an issue of interest or concern to you. The "counselor" practices interpreting what the "client" says, and the client gives feedback about the process and content of the interpretation. It is important to spend at least half an hour on this exercise and to get feedback immediately, before switching roles.

5. In small groups, take turns describing yourselves as though you were an animal or plant of your choice—e.g., "I am a bear. I'm big and furry and love sweet things," or "I'm a

rosebush; I am planted next to a white fence. My roots are deep." Then consider aspects of your respective personifications that reveal aspects of yourselves.

REVIEW OF COUNSELING SKILLS

A. Overview: Counseling goes beyond listening. It:
- Is a process of short duration
- Involves the exploration and discussion of values, beliefs, and attitudes
- Has self-rewarding behavior as its goal

B. Contracts: Involve a specific agreement between people.
- Consider a behavior, its antecedents, and its consequences
- Are fair
- Have clear terms
- Are stated positively
- Are systematic and consistent
- Involve at least one person besides the client
- Specify a goal that is legal, moral behavior
- Are of three types: self-management contracts, contracts for exploration, and contracts regarding counselor responsibility

C. Decision-Making Counseling Steps
1. Define the problem
2. Establish an action plan
3. Clarify values
4. Identify alternatives
5. Discover probable outcomes
6. Eliminate alternatives systematically
7. Start action

D. Confronting means that you:
- Accurately perceive discrepancies in observable behavior (verbal and nonverbal)

- Point out discrepancies in what people are saying
  or doing
- Use "I" statements rather than only "you" statements
- Use understanding responses such as paraphrasing,
  reflecting feelings, and sharing personal reactions
- Avoid evaluative or judgmental responses

E. Interpreting means that you:
- Rename or redefine feelings, thoughts, actions, or
  experiences from a new point of view
- Generate alternatives explanations for the client's
  behavior
- Have the client make interpretations on the basis of
  clues that you provide in feedback
- Are aware of the frame of reference from which you
  shape your interpretations
- Understand the client's world view
- Avoid accusations or moral judgments

4

CRISIS COUNSELING SKILLS

*by Laraine Zappert, Vincent D'Andrea,
Peter Salovey, and Sally Baird*

A *crisis* is an emotionally significant event or radical change in a person's life. The central tenet of crisis intervention theory is that some amount of distress is a normal reaction to such changes. All people experience crisis at some point in their lives.

Many crises seem to occur during periods of life change (e.g., from childhood to adolescence, or from adulthood to old age), during periods of increased external stress (e.g., in times of war, unemployment, or disaster), and during periods of decision making. Such crises are normal in human development.

It is only when the nature or magnitude of a crisis outstrips people's ability to mobilize personal, social, or environmental resources to deal with the stress involved that crisis intervention counseling becomes necessary. At that point, it is vitally important that the crisis counselor be able to provide some structure for the people in crisis, to help them gain a sense of control over their anxiety and confusion.

When people experience a crisis that is out of the realm of their experience or beyond their ordinary coping strategies, they may manifest anxiety and discomfort. Symptoms range from racing thoughts, illogical associations, and pressured speech to heightened emotionality, shortened attention span, and vexing self-doubt. In most instances, as they gain a sense of mastery over the circumstances contributing to the crisis, the accompanying confusion and anxiety clear up without intervention.

What do we mean by coping mechanisms? One of the pioneers of crisis intervention theory, Gerald Caplan (1964), identified the following characteristics of effective coping behavior:

1. Active exploration of reality issues and search for information

2. Free expression of both positive and negative feelings and tolerance of frustration

3. Active invoking of help from others

4. Breaking problems down into manageable bits and working them through one at a time

5. Awareness of the effects of stress and fatigue; pacing efforts and planning accordingly

6. Active mastery of feelings when possible and acceptance of inevitability when not

7. Flexibility and willingness to change approach in service of progress

8. Trust in oneself and others and optimism about outcome of problem(s)

As a crisis counselor, you perform the dual roles of an active listener and an active collaborator. You collaborate in the process of assessing the situation, evaluating the person's resources, suggesting options and alternatives, developing a plan of action, and following up and evaluating the outcome. All of this needs to be done within the framework of thoughtfulness and calm. As Lee Ann Hoff (1978) mentions in her book *People in Crisis*, "The necessity of thinking and planning quickly does not eliminate the necessity of thinking and planning. Action without thought is usually fruitless."

The desired outcome of successful crisis intervention is for clients to achieve a sense of active mastery over their situations. Because people are more effectively available during crises and because they are highly motivated to resolve their situations, growth and development are very much a part of resolving distress. You should align yourself with your client's strengths and resources, help identify and mobilize these assets, and ultimately contribute to the person's sense of self-esteem and efficacy.

STAGES OF CRISIS DEVELOPMENT

Caplan has outlined four phases of crisis development that trace the transformation of anxieties and distress into an acute state. They are as follows:

Phase I
A person faces an unfamiliar or unanticipated stress that causes an increase in anxiety. To deal with the stress, the person attempts to use his or her repertoire of usual coping skills.

Phase II
The person's usual problem-solving skills fail to reduce the stress, and this causes additional anxiety.

Phase III
With the increased anxiety, the person attempts new coping strategies. The options may be limited by the anxiety being experienced.

Phase IV
The person is now in a state of extreme distress. The stresses remain unabated and the person no longer feels able to cope.

Ideally, crisis intervention should occur before Phase IV so that the person does not reach a state of helplessness and despair. If the person does reach a state of acute distress, it is essential that you provide assurance that options and alternatives are still available. You also need to help the person choose those options most appropriate to his or her needs.

CRISIS INTERVENTION

The cardinal rule in helping an individual who is in a state of distress is: *You help primarily by keeping the person focused on the structuring and organizing of the problem.* This helps define possible responses or options. Second in importance are the joint effort involved in organizing the problem and the associated relationship with a person who is a model of reason, knowledge, and mastery in the acute situation.

Basic skills and rules of thumb involved in handling the situation are:

1. Circumscribing the problem and locating it in time and place. This systematically focuses attention on recent relevant history, on what has happened to the client, and on what connections might exist between events and feelings. That is, events in the here and now or in the recent past may somehow have more significance due to the person's emotional state at the time. Helping to inventory in sufficient detail the natural history of a crisis generally has a controlling effect on symptoms. By cataloguing emotional states and the effects of the disorganized behavior or thinking, you go beyond the limits of the experience into other areas where there is good functioning. In this way, the client is able to experience the limits of his or her distress and to gain some control and knowledge.

2. Participating with the client in the organization of the problem. This is extremely important, especially in the

early and more disorganized phase of the crisis. Here you are interested in what important elements of the individual's life have a bearing on the crisis. Explore the potential for change in various aspects of the situation. What can be changed, and what are some ways and techniques for effecting the desired change? Seeing how you analyze and organize the situation by surveying potential problems and various solutions, the client may begin to identify with you as a model and in this way gain greater control.

3. Limiting the duration of the encounter and focusing on growth and development. Throughout the period of problem solving, you should indicate that there will be time limits on working together. In many crisis situations in various settings, visits once or twice weekly of about one-half hour, tapering quickly in length and frequency, seem to work well. Because a high percentage of crises are resolved within 20 days, it is often not necessary to maintain continuous and prolonged contact. You should also indicate that you do not expect to intervene in the problem directly unless, in your judgment, it is necessary. In some instances, it may be advisable to refer the person to a physician if symptoms seem to warrant medical attention; or to a mental health professional, if distress is prolonged.

> *Keep the focus on expanding the client's resources by the process of taking inventory and exploring options. The possibility of growth and development is greater than the possibility of the crisis becoming a more serious one.*

4. Holding the client responsible for day-to-day living. Experience indicates that it's best for people not to remove themselves from work or other occupation during counseling—or to absent themselves only briefly. In this

way, people acknowledge their feelings, including the wish to withdraw, but remain identified with social reality, legitimize their feelings, and still act responsibly. Actively making the decision to remain socially responsible is often a powerful influence in maturation and problem solving.

5. Creating a dynamic and renegotiable plan for dealing with a crisis. Any plan that is developed jointly by you and your client should be flexible. As the crisis situation changes, new options and alternatives may become necessary.

6. Building in a follow-up component. Any intervention plan should include some follow-up provisions that allow you and your client to evaluate the success of an intervention and to make any necessary adjustments.

When the Professional Can Be of Help
In some cases, a crisis or other critical event in a person's life precipitates a more severe disorder. This is especially true when the individual's history includes a previous difficulty either in a school, work, or family context.

The most common problem to be aware of is depression—the feelings of frustration and discouragement that people usually control but that also may persist or develop into a more serious problem. Clients whose depression persists should also see a mental health professional. When an individual is persistently withdrawn, has been missing significant work or school time, or complains about a lack of energy and/or disturbances in sleep or appetite, you should direct that person to a physician or therapist.

Peer Crisis Counseling
Relatively few people will require referral to psychiatrists or other professionals. By keeping in mind the general notions and rules of thumb outlined above, and by discussing and learning

from actual situations, many peer counselors have become quite skillful in providing this kind of help.

CASE 1

A male student comes in to see you. He appears both agitated and depressed. He reports having increasing difficulty studying because he can't keep his mind on his work. His thoughts keep racing, and he is having trouble getting to sleep and staying asleep. He feels as though nothing really matters any more, and he's worried about how this feeling is affecting his schoolwork. Ever since he can remember, he has wanted to be a lawyer, but now he's not sure. When he felt this agitated in the past, he'd taken some of his mother's tranquilizers, and they helped him get some sleep. Since he doesn't have tranquilizers at school, he's starting to drink at night, but it hasn't helped his sleep much, and it leaves him with a bad hangover the next morning.

As a crisis counselor, what is your response?

Some possible approaches:

1. Get a clearer definition of the problem. Get more history regarding the onset of his agitation and depressed feelings. Explore events occurring at the time of onset. (In this case, the onset coincided with his taking the Law School Aptitude Test.)

2. Explore his feelings about significant recent events. Explore how the student feels about the prospect of law school. (He revealed that he was very ambivalent about becoming a lawyer and felt a strong desire to become a musician. He expressed concern about his parents' reaction. He reported that he felt unable to discuss this with his parents but did mention a sister.) Explore his support system. (The student accepted the counselor's suggestion that perhaps he could discuss his career

concerns with his sister and/or an advisor with whom he had a good relationship.)

3. Discuss more appropriate coping strategies to use for insomnia instead of using alcohol.
   a. Discuss the use of relaxation techniques as aids in falling asleep. Provide help in learning the skills and/or provide information on where they can be learned.
   b. If necessary, recommend that the student be evaluated by a physician for short-term sleep medication as well as a more complete diagnostic assessment of his depression.

CASE 2

You receive a phone call from a young man who is upset and concerned about the woman he dates. For the past two weeks or so, she's been very cold and aloof, refusing to answer his phone calls and spending increasing amounts of time alone. When she does speak to him, she claims she needs time to think and be by herself. He wouldn't ordinarily be worried, but in talking with her roommate, he learned that the woman was talking about killing herself. Her roommate and the man are both quite concerned, and they have come to you for help.

As a crisis counselor, what is your response?

Some possible approaches:

1. Ask the man to encourage the woman to come in and see you. While discussing this with him, allow him an opportunity to vent some of his own feelings of anxiety and concern. By providing support and structure for him, you enable him to be more in control of his own feelings and anxieties, and you indirectly help the young woman in crisis. Talking with the man also provides a chance to assess how much support he can provide in the situation and what other resources are available to the woman.

2. Mobilize the best resources for encouraging the woman to come in for a face-to-face meeting. These resources may include the young man or the roommate. It is important not to involve unnecessary people in the process.

3. If the woman will not agree to come in, she may agree to phone you, at which time you could encourage her to come in and talk about how she's been feeling. You can best assess her strengths and resources in a face-to-face meeting and determine the extent to which she is in crisis.

During your first meeting with her, you learn that she's a sophomore, pre-med, with serious plans for a career in medicine. A friend of hers had made a suicide attempt with tranquilizers while in high school. The young man she dates is leaving to begin graduate school in the East in January. She got a positive pregnancy test a week ago, and her religious beliefs oppose abortion.

What are some of your options in developing an intervention plan?

1. Provide ample opportunity for the woman to explore her feelings about her situation: the young man, the abortion, her religious concerns. While she should feel free to discuss these feelings and issues, the contact should not be open-ended. A time-limited contact will avoid obsessive machinations that may heighten her sense of helplessness. As a crisis worker, you may have to be more active than would ordinarily be appropriate in a counseling role. Structuring an interview, providing a time frame, or suggesting alternatives are all part of the repertoire of skills used in crisis intervention.

2. Assess the risk of her attempting suicide. Ask whether the woman is having feelings of wanting to harm herself. It may be necessary to do a full assessment of suicidal risk. This includes finding out whether she has a plan, assessing

its lethality, eliciting admission of prior suicide attempts, and so on, as outlined in this chapter's section on suicide.

3. Explore alternatives. Let her describe and evaluate her options as she sees them, and then perhaps suggest some she has overlooked—e.g., abortion versus adoption versus raising the child, seeking religious counseling on religious issues, and so on.

4. Provide assistance and information about the options chosen. If abortion is the option she chooses, provide help in locating a physician through referral to appropriate services. Although it is important to be helpful during a crisis, it is equally important that the client help develop a plan of action. Do not substitute "doing for" for "doing with." It is essential that a crisis intervention plan enhance the person's sense of active mastery and not foster unnecessary dependence.

5. Arrange for a follow-up visit. A good crisis intervention plan always includes some follow-up to assess and evaluate how well the plan is working and to determine if further counseling is necessary or desired.

Summary—Crisis Intervention

Crisis intervention is a specialized counseling approach used when a person's usual ways of coping with stress become ineffective or begin to break down. Counseling in crisis situations (such as suicide, death, severe loss, or trauma) calls for action on your part, without relieving the client of the responsibility of finally solving the problem. Organizing the problem into components and systematically exploring possible solutions are the key to crisis counseling. Maintaining flexibility about alternatives is important, as is a clear follow-up plan. Awareness of social resources and networks is also important in crisis intervention. In many settings, crisis counselors utilize a team approach for mobilizing resources and sharing the problem solving.

SEXUAL ASSAULT

To provide a structured response to someone who has been raped or assaulted, you need to combine peer counseling skills with specific information and sensitivity about sexual assault. In particular, it is important to understand the prevalence and range of behaviors that encompass sexual assault, to be aware of myths and misconceptions about rape, to know your own biases and the limits of your role, and to be familiar with information and referral resources in your area.

The Sexual Assault Continuum

Sexual assault encompasses a wide range of behaviors that may or may not involve physical contact but that are designed to coerce, humiliate, and control the victim through sexual means. The actions of an obscene phone caller, exhibitionist, or voyeur exist on a continuum that includes sexual harassment, fondling, incest, sodomy, and rape. Each type of assault creates an environment and tolerance for the others, either as single, isolated events or as repeated attacks that may involve several behaviors on the continuum.

This continuum is supported by a popular culture that uses sexual imagery to objectify people and fuels myths that blame the victim. For example, depicting sexual violence—in print, on the screen, in lyrics—can desensitize us to the painful reality of sexual assault. It also distances us: we think rape happens to someone else, someone unlike ourselves.

Myths

It is important to examine your own attitudes about sexual assault and to be aware of personal biases that may affect your ability to be objective when dealing with someone who has been assaulted. Widespread assumptions and attitudes are often embodied in myths such as these:

1. Sexual assault is an act of desire or passion.

2. Men are not sexually assaulted.

3. A woman cannot be raped against her will.

4. Some women are just asking for it.

5. Rapists are strangers who attack at night in desolate places.

6. A woman will lie about sexual assault because she changed her mind about having sex, or because she wants to get revenge.

In reality, perpetrators report various motives for rape; sexual gratification is not the primary one. Rape is a violent act that provides the rapist with a feeling of total control and power over another person. Other motives include expressing anger and revenge—against the victim in particular, women in general, or society at large.

Everyone—regardless of age, ethnicity, gender, income, or social standing—is vulnerable to sexual assault. The ordinariness of the circumstances under which most assaults occur contributes to people's reluctance to identify themselves as victims and to seek help. Due to the added stigma it carries for males, they may be even more reluctant than females to seek support. Dispelling myths in a sensitive manner by providing accurate information can help create a safe place for the survivor to explore feelings without fear of being blamed or shamed for the assault.

Over 80 percent of assaults are perpetrated by an acquaintance in familiar surroundings. Current estimates are that one in three women will be assaulted in her lifetime, and one in five men.

The idea that a woman can avoid rape by using sufficient willpower ignores the violent nature of this crime. So does the misconception that clothing or behavior can provoke, invite, or justify someone else's behavior. This often gives rise to the attitude that we can protect ourselves by not doing anything to "deserve" harassment, assault, or other criminal behavior.

The myth of false reporting is sometimes used as a defense in date rape cases, in which the survivor knows the perpetrator. In fact, rape is one of the most underreported crimes: recent estimates show that only 11 percent of rapes are reported to law enforcement. The percentage of documented false reports is similar to rates of false reports for other violent crimes.

These myths blame the victim and minimize the extreme fear that anyone might feel in the face of intimidation, threats, or physical force. The perpetrator is the only one responsible for any assault.

Crisis Intervention
How to respond appropriately to a client who has been sexually assaulted depends on the type of disclosure. You may want to acknowledge that this can be a difficult or embarrassing subject to talk about, and that obtaining factual information is impor-

tant to assess safety and set priorities for action. You can ask questions calmly and plainly while letting the survivor know that it is okay not to answer or to have only a sketchy idea of what happened.

Crisis intervention counseling is a priority when urgent decisions need to be made and the person's coping skills have been overwhelmed by the assault. During your initial contact with the person, you want to focus on factors of immediate importance to the client's well-being. You do not have to know all the details of the assault to understand the person's situation and to develop a plan of action.

1. When did the assault occur? Establish a time frame and sense of immediacy. The assault may have occurred today, yesterday, a week ago, a year ago, or when the client was a child.

2. Is the survivor in a safe place right now? If you are counseling someone over the phone, you need to establish safety. In 85 percent of cases, the survivor knows the attacker, at least to some degree. Threats, harassment, and even a repeated assault are distinct possibilities. if the caller does not feel safe, the first priority is to work together to come up with ideas of where he or she can go.

3. Does the person need medical attention? Aside from the need to restore a sense of physical well-being, the survivor may have external or internal injuries, may have contracted a sexually transmitted disease, or may be pregnant as a result of the rape. With the person's consent, the local law enforcement agency may request that the hospital or physician conduct a formal medical rape exam. This includes collecting evidence and reporting the findings to law enforcement officials.

4. Has the survivor reported the assault? Whether to report the assault is a major decision. You can help the person

verbalize his or her feelings about reporting. Many survivors feel that reporting the assault validates their experience in an important way, whether or not their offenders are prosecuted. Others emphatically do not want to report the incident. The peer counselor can provide valuable information and referrals about legal options, but it is important that survivors make the final choice about reporting, without feeling pressured by you.

Beyond the initial assessment, rape crisis counseling consists of helping the person regain control by collaborating to develop strategies for the immediate problems presented by the assault. Again, you need to combine information and sensitivity about sexual assault with peer counseling skills, information about resources in your area, and referrals to the helping professions as needed.

Summary—Sexual Assault

Helping someone recover from a sexual assault is intense and challenging for the peer counselor. Listening, counseling, and crisis counseling skills facilitate the client's progress from a position and identity of being a victim to being a survivor. Survivors are people who have regained their personal sense of autonomy and developed a heightened awareness and appreciation of their own unique strengths as well.

DEPRESSION

Depression has often been referred to as "the common cold of mental disorder" and, like the common cold, it occurs in varying intensities. This section discusses some of the symptoms of depression. Keep in mind, however, that "depression" can mean different things to different people. To one individual, being depressed might mean being tired and draggy; to another, it might mean unhappiness coupled with tension or fear. To speak of depression is to speak of a very idiosyncratic notion; we each conceptualize and experience depression in different ways.

This section focuses on the "normal" periods of depression experienced by all of us at different times in our lives. This "normal depressed mood" is typically experienced when we encounter losses such as the breakup of a love relationship, the death of a close relative or friend, a failure at work or school, or a sudden rejection. These events that often leave us depressed are clearly within the range of normal human experience.

This usual sort of depression is very different from the more serious mood disorders diagnosed by psychiatrists and psychologists. Mood disorders—often called major depression and bipolar disorder—are mental disorders that should be treated by professionals. As peer counselors, we are much more concerned with depression as a reaction to traumatic (but normal) life events. Individuals experiencing extreme or long-term depression are best referred to mental health professionals.

What are the common symptoms of depression? They may be divided into four groups: physical, emotional, cognitive, and behavioral. The most common physical symptoms of depression are changes in eating and sleeping patterns. Although depressed individuals occasionally eat more than they otherwise would, depression is generally characterized by a lack of interest in food and a weight loss that can sometimes be alarming. Sleeping habits may also be disrupted. The depressed person might have difficulty falling asleep, sleep irregularly, awaken early in the morning, or occasionally not be able to get out of bed at all. Fatigue is the most common complaint of depressed individuals. Other physical symptoms that can accompany depression include constipation, frequent urination, loss of interest in sex, dizziness, and headaches.

The emotional, or *affective*, symptoms of depression are also easily recognized. Depressed people feel helpless, hopeless, and generally unhappy. They may also feel worthless, guilty, lonely, ashamed, or useless. Sadness, however, is the most common affective state and is usually accompanied by crying. The depressed person's day is characterized by these feelings of sadness, which are usually most intense in the morning hours. Some depressed individuals also feel anxious or agitated; this is, in fact, quite common. Also, depressed people often experience little gratification. Work, hobbies, recreational activities, and close friends no longer seem exciting or interesting.

Thoughts that accompany depression are particularly apparent to the peer counselor, because they are generally quite evident in the depressed person's conversation. The depressed person often has a very negative self-image, considering him- or herself inadequate or incompetent. Past failures or disappointments may be exaggerated and thought of as highly significant. These thoughts are often accompanied by self-blame and guilt for one's troubles, and for the problems of others, for which the depressed person mistakenly takes responsibility. Finally, the depressed person thinks about the future with great pessimism. The smallest obstacles seem like great hurdles; potential gains seem like dreaded failures.

Depression is associated with some obvious changes in behavior. Depressed persons are often very passive, having little motivation to initiate any kind of activity. In severe cases, routine tasks such as grooming or changing clothes are difficult to initiate. Depressed individuals also can suffer from psychomotor retardation and lethargy. They walk and speak slowly and react to stimuli after long delays. Depressed people are slow to initiate physical and mental activity; they seem to move slowly and avoid problem-solving tasks. This avoidance seems to result from acute indecisiveness. Decisions seem overwhelming; outcomes appear frightening.

EXAMPLE

Lately, Tomas hasn't had much of an appetite. He has turned down a couple of good offers to go out for food and fun with friends, saying that he has a lot of work. He acknowledges to himself that he feels pressured and unsociable. Without intending to, it seems he is hiding his true feelings so as not to "bother" his friends. When he sits down to work, he is unable to concentrate for more than a few minutes. He feels bored, and he wishes his life were more interesting. He also wishes that people would drop by to say hello more often. He wonders what it is about him that puts people off. He's been doing a lot of introspection during the last several days, and it makes him sleepy. He takes naps instead of working—another recent habit.

Tomas's mother is in a dilemma. She is agonizing over whether to divorce his father. The lines of communication between her and her husband have been rapidly closing up. She also doesn't like the fact that her husband pushes Tomas so hard about succeeding in life. Tomas is the only one she can talk to; he seems to be both understanding and objective.

As a peer counselor, how can you best deal with depressed clients?

1. Discover more precisely what an individual means when he or she says, "I'm depressed." As mentioned, different people experience depression differently. Is the person anxious? Immobile? Feeling guilty? Fatigued? Cynical? Helpless? What specific thoughts, feelings, and behaviors does this person label as "being depressed"? It is important to focus on *specific problems*. If the person says "I'm so depressed," narrow down what is wrong, using questions such as: "What specifically is bothering you?"

2. Explore events in the depressed person's life that are controllable (such as what to do each day) rather than events that he or she cannot control (such as ending world hunger single-handedly).

3. Concentrate on small steps that the individual can actually take. Motivating the person to do small tasks—

writing a letter, doing the laundry, or going to the supermarket—can sometimes help the person begin to regain a sense of personal worth and efficacy.

4. Use a step-by-step approach to motivate the client to initiate larger tasks. Break complicated tasks, such as finding a job or changing living situations, into small subtasks, and ask how he or she would go about starting some of these smaller tasks.

5. Another approach that can motivate depressed individuals is behavioral contracting (see chapter 3). Make an agreement that the person will accomplish certain tasks, and encourage the use of self-reward for completing the task. For example, "Would you agree to do X and call me when you do it?" Try to find what kinds of things the person enjoys doing, and pair them with the accomplishment of more mundane, yet important, tasks. It is very important that you give your client much positive feedback for even the smallest steps in the right direction.

Using these principles as a starting point, let's imagine how a counseling session with Tomas, the person in the scenario, might proceed.

Tomas has decided to speak with apeer counselor, so he walks over to the counseling center.

Tomas: *Do you have a few minutes? I'd like to talk.*

You: *Sure. What's on your mind?*

Tomas: *Well, I'm not able to concentrate on my work, and I don't seem to care about much at all.*

You: *So, you're having trouble concentrating and caring. And how are you feeling?*

Tomas: *I feel sort of numb and a little depressed.*

You: *Numb and depressed . . ... What do you mean by depressed?*

Tomas: *I think I should be enjoying myself, but I can't generate any interest in having fun.*

You: *And how do you feel about that?*

Tomas: *Like everything is kind of futile and not worth the hassle of working out.*

You should continue to elicit feelings from Tomas. He says he's depressed, but remember: for each person, depression is a unique set of thoughts, feelings and behaviors. After talking about Tomas's feelings some, try to focus on what *specifically* is bothering him.

You: *So everything seems futile. What do you mean by "everything"?*

Tomas: *My friends want me to have a good time with them, but I don't think it'll help me feel any better. I used to like my classes, but school is seeming more and more artificial and pointless. I can't even return my overdue library books . . . just too much hassle.*

You: *Your friends are trying to cheer you up?*

Tomas: *Yes, but they don't know how depressed I really am, and I don't think they'll be able to.*

You: *You mentioned that school seemed "artificial." Could you say more about that?*

Tomas: *It seems that the more intense classes get, the less I can see their relation to the real world.*

You: *I hear what you're saying, and we will talk about it some more. The intensity of school life can be very frustrating. What else, outside of school, is going on in your life?*

Tomas: *I feel sort of stuck between my parents. They aren't talking to each other—they say it all to me. My mom thinks that my dad doesn't care about her, and it's tearing him up, but he can't tell her. He's sort of like me . . . very sensitive, but he makes people think he's always objective and logical. I just try to listen to them both because I know they need a sounding board—and I'm it.*

So, Tomas is feeling depressed, and his depression revolves around school and a pending crisis at home that is being dumped on him. At this point, you should continue to explore both of these issues with him: his parents and school. When you sense he has been able to disclose his thoughts and feelings fully, try to move the conversation toward those things that still give him pleasure. What could he be doing to make himself feel better and thus be better able to cope with his parents and with his schoolwork?

You: *You've made things pretty clear for me, Tomas. I understand why you are feeling depressed. What kinds of things do you still enjoy doing?*

Tomas: *When I'm not sleeping, I've been doing a lot of read-ing. I'm afraid I'm sort of retreating that way, though. That bothers me.*

You: *How does it bother you?*

Tomas: *It seems like I should be doing something more constructive.*

You: *What kinds of things would be more constructive?*

Tomas: *Organizing my studies or doing my laundry or practicing the violin or something.*

You: *Okay, so those would be constructive things to do . . . but would they make you feel better?*

Tomas: *I've wanted to just go out and play on these nice days, shoot some baskets or throw a Frisbee. But when I've got that kind of energy, I feel I ought to study, so I just stay inside.*

At this point, you and Tomas should discuss some specific ways in which he can deal with his parents. What could he tell them? How should he respond to their demands without feeling guilty? How can he help them? Where should he draw the line? Also, you may want to discuss his frustrations about school. What could he be doing to make his school experience more meaningful?

Finally, it is time to wrap things up for this session. He feels like he got a lot off his chest and would like to talk some more next week. It is probably a good idea to end on a positive note with some kind of contract specifying behaviors he should focus on in the coming week.

Tomas: *I'm glad you were so easy to talk to. I feel a lot better. Can I stop by again in a few days to let you know how I'm feeling?*

You: *Okay I agree to talk in a few days. . . . In the meantime, would you be willing to do a few things?*

Tomas: *Like what?*

You: *Well, how about getting a few of those little things done that have been on your mind?*

Tomas: *Like my laundry, and returning those books to the library? Okay. Sounds pretty easy right now.*

You: *Sounds great to me. And when you finish that, why don't you go out and shoot some hoops for an hour or two, and then I'll see you again on Friday. Okay with you?*

Tomas: *Great. It'll sure feel good to clear up some of these hassles and get some exercise.*

You: *Okay. See you Friday!*

Tomas: *Bye.*

This entire process should take about an hour. Don't rush things—they will unfold with only a little prompting. In this session, you have:

Elicited Tomas's feelings

Gotten a handle on how he feels when he says he's depressed

Discovered some causes for his depression

Discussed some strategies by which he can deal with his problems

Motivated him to make some small steps toward resuming his "normal" lifestyle

Ended on a positive note. Tomas feels better and the two of you have reached an agreement whereby he will start getting his life back together, reward himself with a pleasurable activity, and talk to you again in a few days.

This supportive, problem-solving approach is suitable with many people who manifest depressed feelings and thinking. If Tomas reported continued inability to concentrate, if he felt increasingly hopeless and guilty, if he were waking up early and unable to get back to sleep, a consultation would be in order. In particular, if he began to have thoughts of harming himself in some way, a no-suicide contract would be called for, as well as discussion with a referral to a professional. This issue is discussed in the following section on suicide.

Summary—Depression

- An approach based on good listening and supportive problem-solving, and which focuses on feelings and behavior change, can be very helpful to many persons experiencing depression.

- Eliciting accurate and complete information is important.

- Familiarity with the varied expressions of depression is helpful in estimating the seriousness of the problem.

SUICIDE

Although suicide calls to peer counselors are relatively uncommon compared to other types of counseling calls, suicide is not an infrequent occurrence. About 30,000 suicides are reported each year in this country with possibly an additional 50,000 unreported or misclassified.* In the entire population of the United States, suicide is the eighth most frequent cause of death. Among 15- to 19-year-olds, it is the *third* leading cause of death; and among college students, it is second only to automobile accidents.

---

*Some automobile accidents, plane colisions, drownings, and deaths of the terminally ill are actually suicides.

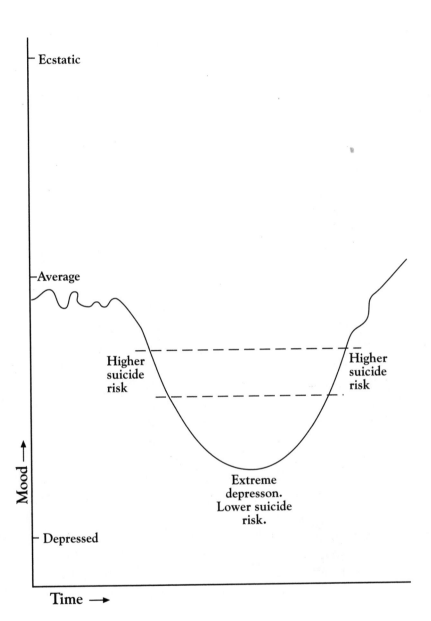

Fifteen out of every 100,000 students kill themselves each year.* And since there are about ten times as many suicide attempts as completed suicides, experts estimate that in the United States 5 million people are alive today who have attempted suicide.

Certain segments of the population seem particularly suicide-prone. Divorced and widowed men and women have particularly high rates of suicide. Although women are three times more likely to attempt suicide than men, men succeed in killing themselves three times more often than women. Typically, suicide attempters are young (ages 20 to 30) females, while committers are older (over 40) males. These sex differences are probably due to the different methods that men and women use in attempting suicide. While men often use guns or jump off buildings, women typically overdose with pills or cut their wrists. As it takes longer to die from taking a drug overdose or slashing one's wrists than from shooting oneself or jumping from a building, women who attempt suicide are often discovered still alive and rushed to hospitals.

Some individuals, particularly adolescents, commit suicide to punish others. Often they are trying to manipulate others (usually parents) into feeling guilty and inadequate. This motive for suicide is called the "ultimate revenge." Some individuals kill themselves because of extreme anger. Occasionally, when people feel they have been abused by a loved one, they want to kill that person. At times, they direct this "murder" impulse toward themselves. A third, although rare, cause of suicide is psychotic behavior, such as trying to fly out of a window. A fourth reason that some people commit suicide is a desire to determine their own destiny. For example, a terminally ill patient may save her sleeping pills by hiding them under her mattress. Then, after several weeks, she takes them all at once, reasoning that she doesn't want to lie around waiting for a

*The rate of suicide among nonstudents of the same age is lower: 10 per 100,000.

painful death from cancer. Another motive for suicide is the "trial by ordeal." In this instance, individuals are "testing fate," figuring that if they are supposed to live, they'll just wake up; if they're not supposed to live, they won't.

The most common motive for suicide, however, is a complete absence of other alternatives, and this is the most useful way for peer counselors to conceptualize suicide. An individual cannot imagine any other way to avoid his or her "painful" life, and believes that it is impossible to change. The person feels out of options, hopeless, and helpless.

Suicide is often the result of severe or prolonged depression. Of course, most depressed individuals do not try to kill themselves, and not all victims of suicide are depressed before killing themselves. In fact, very severely depressed individuals often do not have the energy or motivation to take their own lives. A person who is somewhat depressed and sinking rapidly is most vulnerable to suicide. The person in the depths of depression generally is not.

Suicide Facts

Expected incidence: 10/100,000 population ages 18 to 25
Student incidence: 15/100,000 student population

In the 15- to 19-year-old age group, suicide ranks as the third most frequent cause of death (after automobile accidents and cancer).

In the U.S. population, suicide is the eighth most frequent cause of death. About 30,000 Americans commit suicide each year, with estimates ranging to 50,000 per year.

Profiles

	Attempters	Committers
Sex	Female (F:M = 3:1)	Male ("older, white, unemployed male in poor health, divorced and living alone") (M:F = 3:1)
Age	20-30	40+
Method	Barbiturates	Gunshot
Reason	Marital problems, depression	Health, marital problems, depression, psychosis, alcoholism

Twelve percent of all suicide attempts are by adolescents. Ninety percent of these attempts are by females.

The following are typical indicators that a person may be considering suicide:

- Loss
- Social isolation
- Suicidal act as communication
- No other options perceived
- Poor interpersonal capacities
- Marital isolation
- Disturbed communication
- Help rejection

Sources: U.S. Department of Health and Human Services, National Center for Health Statistics (1991). *Health United States 1990.* Washington: U.S. Government Printing Office.
McIntire, M. S. & Angle, C. R. (1980). *Suicide attempts in children and youth.* New York: Harper & Row, pp. 1-13.

Counseling the Suicidal Person

For most peer counselors, suicide counseling occurs on the telephone rather than face to face. The procedure described in this chapter was specifically designed for telephone counseling, and it might be useful to keep a copy of the checklist near your hotline for easy reference. However, you can also use the procedure for face-to-face interaction. (Another exercise in using these steps is to review Appendix D, which is a transcript of telephone counseling with a suicidal man.)

Step 1: Define the Problem

If you suspect that the person you are talking to may be thinking of suicide, you should frankly ask whether he or she is considering suicide as an option. Counselors are often afraid to ask this question. They worry that they might be putting ideas into their clients' heads. Nonsense! No one will ever answer the question with, "No, I wasn't considering suicide. But that's a good idea, I think I will kill myself. Thanks."

An individual who is considering suicide will appreciate your frank discussion of the topic. If the person is not considering suicide, you can simply continue with your usual counseling strategies.

Often clients will give you clues that they are seriously considering suicide. If you detect any of these clues, ask, "Is suicide an option that you are considering?" For instance, suicide may be a consideration if the person:

Has recently made out a will
Has recently bought a gun
Has shipped the kids off to a relative for the weekend
Has put the dog in a kennel
Has written several close, personal letters to old friends and
   relatives

Remember, if suicide seems at all possible, ASK!

One thing to keep in mind is that at least part of the person does not want to die. He or she probably has not called you to say good-bye, but rather is reaching out, hoping to find an alternative.

Step 2: Assess Lethality

It is very important that you discover how close the person actually is to killing him- or herself. If the person has already taken pills or slashed wrists, tracing the call may take too long. Instead, do what you can to find out the person's location and then call the police or paramedics.

If the person has not actually harmed him- or herself (and this is generally the case), you must find out two things: (1) what is currently going on in the person's life, and (2) how much thought has he or she given to suicide—i.e., does he or she have a plan, an easily available means, etc.? Try to find out if the person has recently undergone any major changes or had any particularly stressful experiences. For example, has a close friend or relative died recently? Is the person suffering from a painful physical illness? Has the person recently lost a job or been under considerable financial stress? Has the person recently moved to a new place?

It is also useful to find out the person's "suicidal history." Is suicide something he or she frequently thinks about? Has the person attempted suicide before? This last question is very important. Repeated attempters have the highest suicide rate of all: eight or nine out of ten ultimately kill themselves.

Finally, it is very important to find out how real the act of suicide is. How does this individual plan to kill him- or herself? Where are the pills (or gun, or whatever)? Is the person under the influence of drugs or alcohol? Is he or she alone? Try to get this information as quickly as possible. But it is important not to make the person feel as if he or she is getting the third degree. Continue to use your counseling skills: show accurate empathy, paraphrase accurately, and reflect feelings.

Step 3: Get Information and Reduce Lethality

It is usually not difficult to find out the first name of your client. However, other pieces of personal information may not come as easily. If possible, get the person's phone number. Explain that you are not sending out the police (assuming that the person has not harmed him- or herself) but that you want the phone number for your own use, so that you can call back if you don't hear from the caller after an agreed-upon period of time.

It is important to determine if the person is alone or if there is anyone else who could be trusted. Is the caller seeing a therapist? Are there any close friends or relatives nearby? Neighbors? Coworkers? Try to determine what kind of support system exists for your client.

Finally, try to convince the person (again using counseling skills) to reduce the lethality of the situation—that is, to flush the pills down the toilet, unload the gun, or give the razor to a neighbor.

Step 4: Build Trust and Rapport

Before alternatives and solutions can be considered, you must allow the suicidal person to vent any pent-up feelings and thoughts. You might be the first human contact for this person in several days, so it is important not to rush. Rather, use your counseling skills—ask open questions, paraphrase, work with feelings—to try to hear and understand what the person is saying. Validate his or her pain; recognize that life might be rough. Show caring and concern; explain that you really are concerned that the person might hurt him- or herself. This is no time to understate the client's feelings. It is important to paraphrase accurately. For example, if someone says, "I'm so confused and scared, I want to end it all," don't just say, "So things are a little tough right now." Remember, accurate empathy is very important.

If the person is crying uncontrollably, just listen for a while. Reassure the caller that it's okay to cry, that you won't hang up, that it's all right to get some of the feelings out. If the person can't stop crying and is feeling out of control, help him or her stop—be firm and supportive. Say, "Take it easy, it's difficult for me to hear you. I can't understand you. Let's slow down for a minute." Be assertive, yet gentle. Continue to let the person talk about how he or she is feeling.

Step 5: Deal with the Problem and Generate Alternatives
After the person has talked about bad feelings for a while, it is important to turn the conversation gently toward more positive things. Appeal to the side of the person that wants to continue to live. First, offer support and encouragement by helping the person reinterpret the situation in a positive manner—talk about his or her courage in calling and being willing to share such deep feelings with you. Then try to get a handle on the situation: try to find out how long this individual has been considering suicide and what precipitated the feelings of wanting to die. Talk about these thoughts as long as the person wishes, but try to stay with the situation as it exists here and now.

Next, discuss the options or alternatives this person might have. How has he or she handled similar situations in the past? What is needed to develop or build a support system? Who can the person call for support and comfort? Discuss what can be done to change the current situation; find out what the caller is doing or can do to take care of him- or herself. Try to encourage the person to continue daily activities and to take things slowly, one step at a time.

Step 6: Terminate the Session
This is the most important part of suicide counseling: negotiating a no-suicide contract and convincing the person to obtain some kind of follow-up help.

The no-suicide contract is an explicit agreement between you and a suicidal person that he or she will not hurt himself or herself before speaking with you or another professional. Have the person actually say, "I will not kill myself without talking to you first." Then try to establish a time frame for the contract—have the person agree to call you back to check in after a specific interval of time, such as 24 hours.* Sometimes it is necessary to get a contract for just an hour or two and then have the person call back (Drye et al., 1973).

After making a no-suicide contract, refer the person to professional help. Ask the person to call and tell you after contacting that referral. Reinforce the referral—encourage the person to complain (if things aren't going well) directly to the therapist.

Finally, if your support is not accepted and the person refuses to make a no-suicide contract, *don't hang up*. Buy time; talk some more. Go back to step 4 and move through the procedure again. If, as rarely happens, the person refuses all help and actually decides to kill him- or herself, you can try deterring the person with guilt by saying things such as:

"You're copping out; you're taking the easy way out."

"How will your children feel knowing that Mommy [Daddy] killed herself [himself]? Your children will live a life of guilt and pain. Who will raise them?"

"I know you could kill yourself. But give yourself one last chance. It's your life!"

Let us warn you: don't use these obvious manipulations unless you are convinced that there is no other way to get the person to save his or her life.

After dealing with a suicide call, even if the outcome is good, *you* might consider talking to another counselor or professional about your feelings. If you use the procedure outlined above, you will know that you've done everything you could to prevent a suicide. But remember, it is also important to take

---

*If you did get the person's phone number and then don't get a call at the agreed time, you should not hesitate to call him or her.

care of yourself; if you are feeling at all guilty, unsettled, manipulated, or anxious, talk to someone about it. Support for suicide
counselors is very important. Don't let your feelings and
thoughts about suicide end when you hang up the phone; share
them with others.

Suicide Checklist
This checklist reviews the preceding section.

1. Define the problem. Remember, if at least a part of the
   person didn't want help, he or she wouldn't call.
   A. A suicide call is a "cry for help" from the part of the
      person that wants to live. This part is fighting other
      parts that want to die, give up, avoid pain.
   B. Possible motives for suicide vary.
      1) Manipulation—the ultimate revenge
      2) Anger—misdirected murder (particularly after abuse
         from a loved one)
      3) Psychosis—distorted reality
      4) Self-determination—"I'm not going to wait for a
         painful death"
      5) Trial by ordeal—"If I'm supposed to live, I'll just
         wake up"
      6) Limited alternatives—the caller does not know how
         else to avoid a painful life and does not believe it's
         possible to change those life circumstances.

2. Assess lethality.
   A. Identify recent major changes and/or stresses in the
      person's life, which increase the likelihood of suicide.
      1) Loss of loved one (death, divorce, separation)
      2) Physical illness (particularly a fatal one)
      3) Loss of job (fired, retired)
      4) Financial stress
      5) Moved to new place (house, town, etc.)
      6) No support systems: family, friends who listen
      7) Hopelessness

B. Determine how much thought the person has given to a suicide attempt and whether his or her immediate environment contains specific tools of suicide.
1) Is thinking about suicide—especially impulsively?
2) Has attempted suicide previously?
3) Has a plan (is giving away possessions, etc.)?
4) Has the means available (knows where to get pills, gun, etc.)?
5) Is intoxicated with drugs or alcohol?
6) Is alone and has the means immediately available?
7) What are the speed and reversibility of method?

3. Get information in a natural way (in the course of conversation, not in a forced way) and reduce lethality.
A. Anyone else there?
B. Therapist, relatives, friends (support system) in the area?
C. Reduce lethality (have caller get rid of pills, gun, etc.)
D. First name? (Particularly important with drug overdose)
E. Phone number?
F. Full name?
G. Address?

4. Build trust and rapport, and encourage the caller to vent emotions.
A. Support the person within limits:
1) *Yelling, screaming, ranting, raving*—Say in an assertive, supportive manner: "Take it easy. It's difficult for me to hear you. I can't understand you. Let's slow down now."
2) *Crying, sobbing*—Gently say, "I'm listening to you. It's okay. I won't go away. Go ahead and take some time to cry—get some of it out."
3) *Uncontrollable crying, loss of control*—Help the caller stop and regain self-control. (See the preceding Step 4A1.)

4) *Anger*—The person is not angry at you! Don't take it personally: "I'm trying to listen, but it's hard when you yell at me. I know you're angry, and you have a right to be. But I want to hear you, and it's hard when you direct your anger at me."

B. Listen, explore, and acknowledge.

1) Build rapport. Facilitate the venting of feelings. Hear and understand what the person is saying.

2) Validate. Recognize that the person's hurt and pain are real. "Yes, it is painful and rough . . . right now."

3) Clarify the state of depression. Ask the person directly if suicide is one of the alternatives that he or she is thinking about.

5. Deal with the problem and generate alternatives.

A. Reinforce the person for having the courage to call.

B. Reinterpret the situation in a positive manner.

C. Reinterpret the caller's self-image as having worth. "To be in this much pain, you must feel deeply." "People who allow themselves to feel that deeply are very special, indeed!"

D. "What precipitated these feelings of wanting to kill yourself?"

E. "How long has this situation existed?"

F. "What kinds of things have you tried or thought of?"

G. "What does this situation or feeling mean?"

H. "How have you [your friends] handled similar situations in the past?"

I. "How can you build a support system?"

1) "Who can help you through this time? [People can't help if they don't know.]"

2) "If not family or friends—or partial support from them—then how about a counselor, agency, or self-help group?" (e.g., AA, Suiciders Anonymous)

J. "How can you change your situation and/or feeling now?"

6. Terminate the session. Make a no-suicide contract and refer the caller to professional help.

A. If support is accepted, develop a plan of action.

1) Contract: a promise not to harm self, and to remove suicidal means to a "safer place."

2) Appointment with a therapist, agency, etc.

3) Calling a friend or relative to come spend the night.

4) A few days' rest in the hospital (if necessary).

5) Contact the next day, after the plan has been going, to make sure that the person's support system has begun to form. At that time, make it clear that you are glad that the caller is taking care of him- or herself, and that you could help in this crisis. Repeat that the hotline is available on a 24-hour basis, as needed.

B. If support is not accepted:

1) Buy time for the person. Keep talking.

2) If the person has harmed him- or herself, CALL THE POLICE.

C. Let's say all supportive efforts fail. You have heard and understood what the person is trying to say, you have established that you are interested and genuinely concerned, and you have taken the time to form a positive relationship. If none of this works, try to dissuade the person as supportively, positively, and truthfully as possible:

1) Suggest that the person is copping out—taking the easy way out.

2) Say, "Your children will grow up with guilt and pain. And who will raise them?"

3) Say, "You're not being fair to yourself. You could live in this world and experience some fun and happiness. Tomorrow usually feels better. Try it. you can kill yourself another time."

4) Existential reality: "You can kill yourself. BUT your life doesn't have to be absurd, unfair, painful. You're

bright and sensitive, and have more strength and courage than you give yourself credit for. With some help, you can learn better how to deal with life."

Exercise 1. Test Your Suicide I.Q.

TRUE or FALSE:

1. People who attempt suicide rarely talk about it.

2. Suicidal tendencies are not inherited.

3. People who attempt suicide never *really* want to die.

4. All people who attempt suicide are psychotic.

5. If a person seems calm after they talk about suicide, they are over the crisis.

6. More men than women complete suicide.

7. Most people leave notes of intent or cause.

8. Suicide is usually done for revenge against another person.

9. Once truly suicidal, people will be suicidal the rest of their lives.

10. All of the people in this room are capable of being suicidal if they are pushed far enough.

Exercise 2

Students should consider the following statements. Discussion should be held in class or in small groups.

If you were in these situations, would you consider ending your life?

Answers to Exercise 1. 1:F. 2:T. 3:F. 4:F. 5:F. 6:T. 7:T. 8:F. 9:F. 10:T.

- Incurably ill, middle income, and facing a long, painful death
- Just had all your loved ones die in an auto accident
- Broke up with your spouse through divorce
- Find no meaning to your life

EXERCISE 3

If a videotaped suicide crisis call is available, review it in class. As an outline for the viewing and discussion, use the assessment scheme suggested in this chapter. If no tape is available, review and discuss Appendix D.

REVIEW OF CRISIS COUNSELING SKILLS

A. Crisis Counseling
  1. Crises are normal reactions to sudden changes or unanticipated, stressful events.
  2. In crisis, a person's usual coping behavior is strained or begins to break down.
  3. As the counselor, you are an active listener and collaborator, encouraging your client to:
     a. Assess the situation, setting it in context
     b. Evaluate resources
     c. Explore options and additional resources
     d. Make a joint effort with you in organizing the problem and systematically exploring possible responses or options
  4. Follow-up provisions allow you to evaluate interventions.
  5. You are alert to unusual anxiety, depression, or disorganization in your client.

B. Depression
  1. Symptoms
     a. Physical—changes in eating and sleeping patterns, fatigue, constipation, frequent urination, no interest in sex, dizziness, headaches

     b. Emotional—sadness, helplessness, hopelessness, crying, melancholia, anxiety (occasionally), guilt

     c. Cognitive—negative view of self, others, and the future; self-blame, pessimism

     d. Behavioral—passiveness, lack of motivation, no initiation of activities, psychomotor retardation and lethargy

  2. Counseling

     a. Focus on specific problems rather than generalized sadness.

     b. Explore events that are "controllable" by the client.

     c. Initiate small tasks, small steps the person can actually take.

     d. Initiate larger tasks by breaking them down into smaller subtasks.

     e. Use behavioral contracting.

C. Suicide

  1. Define the problem—Is there a motive for suicide? Is suicide an option being considered?

  2. Assess lethality—Is a method easily available? What method? Has there been much "suicide planning"? Has the person experienced recent losses or traumas? Does the person have a suicidal history?

  3. Get more information, reduce lethality—Ask about the caller's name and phone number, support systems; have the person remove weapon, pills, etc. from home.

  4. Build trust, help the person vent emotions—Validate client's negative feelings, reflect the feelings, show accurate empathy.

  5. Deal with the problem, generate alternatives—Reinforce and reinterpret the situation positively, and help client to realize that alternatives are available.

  6. Terminate session—Establish no-suicide contract, refer the person for counseling, and follow up.

PART II

ETHICS

5

Ethical Considerations in Peer Counseling

by Thom Cleland

What is help? Certainly it is more than altruism. In Steinbeck's Sweet Thursday, *Hazel, in his effort to help a wounded gull, chases it into the sea to drown.*

—Joann Chenault

This chapter is not intended to be a comprehensive synthesis or even a review of different ethical model systems. Hopefully, however, it will serve as an introduction to the breadth, variety, and vigor of ethical thought. With these building blocks, it may help establish an inclusive, functional ethical structure for the peer counseling paraprofession.

In this spirit, this chapter synthesizes an ethical schema structured around a system of rules appropriate to professional and paraprofessional organizations yet devoted to the context-awareness and focus on care and responsibility that are central to counseling. Formal, abstract ethical principles and codes provide for a degree of desirable universality within a professional or paraprofessional community. Such rules are important guides for both training and practice. However, as a peer counselor, you must remember that your work is fundamentally concrete and contextual: real people, real feelings, real lives will be affected by your ethical decisions. There is no substitute for an individual, personal commitment to principled action. Your understanding and practice of ethical behavior must become as much a part of you as the caring that attracted you to peer counseling in the first place.

INTRODUCTION

What are ethics? This is the first question in any discourse on ethics or morality, whether personal or professional. It is important to recognize at the outset that standards of ethics and morality are by no means universal. In the face of abundant diversity, maintaining ethical behavior is an ongoing, interactive process. Different communities—including professional communities as well as those based on culture, gender, lifestyle, or other commonalities—have developed ethics for themselves in an effort to ensure the community's smooth functioning. These ethics also promote harmony and consistency in the actions and responses of individuals within those communities. In general, as Robert Brown (1985) notes, "appropriate ethical behavior is often determined by relating it to what is thought to be the common good, which is usually influenced by community norms."* However, as Brown also notes, different communities may profess different understandings of ethical behavior, such that "when the norms of . . . different communities conflict, individuals are confronted with a dilemma" (p. 70).

Professional and paraprofessional institutions often establish formal codes of ethics that serve to guide the behaviors of individual community members. Such codes also serve to

---

*Ethical standards also can vary with time. As an example, Alves (1959, p. 112) notes that early in the development of social case work in the United States, "It was the caseworker's opinion of what was in the best interest of the client, rather than the client's, which was the criterion. Almost every statement of ethical standards or code of ethics has some such statement as 'Case records should be open to workers of agencies of similar standing who may be interested in the case.' . . . Never is mention found of an obligation of seeking client's consent" [sic].

help define the nature of the profession itself, and to provide a degree of consistency in the behavior of member professionals. Indeed, Winston and Dagley (1985, p. 49) have noted that "the existence of an enforceable code of ethics is at the very core of what it means to be a [para]profession." Fuqua and Newman (1989, p. 92) further declare that "any profession has a fundamental responsibility for establishing ethical standards for practice and for monitoring adherence to those standards." By their very nature, such codes have tended to develop from philosophical systems that describe ethical behavior in terms of a set of abstract principles, or rules. One obvious example of such an ethical rule is the Hippocratic admonition to the medical profession: "Above all, do no harm."

Other ethical theories concern themselves less with systems of abstract rules for behavior and focus more on concrete judgments of choices and consequences. For example, Carol Gilligan (1982) has described an "ethic of care." This theory was drawn from her studies of moral thought and choices among women, as an alternative to the rules-based "ethic of justice" derived from the largely male-dominated European tradition. Patricia Hill Collins (1989) has outlined ethics of care and personal accountability derived from a fundamentally Afrocentric epistemology. Collins' work both presents a strong challenge to European (and particularly masculine) understandings of appropriate and moral behavior and has particularly significant implications for the paraprofessional ethics of peer counseling. Still other communities—ethnic, professional, cultural, philosophical—also have their own mores and ethical constructs to contribute to any normative discourse on moral behavior.

Differences in how people perceive and enact moral behavior provide a special challenge for ethics in peer counseling. It is part of our mandate to be accessible to any potential client, regardless of what communities he may participate in or what values she may hold. It is well established that a peer counselor must be sensitive to the client's particular situation and needs. This understanding is absolutely fundamental to a paraprofessional ethic that is truly accessible and pluralistic. Such an ethic must not base itself so heavily on the mores of one community that it marginalizes and thus inadvertently excludes members of other communities. The role of paraprofessional ethics in a peer counseling relationship subsumes not only the peer counselor's treatment of the client, but also the approach taken in concert with the client to address that person's problems. The two are intertwined.

This chapter therefore frames ethical considerations for peer counseling within a model developed by Karen Kitchener (1985). This three-tiered model of ethical decision making is powerful both in its specificity and its flexibility. It is suitable for the construction of formal ethical codes supported by five core principles, and yet meaningfully incorporates and expresses the moral contributions of disparate ethical theories. This is particularly true for those derived from various gender and cultural perspectives.

The most specific of the three levels of Kitchener's model is that of the ethical code, or rules. As noted, formal ethical codes are appropriate to professional organizations and often serve to define the scope of the profession itself as well as appropriate behavior for members. A code of ethics for a peer counseling center is an essential part of both training and practice. However, no single code of ethics, however profound, is capable of unambiguously addressing all of the wide variety of problems, situational complexities, and personal principles that different clients will bring you. Rather than imposing a litany of formal rules which real-world peer counselors must occasionally bend in order to help clients successfully, the healthy ethical code supports itself on a deeper framework. That deeper framework allows people to recognize that these exceptional cases are an intrinsic part of acting ethically, and not an "understandable deviation" from the code. In short, a code must help guide and educate you as a peer counselor without detracting from your effectiveness in what is fundamentally an intensely personal process.

Ethical principles, the next level, are the general framework upon which ethical codes are built. They both provide philosophical justification for ethical rules and afford ethical guidance whenever specific written codes are ambiguous or silent. Kitchener elaborates on five principles: respect for autonomy, nonmaleficence (doing no harm), beneficence (benefiting others), justice, and fidelity. Exactly how these principles should be considered and weighed against one another in a given situation is occasionally a dilemma, however. It is in these cases that the third level, ethical theory, must be considered.

Ethical theory constitutes the overarching principles of what it means to act morally, and a comprehensive discussion is beyond the scope of this chapter. Suffice it to say that ethical theories as illustrated by Gilligan (1982), Collins (1985), and Abelson and Nielson (1967) all converge in the desire to understand and thus promote moral behavior. In the context of peer counseling, ethical theory informs how we apply Kitchener's five principles, particularly in situations when they conflict.

As a peer counselor, you need to recognize that people can legitimately differ in their sense of ethical behavior. How, then, should you employ your own ethic in the context presented by a given client? In particular, a respect for potential differences in moral understanding is essential for effective cross-ethnic and cross-gender peer counseling. At a minimum, you must remain respectful of the different weightings of principles that individual clients may conduct.

In short, paraprofessional ethics are much more than a list of rules, particularly in the helping professions. Ethics is a growing, dynamic, and conflict-laden body of thought, enriched by the multitude of voices and experiences that underlie it. To be ethical is a highly demanding and complex task, yet it is nearly synonymous with the practice of peer counseling. In a sense, ethics are central being able to care successfully. To deal productively with your clients' dilemmas, you must have an understanding, even a developed intuition, of paraprofessional ethics.

ETHICAL THEORY

As noted, comprehensive discussion of ethical theories and their applicability to the needs of peer counselors and clients is beyond the scope of this chapter. However, brief treatment of a few selected topics follows, to highlight some elements of ethical fundamentals that are particularly relevant to the needs of peer counselors and the helping professions. For a greater understanding of the breadth and scope of ethical considerations in a complex, multicultural, and evolving world, I unambiguously encourage you to consult the literature. Professional ethics, gender and ethnic studies, and the counseling and student-services literature are all especially applicable. Even more important, of course, are the personal insight and experience you can gain directly only by interacting with other people.

Power

It is a foundation of the peer counseling paraprofession that clients are equals—not patients—and that the peer counselor bears no personal responsibility for their conduct or betterment. Rather, you serve as a caregiver and resource to help your clients sort out their own feelings and determine their own solutions to the problems facing them.

While these principled limitations on your role as a peer counselor are fundamental in paraprofessional training, the distinction may well be lost on the person seeking help. In a majority of situations, the very act of seeking out a peer counselor is an admission of a need or desire for help, and it includes some degree of vulnerability. However unwanted, however inappropriate, it is often a reality that a peer counselor wields a significant amount of power in any counseling relationship. This means a peer counselor is at times capable of doing significant harm to the client through action or inaction. As Chenault (1969, p. 90) points out:

> The question of the nature of our influence is of vital importance in a culture where professional words are associated with wisdom and truth . . . . In spite of our protestations that the client always retains the ultimate responsibility for his own decisions, we must question the degree to which we, intentionally or not, usurp that responsibility through the nature of our influence.

The very declaration that peer counselors are the equals of clients and not their caretakers is a fundamentally ethical statement. It essentially amounts to a refusal to wield power over another even when such power is easily within reach. Peer counselors—and their trainers and supervisors—must remember: no matter how boldly the word *peer* is highlighted in our paraprofession, it still adjoins the word *counselor*. The latter represents a position of power. As a peer counselor, you usually have the power to set the tone of the counseling session, determine the focus of conversation, and even to guide the client toward decisions that you believe are correct. These are by no means inherently unethical practices. Employed appropriately, they can be essential tools in resolving people's difficulties. However, the potential clearly exists for abuse. It is the client whose needs are being addressed and who must live with the decision and its consequences.

The peer counselor's power also ultimately involves the issue of accessibility. Guidance incongruous with people's personal priorities and needs is certainly unhelpful and may be durably alienating to your clients and those with whom they share their thoughts. It is incumbent on the peer counseling community to earn and maintain a reputation for understanding and respecting their clients' personal ethics and autonomy. This respect for the client acknowledges the relative vulnerability of many who request counseling as well as the peer counselor's ability to alienate or even do serious harm. It is our primary ethical responsibility both to admit this and to refuse to exercise inappropriate power.

Example 1

Danielle has been counseling Ray following a difficult breakup with his girlfriend which left him feeling devastated and depressed. He comes to trust Danielle quickly, begins to linger after appointments, and occasionally drops in between his scheduled sessions. He appears to be recovering from his breakup very well, reports being much more able to concentrate in class, and recently aced an exam. As Ray's attentions increase, Danielle becomes concerned that he is coming to see her as a replacement for his ex-girlfriend, though she is not entirely certain. She likes Ray but is not interested in dating him, and she worries that to discourage his interest would undo all the progress he has made while talking with her. To encourage it or permit it to continue would just amplify the eventual impact of her lack of interest. What ethical courses of action are open to Danielle? Would they differ if she were interested in dating Ray? If so, how?

Example 2

Xavier is counseling Roberto, who is having a family crisis. His mother, an immigrant to the United States, is threatening to leave his father and return to her native country. During the course of counseling, Xavier learns that Roberto's childhood was punctuated by travels back and forth between the United States and his mother's place of birth, both with and without his father's approval. Xavier becomes interested in Roberto's experiences growing up. As Xavier's thesis project concerns the impact of immigration on family structure and cohesiveness, and he thinks it would be good for Roberto to talk about these topics (particularly with someone like himself who has studied the issues involved), he begins asking Roberto several questions about his upbringing and the nature of his relationships with his extended family over time.

EXAMPLE 3

Ariela is counseling Vonda about difficulties within her family. Vonda describes her parents as controlling and manipulative. They are threatening to withhold tuition assistance unless Vonda continues on a pre-med track. Vonda has found biological research more interesting but is intimidated by her parents' insistence. Ariela identifies with Vonda's situation, having recently succeeded in convincing her own highly skeptical father to accept her shift from literature into mathematics. She therefore begins to ask Vonda some questions intended to lead her to some realizations about how to connect with authoritarian parents.

Ethical Standards and Moral Reasoning

An ethical standard for any profession or paraprofessional community serves many purposes. For those initially entering the field, it serves as a guide to the minimum standards of conduct and impresses on them the need for such standards to perpetuate the integrity of the community. It also clarifies each member's duties and responsibilities. For those already within the field, the standard serves as a set of guidelines for practical decisions that must be made during the course of service. Such guidelines can be particularly helpful in those decisions in which pressure or motivation exists to make an unethical choice.

Such a standard also provides protection to the individual peer counselor. That is, the established code of the peer counseling institution and the support of colleagues stand behind the ethical choices made by the peer counselor if and when others question those decisions. A formal ethical standard shifts some responsibility for ethical decision-making from the individual peer counselor to the institution. This provides a degree of consistency among peer counselors and thus fosters greater client trust in the integrity of peer counseling in general.

It would seem, then, that the goals of an ethical standard would be best served by a universal, all-encompassing code of rules. As Huston (1984, p. 823) notes, there is "low ethical consensus on dilemmas about situations that [are not addressed by a code]." As Winston and Dagley (1985, p. 60) note:

> Many standards statements have built-in conflicts or inconsistencies. While it is probably impossible to eliminate all internal inconsistencies, means should be provided to guide users in resolving conflicting mandates or principles.

Kitchener's five ethical principles certainly serve this purpose: to inform the application of ethical codes whenever they may conflict. However, ethical principles suffer the same limitation as ethical codes. Not only may they conflict with one another in certain situations, but the ethical resolution of these conflicts is often highly dependent on context and the particular situation at hand. Kitchener herself (1985, p. 27) states that

> most contemporary oral philosophers . . . would agree that following moral principles absolutely would in some cases lead to immoral acts. For example, if truth-telling were considered absolute, it could lead to the death of an innocent person if information was requested on the whereabouts of a Jew in Nazi Germany.

This limitation does not mean that principles are irrelevant or that all ethical values are entirely personal, subjective, and morally equivalent. The middle road between absolutism and subjectivism, upon which most modern ethics are based, considers ethical principles as *prima facie* binding. Kitchener (1985, p. 27) provides an excellent, concise definition:

> The meaning of the term prima facie comes from law, where it means that something—for example, a principle—establishes

an obligation unless there are circumstances or other obligations that are stronger. In this case, it means that ethical principles are more than convenient guidelines but less than absolutes. They are always ethically relevant, and they can be overturned only by stronger ethical obligations. In the case of telling a lie to save a life in Nazi Germany, truth telling remains ethically important, but saving a life is more important.

The *prima facie* standard, while establishing the validity and utility of formal ethical codes, recognizes the limitations of such codes and therefore imposes final responsibility for ethical behavior on the individual:

Viewing ethical principles as prima facie valid does not relieve professionals from the burden of decision-making in ethical cases. Instead, it plants the responsibility firmly on their shoulders, where justifiably it should lie, since professionals must ultimately answer for the consequences of their own decisions. [Kitchener, 1985, p. 28]

There is increasing recognition of these context-oriented and personal moral development issues within the professional counseling community. Fuqua and Newman (1989, p. 89, citing Wicker, 1985) suggest:

Conceptual frameworks or theoretical systems are often strengthened by placing problems and questions within larger contexts. When applied to ethics theory, this recommendation will require that ethical judgment and decision making be conceptualized within a complicated context of counselor, client, situational, and setting factors that are embedded in broader professional and social realms. Theory must ultimately address these various components and the potential patterns of interaction among them.

Furthermore, they highlight Tennyson and Strom's (1986) concept of "responsibleness" as potentially (hopefully!) a more fundamental basis for why professionals and paraprofessionals make the ethical decisions they do. In that concept, "responsibleness comes from within, and the person responds not out of duty alone, but because he or she decides a certain response is right" (p. 299).

This ultimate reliance on the personal responsibility of individuals, even when guided by comprehensive formal codes of ethics, is consistent with the efforts of scholars such as Collins and Gilligan to question and subsequently reconstruct "rules-based" ethical structure. Gilligan's (1982) ethic of care developed out of her studies of moral decisions among women and moral development in children (one should note that her subjects were primarily white and middle class). She describes a moral reasoning quite distinct from the traditional, "masculine" conception of ethics. As Delworth and Seeman (1984, p. 489) describe:

> Basically, Gilligan (1982) stated that a woman's conception of morality concerns the ethics or activity of care, which centers moral development around the understanding of responsibility and relationships in context. The conception of morality as fairness, typical of men, ties moral development to the understanding of rights and rules.

The point here for peer counselors is not to presume any particular gender affiliation for structures of moral reasoning.* Rather, you need to understand that ethical theories may be built on distinctly different foundations and employ separate processes of ethical reasoning.

Gilligan highlights a clear, albeit simple, illustration of the contrasting processes underlying ethics-as-fairness and ethics-as-care. She employs Kohlberg's (1969) classic dilemma of Heinz and the drug. The individual must judge whether a

---

*Though that presumption is not integral to Gilligan's thesis, the implications of "difference feminism" have sparked considerable debate among her critics and among feminist scholars (cf. Brabek, 1989; Larrabee, 1993; and particularly Pollitt, 1992).

man named Heinz should steal a drug that he cannot afford to buy to save the life of his wife. One person, Jake, frames the dilemma logically, as a conflict between life and property. Choosing life as the moral priority, Jake decides that Heinz has a right to steal the drug. As Jake considers this the rational response, he further assumes that any reasonable person—e.g., the judge before whom he will presumably be taken in trial—would agree. In contrast, another person, Amy, replies more ambiguously:

> *"If he stole the drug, he might save his wife then, but if he did, he might have to go to jail, and then his wife might get sicker again, and he couldn't get more of the drug, and it might not be good. So, they should really just talk it out and find some other way to make the money."* [Gilligan, 1982, p. 28]

Abstract debate regarding property, law, and rights are not a prominent part of Amy's reasoning. Indeed, she does not use those terms at all in considering Kohlberg's "self-contained problem in moral logic" (Gilligan, p. 29). Indeed, Amy and Jake conceive the primary moral issues at stake in qualitatively different ways. They build different questions (and subsequently different decisions) out of seemingly identical situations. Thus, "she finds the puzzle in the dilemma to lie in the failure of the druggist to respond to the wife" (p. 29), rather than in terms of weighing the values of property and life. As Gilligan writes (p. 30–31):

> *Amy's judgments contain the insights central to an ethic of care, just as Jake's judgments reflect the logic of the justice approach. Her incipient awareness of the "method of truth," the central tenet of nonviolent conflict resolution, and her belief in the restorative activity of care, lead her to see the actors in the dilemma arrayed not as opponents in a contest of rights but as members of a network of relationships on*

whose continuation they all depend. Consequently her solu-
tion to the dilemma lies in activating the network by commu-
nications, securing the inclusion of the wife by strengthening
rather than severing connections.

As noted, the ethic of care is not solely female (as Gilligan recognizes), nor is it entirely a novel creation of modern feminism.
Patricia Hill Collins (1989) describes ethics of care and personal accountability derived from traditional African humanism
and supplemented by the feminist critique of rules-based ethical
systems. This Afrocentric ethic of caring is founded on three
core components: an emphasis on individual uniqueness and
expressiveness, the appropriateness of emotion in any dialogue,
and the development of a capacity for empathy. These principles are reflected in the feminist concept of "connected knowing," presenting a fundamental challenge to the medical model
out of which the counseling professions grew. Whereas *separate
knowing,* reflected in the medical model and in most professional ethical codes, attempts to "subtract the personality of an
individual from his or her ideas" (Collins, 1989, p. 767) because
that person's personality, personal history, or other predilec-
tions are seen as inappropriately biasing those ideas, *connected
knowing* considers personal nature and opinions as important
components of an individual's ideas.

Collins' concomitant ethic of personal accountability is
even more forthright. It is, as Kochman (1981) writes: "*essential*
for individuals to have personal positions in issues and assume
full responsibility for arguing their validity" (cited in Collins,
1989, p. 768; emphasis added). As a peer counselor, you cannot
be detached and impersonal and still retain a respectable role as
counselor; your capacity for empathy intertwines with personal
and emotional expression. This ethic rejects

Eurocentric masculinist beliefs that probing into an individu-
al's personal viewpoints is outside the boundaries of discus-
sion. Rather, all views expressed and actions taken are

thought to derive from a central set of core beliefs that cannot be other than personal. From this perspective, knowledge claims made by individuals respected for their moral and ethical values will carry more weight than those offered by less respected figures. [Collins, 1989, p. 769]

What does this mean to you as a peer counselor? First of all, it does *not* mean that a person's sense of ethics is a necessary function of gender, race, or culture. As Gilligan emphasizes (1986, p. 327), "the contrasts between male and female voices are presented [in her work] to highlight a distinction between two modes of thought and to focus a problem of interpretations rather than to represent a generalization about either sex."

What these ethics of care do offer you is a moral framework that may be more suited to many of the immediate needs of the helping professions than an ethic based on rights and rules. The focus on concrete experience and the awareness of immediate context and consequences on which the ethics of care are founded are vital to the practice of peer counseling. It is usually not your role to adjudicate conflicts of rights between people. You are not an arbitrator of disputes, but rather a helper to people who may be suffering due to such disputes or other personal difficulties. Your primary goal is to help your clients feel better, more self-assured and confident, more capable of resolving their own disputes. An understanding of ethics that centers primarily on care has a lot to offer the peer counseling paraprofession.

Note that an ethic of care does not invalidate or reject commonly recognized ethical principles, whether or not they are formalized like those of Kitchener (1985). Rather, it expresses them in a qualitatively different way. Indeed, Gilligan (1982, pp. 62–63) stresses the need for an ethics both of justice and of care. Zella Luria (1986, p. 320) echoes this by proposing that "a reasonable goal seems to me to make women—and men—able to choose when to be caring and related and when to be concerned with abstract issues."

It is important to recognize that these alternatives are not mutually exclusive. Notably, Gilligan (1982, 1986) presents many instances in which judgments of fairness and of care are intertwined (see also Luria, 1986; Lyons, 1983; Johnston, 1985; Waithe, 1989). Likewise, it is vital to recognize the validity of each of these alternative structures and to construct the ethical principles of any professional or paraprofessional community with respect for the role of both. Each ethic highlights important considerations that the peer counseling community needs to recognize. This diversity of sources does not weaken the force of these principles; rather, it enhances their validity by broadening their applicability. As Kitchener (1985, p. 28) reminds us:

> while the principles do not provide absolute answers, neither do they lead to nihilism, for they provide consistent, cross-situational advice on which ethical actions and decisions are based.

That is, ethical codes and principles provide a framework that is useful because it enhances the efficacy of peer counseling. Ethics can be thought of as the education of your integrity. As such, ethics serve as the structure by which you can translate "meaning well" into successfully "doing well"—the very essence of peer counselor training. This is why ethics are at the heart of what it means to be a peer counselor. The present challenge, therefore, is to construct a set of paraprofessional codes and principles sufficient to define and guide the peer counseling community while putting primary import on the diverse needs of individual clients and their situations.

Example 4

A client has just confided in Beverly, a peer counselor at a rural university, that she was recently acquaintance-raped during a party on campus. Unbeknownst to the client, Beverly herself had been similarly raped a year earlier. Beverly wonders to herself whether her experience constitutes an emotional conflict and a threat to her impartiality, perhaps a threat to her ability to respond to the client's own needs. Or is the shared experience actually an asset, a point of solidarity and personal credibility that increases her ability to respond to her client's feelings? Should she continue the counseling relationship as is? Share her own experience and continue the counseling relationship from there? Arrange for the woman to talk with another peer counselor instead? And should Beverly's response be any different if her client were male?

Is there an unambiguous answer to Beverly's concern? If not, what might determine the best course of action for her? Might different ethical frameworks suggest different courses of action? If so, what might this mean for a counseling ethic? What situational variables might influence what the ethical choice would be? Does too much context-sensitivity invalidate the concept of ethical principle?

EXAMPLE 5

Kitchener (1985) notes that many twentieth-century ethicists suggest that all ethical decisions should be ultimately universalizable and generalizable. However, Collins (1989, p. 773) concludes her articulation of the ethics of care by stating: "Rather than trying to synthesize competing world views that, at this point in time, may defy reconciliation, [our] task is to point out common themes and concerns."

How might these views—and the ethical schemas themselves—be reconciled? Does each of these moral frameworks have something valuable that should be preserved? How might they be combined, if at all, to yield a robust, more universal ethical schema (for peer counseling or otherwise)?

ETHICAL PRINCIPLES

Part of the elegance of Kitchener's formulation of ethical principles is that it provides the solid structure required of a professional ethical standard while largely avoiding commitment to a particular manner of thinking about ethics. That is, the principles may be understood and employed both in terms of rules and justice, and of care and responsibility. They lend themselves to principled ethical thought and also provide guidance for the concrete and highly personal moral judgments of the individual peer counselor. Again, please note that the following principles, while sound, are not absolutes. Certain situations can present a basic conflict between these principles that individuals must resolve.

Autonomy

The principle of autonomy asserts that human beings have the right to make decisions and act on them in an independent fashion. This is limited, of course, by the constraints of law and the obligation to preserve the rights of others. It also subsumes freedom of thought and choice. In peer counseling, autonomy is a direct obligation of your position as a paraprofessional as well as a general ethical principle. Those cases in which other principles dictate the suspension of autonomy under *prima facie* considerations (such as a client hysterically threatening suicide or homicide) are serious. You must discuss them with professional staff as soon as possible. The criteria for competence or incompetence of a client's judgment are hazy at best. Only acute crisis situations should warrant any action other than complete respect for autonomy.

Nonmaleficence (Doing no harm)

Perhaps the most fundamental of the five principles is the obligation to commit no action that will result or run a high risk of resulting in harm to oneself or another. Such harm can be physical or psychological. In crisis cases, this ethic is prone to conflict with autonomy. For instance, suppose a client is threatening suicide and demands to leave the counseling session. In such a case, you must be prepared to make a *prima facie* judgment of ethical theory, which may result in suspending the client's autonomy until the crisis passes.

Another conflict can arise when avoiding harm to one person results in harm to another. This situation also requires recourse to ethical theory to resolve potential conflicts with the principles of justice and fidelity.

Under routine circumstances, the imperative of nonmaleficence is perhaps best displayed in the need not to judge. One reason people come to peer counselors is to tell their own side and sort out their feelings, behavior, and reasoning. To pass judgment is to obstruct fulfillment of this need, and thus undermine a vital part of the peer counseling creed. Nonmaleficence is the foundation upon which any counseling ethic must be constructed.

Beneficence (Benefiting others)

If nonmaleficence is the fundamental requirement of the peer counseling ethic, beneficence is the creed. The entire reason for the existence of peer counseling is to benefit those who come in need of the service. Beneficence is not owed solely to the client, however. In addition, your duty is to take into account the welfare of anyone and everyone who may be affected by your decisions. Notably, this includes yourself. While the principle of fidelity highlights the primary responsibility that you assume to protect the welfare of your clients, beneficence requires consideration of others' rights as well. One situation in which this becomes important is when a client makes fulfillable threats, whether overt or veiled, toward a third party.

It is also important that beneficence not serve as a guise under which you attempt to guide a client toward a decision that you believe is correct. This is a tempting shortcut and an easy misuse of power. While your role in guidance and clarification of the person's feelings is important, you take it too far if your ideas begin to replace, rather than supplement, those of your client. The deeper beneficence results when your clients formulate their own solutions and grow in the process.

Justice

Justice refers to the belief that individuals should be treated fairly, often balancing the rights of one person or group against those of another. It subsumes impartiality, equality, and reciprocity (to treat others as you would be treated). Justice is relevant to peer counseling in two primary ways. One concerns the counselor–client relationship. Impartiality affects your response to the client considerably; you must not take sides. Just as you must not judge the client, neither must you openly side with (or against) the client. This could, for instance, encourage clients to transfer responsibility for their feelings to their adversary, thus hindering resolution of those feelings. Such judgments are counterproductive.

The other mandate of justice concerns people outside the counseling relationship. By the principle of fidelity, the welfare of the client is foremost among your concerns; however, the rights of all involved are at stake and must be respected. Justice offers a universal, contextual perspective; all people involved are to be treated equally and fairly. At the same time, it is your special duty of fidelity to ensure that the needs of your client are met in the process.

Fidelity

Fidelity encompasses your special obligation to be faithful to your client, over and above your duty to maximize universal benefit for all. This particularly incorporates the obligations of confidentiality and informed consent. That is, your client's needs are primary. If the situation is so complex as to threaten the rights of others involved, you must examine your role in the proceedings, mediate any conflict of principles, and come to a productive conclusion regarding your *prima facie* obligations to your client, other parties, and the law.

Fidelity also encompasses the respect, loyalty, truthfulness, and integrity of the counselor–client relationship. This includes assuring your clients that:

- You will not exploit or deceive them.

- Their statements are confidential.

- You will faithfully follow the ethical principles of peer counseling.

- You will fully inform them about any related issues that may concern them, so that they may make appropriate and informed decisions.

In particular, it is imperative that you not in any way misuse your potentially considerable influence on clients. Fidelity establishes the necessary element of trust within the counseling relationship.

As previously noted, these five principles are *prima facie* binding. They cannot be enforced as absolutes, yet are considerably more than guidelines. On occasion, these principles may conflict. For example, if a client is threatening immediate harm to self or others, this situation may mandate the temporary suspension of autonomy. Or if a client has committed a crime, you may need to weigh confidentiality and fidelity to the client versus justice and beneficence to the community at large.

In your day-to-day work, however, situations rarely arise that tax the straightforward standards of basic peer counselor training. A robust ethical framework serves as a guide for those rare situations. It is a frame of mind for the practicing peer counselor, a substrate for the training of new peer counselors, and a unifying principle for the peer counseling paraprofession.

Example 6

Consider each of these two situations (two paragraphs ago), in which ethical principles conflict. How might the conflicts be resolved under a rules/justice-based ethical framework? Under an ethic of care? To what degree does it depend on the specific details of the situation? To what extent do the two approaches concur about what the peer counselor should do? If a difference exists, what might it mean? What do you think is the most ethical response in these two situations?

Example 7

In these situations and others, discuss the potential conflicts between fidelity and law. What is the peer counselor's duty to and/or role within the legal system?

Example 8

Theo is counseling June, who has just tested positive for HIV. She claims to be certain the test is in error but expresses concern that she could have spread the virus to a number of her friends, if she was indeed positive. She does not want to identify her partners to any third party and is terrified of confronting them with the information personally. What are Theo's responsibilities with this information? What are some ethical limitations on his actions? In a worst-case scenario in which June absolutely refuses to offer any more information and terminates the counseling relationship, what is the ethical course of action for Theo?

Example 9

Jeremy has confided in his peer counselor, Rui-yun, that he and two unnamed others were responsible for the recent serious vandalism of the campus theater. Two student productions were consequently canceled while repairs took place. One of these productions was directed by an unnamed drama student who is a bitter personal enemy of Jeremy. Jeremy has been Rui-yun's long-term client and has slowly come to place a great deal of trust in her. He has had many difficulties adjusting to academic life, some of which stem from unhappy interactions with this particular drama student. By and large, the counseling relationship has been very productive and helpful to Jeremy.

In light of this situation, what are Rui-yun's responsibilities? What course of action should she take? Would it make any difference if:

a) A theft was involved as well?
b) No personal enemies were involved, just destructiveness while drunk?
c) A prominent media and police campaign were under way to catch and prosecute the vandals, perhaps including a reward?
d) A personal crime, such as assault or rape, was committed in concert with the property crimes?
e) Jeremy was a new client or was making little progress or effort?

Example 10

Emily is separately counseling two women, Consuela and Annette, who are both having difficulties in their relationships with their lovers. Over some time, after both counseling relationships are well established, it becomes apparent to Emily that the two women are talking about each other. Are there ethical problems or conflicts with Emily maintaining both counseling relationships? Are there potential advantages to doing so? Considering these, what might Emily's principled response be? What factors might influence the ethical course of action?

Example 11

Taiji is counseling Mark, whose boyfriend has recently left him for a woman. Sometimes Mark shows remarkable resilience, talking about classes and social life, while during other sessions he becomes very depressed and angry at his ex. Recently he has made some statements that Taiji fears may be veiled threats. How might Taiji approach this? What if:

a) Mark's threats were very clear and fulfillable?
b) Mark "seemed like" a basically nonviolent person? A violence-prone person?
c) Taiji was acquainted with or friends with Mark's ex?

EXAMPLE 12

Yvonne is talking over the phone with a man who claims his name is Bob. He is calling for the first time. Having lost his family recently, he is very depressed and is threatening suicide. What is Yvonne's obligation, in light of her implicit contract with this client, to respect his autonomy and confidentiality or to have the call traced? How do you gauge whether a client like Bob will actually attempt suicide? Would your judgment be any different if the caller was a woman? If the caller's depression were due to other causes (e.g., drugs or financial difficulties)?

ETHICAL CODES

Ethical codes, or rules, present a clear framework of rights and wrongs within important aspects of peer counseling. They are specific and prescribe conduct in particular situations, serving as precedents and guidelines for sufficiently similar situations. In addition, as noted earlier, such codes also define the purpose and policies of the peer counseling institution and the role of the individual paraprofessional within that institution.

A good code should certainly make clear the basic ethical responses of a peer counselor to those situations that most commonly arise. Only situations with intrinsic ethical conflicts or those not adequately considered by the appropriate ethical code necessitate your resorting to ethical principles to deliberate a moral decision. As a model, a sample code of ethics for a peer counseling center follows. It is based on the 1989 *Ethical Principles of Psychologists* of the American Psychological Association.

An Ethical Code for Peer Counselors

A. Responsibility

1. As peer counselors, we are responsible for being aware of our own capacities and limitations. We are aware of our paraprofessional, rather than professional, status. And we are aware that our clients are peers, not patients.

2. As peer counselors, we will make our clients aware of our limitations if and when a limit becomes restrictive. We will take measures to correct this restriction, including referring the client to another peer counselor or to professional staff. We will avoid or similarly resolve relationships and situations that create a conflict of interest.

3. We will discuss institutional or paraprofessional problems, should they arise, with peer counseling center or professional staff, whichever is appropriate.

4. We are aware of our capacity to affect the lives of others, and we are alert to personal, social, organizational, financial, or political situations and pressures that might lead to misuse of our influence. As peer counselors, we are individually accountable for our influence and potential influence on our clients and for adherence to paraprofessional ethical standards in this regard. This does not imply a responsibility for clients' problems.

5. We are responsible for the integrity and reputation of this peer counseling center, and shall conduct ourselves in our counseling roles accordingly. This includes our responsibility to be prepared and capable during our working hours at the peer counseling center.

B. Competence

1. As peer counselors, we have a responsibility to maintain a minimum level of practical competence, including routine reviews of known processes and techniques, and continuing practice and interaction with staff.

2. We have a further responsibility to expand our knowledge and capacities by continuing education, whether via workshops or simply continuing interest and interaction with colleagues and professional staff.

3. We will accurately represent our competence and areas of ability. We will refer clients whose needs would be better served by referral to another counselor. When we feel the need for guidance, particularly about client problems of a serious nature or especially demanding of confidentiality, we will consult professional staff. In such a case, we will keep the identity of the client confidential unless professional counseling center staff directly and legitimately request otherwise.

4. As peer counselors, we recognize differences among people, such as those that may be associated with age, gender, sexual orientation, socioeconomic and ethnic backgrounds, or with upbringing. When necessary, we will obtain training, experience, or counsel to ensure our own competence to counsel such persons.

5. As peer counselors, we have a responsibility to maintain interaction and communication with other active paraprofessional staff.

C. Moral and Legal Standards

1. Although the peer counseling paraprofession is not formally covered by law, this peer counseling center operates under the auspices of the legally licensed professional staff of the [name of your center].

2. As peer counselors, we realize that counseling sessions are for the client's benefit. Consequently, we know that without informed consent and prior arrangement, it is unethical to design counseling methods to satisfy our curiosity or to use the client or data on the client for any ulterior purpose, such as class work.

3. Members of this peer counseling center do not discriminate on the basis of race, color, creed, national

origin, religious affiliation, gender, disability, or sexual orientation.

4. As peer counselors, we are obligated to uphold all the legal and civil rights of our clients. We may make exceptions to this principle in the case of acute crisis, such as barring the exit of a suicidal client. In such cases, we will adhere to ethical principles rigorously during the course of the emergency.

5. We are aware of counseling center and peer counseling center ethical standards, and we consistently practice them. We are required to behave in accordance with this center's standards while operating under its auspices.

D. Public Statements

1. Public statements, such as advertising, made by the peer counseling center staff shall be truthful, nonmisleading, and maintain confidentiality.

2. No such publication shall refer to any client or information regarding any client, with or without names, without the informed consent of the client and all parties involved.

E. Confidentiality

1. We inform our prospective clients of the requirements and legal limits of confidentiality as practiced by this peer counseling center. Information about a client is confidential and in most cases shall be released to no other party without the informed consent of the client. While some cases may require consultation with other paraprofessional staff, such consultations shall be solely for the purpose of improving services to the client. The identities of clients shall always be kept confidential except upon direct, legitimate request of professional counseling center staff.

2. Clients are entitled to information regarding any professional or paraprofessional communication regarding them. Such information may be released to the client at

the option of the peer counselor, given the permission of all sources consulted.

3. As peer counselors, we are obligated to inform professional staff about certain cases. These include any case in which the client has committed a crime involving one or more victims, in which the client shows signs of severe mental or emotional disorder, or in which the client perceptibly makes serious and fulfillable threats against a third party, whether overt or veiled.

F. Welfare of the Client

1. As peer counselors, we shall be continually aware of our potentially influential position with respect to clients and shall ensure that we do not misuse this power in any way.

2. We avoid conflicting or dual relationships with current clients to avoid impairment of paraprofessional judgment, the potential exploitation of the client, or the appearance of either.

3. We consider it unethical to pursue, develop, or engage in intense emotional involvement with a current client outside the counseling relationship, particularly sexual involvement.

4. If for any reason a client is consistently failing to benefit noticeably from the counseling relationship, we are obligated to take steps to correct this. We may either refer the client to a colleague or confront the client with this observation and subsequently modify or terminate the counseling relationship.

5. In all cases, we maintain respect for our clients as peers, not as patients.

6. We are volunteers, and as such do not accept compensation for our services from any source while operating under the auspices of this peer counseling center.

7. Should a conflict of loyalties arise on our part, as peer counselors, we are obligated to inform all involved parties of the conflict and the way in which we plan to resolve it.

G. Paraprofessional Relationships
   1. As peer counselors, we are responsible for the integrity of
      this peer counseling center. We will endeavor to uphold
      this integrity and the reputation of this center.
   2. We are open to constructive criticism from colleagues
      and professional staff, with the intent of improving our
      capabilities as peer counselors.
   3. Experienced peer counselors involved in the training or
      supervision of other peer counselors accept the obligation
      to facilitate the development of these individuals as peer
      counselors. In this context, we provide appropriate
      working conditions, timely evaluations, constructive
      consultation, and opportunities for experience consistent
      with ethical requirements and this peer counseling
      center's resources and policies.
   4. As peer counselors, we do not exploit our counseling or
      supervisory relationships, sexually or otherwise. We do
      not condone or engage in sexual harassment, defined as
      deliberate or repeated comments, gestures, or physical
      contacts of a sexual nature that are unwanted by the
      recipient.
   5. As staff members of this peer counseling center, we
      operate within the context of this center and its activities.
   6. Should we become aware of misconduct on the part of a
      colleague, we will constructively confront that colleague
      with our assessment of the situation and identify its
      unethical nature. This informal resolution is appropriate
      when the misconduct is of a minor nature and/or appears
      to be due to a lack of sensitivity, knowledge, or experi-
      ence. In the event that such behavior persists or is of a
      more serious nature, we will notify the peer counseling
      center staff leader(s) and/or professional staff.

H. Utilization of Techniques
   1. Before using any peer counseling technique, we will be trained and well versed in its administration. We do this to maintain client confidence and a professional atmosphere.
   2. As peer counselors, we ensure that the client's right to a full explanation of the theory and administration of a counseling technique is upheld.
   3. We ensure that the client fully and properly understands the results of a utilized counseling technique. It is particularly imperative that the client understand the limits of the technique's accuracy and scope.
   4. As members of this peer counseling center, we will use only those techniques approved by the center and by professional staff.

PART III

SPECIAL PERSPECTIVES

Introduction to Part III

The following chapters present material aimed at assisting peer counselors who are working with specific cultural and ethnic issues, with matters related to sexual orientation, or as resident staff in college dormitories.

In Part I, the section on interpretation reviewed the importance of belief patterns and personal points of view. The ways in which cultural points of view and ethnic traditions affect African-Americans, Asian/Pacific Americans, and Chicanos often represent puzzling dilemmas to counselors from the Anglo culture. In working with an individual from a different cultural background and world view, peer counselors find that customary ways of framing, thinking, and solving personal problems are sometimes hampered by a lack of instinctive understanding and empathy as well as unavoidable biases based on life experiences. These matters are addressed in the following chapter.

Chapter 7 presents information and perspectives regarding how to work with peers around issues relating to sexual orientation.

Chapter 8 addresses resident advisors (RAs), who often do not receive focused training or consultation to help them counsel other students around academic and personal issues. The chapter therefore provides information and material to help readers develop skills in this specialized form of peer counseling. A new section deals specifically with the issues around RAs referring other students for professional consultation.

6

CULTURAL AND ETHNIC PERSPECTIVES

AFRICAN-AMERICAN CULTURAL ATTRIBUTES
AND THEIR IMPLICATIONS FOR COUNSELING
AFRICAN-AMERICAN CLIENTS
by Sam Edwards, Jr.

Culture exerts strong influences on the personality. Composed of the "values, attitudes, customs, beliefs, and habits that are shared by members of a society" (Parrillo, 1980), culture affects everything from our unconscious to our thinking to our behavior. It determines how we see the world and how we react to it. It helps us understand other people, choose our friends, and distinguish ourselves from embers of other cultures. It also affects our patterns of interaction, choices of occupational goals, and definitions of success and of good and bad. It gives us directions for coping with and resolving personal problems. Comprising learned attributes that are parts of our personality, culture is a highly dynamic force.

This section focuses on some of the African-American cultural attributes that may influence the counseling relationship and/or may become activated in conjunction with the counseling situation. It discusses selected cultural attitudes, values, and beliefs, along with their implications for enhancing counseling. Further, this section makes efforts to add to your cognitive and emotional understanding of African-American clients from an essentially cultural perspective. It is important that you combine sensitivity and empathy with the intellectual application of peer counseling techniques.

The Cultural Belief that Blacks Are a Strong People

Among the many facets in the African-American culture is the belief that blacks are a strong people. This may be a scar left by oppression. It may be rooted in the culture of slavery, wherein owners valued blacks for their physical labor and stamina. In the agrarian society of the South, blacks comprised the bulk of the work force. Forced to function as if they were strong animals or powerful machines, they were expected to reproduce strong offspring.

Having the basic psychological needs for some form of validation of their self-worth as human beings, blacks probably began concentrating on their physical stamina. It was an asset that whites and society needed to be successful, and blacks probably idealized and identified themselves with it. One may speculate that their real or imagined physical abilities were sources of pride, inspiration, and comfort. That they were directly or indirectly rewarded for strength may have led to the idea that blacks are a strong people and that being strong is good. Like any aspect of culture, it was probably transmitted from one generation to another.

As cultural beliefs often do, this concept lacks a specific definition. Nonetheless, many blacks today share and understand it. When carefully examined, it denotes several abstract qualities:

- Racial pride based on the achievement of survival through severe periods of oppression

- Strength of emotional constitution to endure and persevere under untoward socioeconomic pressures

- Physical stamina

- Collective racial power to exert social influence

In many variations, the belief is embedded in the African-American culture. Black folklore abounds with tales of sexually prodigious African-American men. Some blues songs are rich with statements pertaining to the sexual might of blacks. Some poems speak about survival capacities and perseverance under adversity. John Henry and Jack Johnson, who are African-American cultural heroes, are symbolic of the physical stamina and pride of blacks.

In addition to its manifestations in various forms of African-American art and folklore, this belief is evident in the daily interactions of blacks. Ministers sometimes preach about blacks as a strong people who have come through dark, trying times. In discussions among themselves, blacks boast that they are stronger than white people. A favorite notion is that white people would have "cracked up" under the pressures that blacks have had to bear. Many blacks unhesitatingly expect that African-American prizefighters and football players will perform better than white ones. The whites who are exceptional are often thought to have acquired their assets from blacks. Writers may appeal to the belief in strength when they call on blacks to take collective actions.

Implications for Counseling

The notion that blacks are a strong people may exert considerable influence in the counseling situation or on decisions about seeking counseling. It defines and inhibits the expression of "weaknesses." It defines and mandates manifestations of "strength." Most often, members of the African-American community perceive having personal problems and seeking counseling as significant weaknesses. Blacks often interpret being continuously able to withstand or resolve problems as strength.

The belief discourages seeking or accepting help. Many blacks who need counseling will avoid getting it. Rather, they are likely to conceal problems while attempting to resolve them alone. Many may strongly devalue and feel hostile toward and threatened by counseling services. They experience tremendous feelings of shame and humiliation when facing personal problems. This also contributes to diligently avoiding counseling.

However, some do obtain it. With them, you may need to be alert to cultural patterns of behavior. Blacks may express, reveal, and conceal problems and feelings through familiar cultural patterns. They may model problems and emotions after culturally based images of strength: cool calmness ("Be cool, man"), controlled detachment, intimidating sullenness, postures of questioning your knowledge and understanding of blacks, and threats of physical violence. While you may see them as normal, some of these behaviors may indicate problems, feelings related to those problems, or feelings about seeking help.

It is essential that you be able to sense and appreciate the content of the cultural forms of responses. The failure to be aware of the person's feelings and problems may encourage your client to perceive you as too weak to help him or her. Further, if you fail to "see through" forms of cultural responses, you may find it harder to accept and be empathic toward African-American clients. Empathy and acceptance may be the factors that enable the client to accept help and feel safe enough in the session to relinquish culturally based patterns of behavior that conceal or constitute the problems.

It is also crucial that you bear in mind that the belief that blacks are a strong people is probably the parent of the idea that African-Americans do not commit suicide. Some blacks have the notion that suicide is a behavior of whites, or of blacks who have adopted the values of whites. However, the notion is incorrect.

Studies suggest that suicide is a serious problem among blacks. Hendin (1969) observes that "in New York, suicide is twice as frequent among Negro men between 20 and 35 as it is among white men of the same age." He explains that, between the ages of 20 and 35, suicide is actually more of a problem among blacks of both sexes than it is among whites of the same ages. The Crisis (1981) reports that Chunn has found that "suicide has reached epidemic proportions among blacks from ages 15 to 29 and is the leading cause of death today in that group." The African-American researcher is further quoted as saying that a "marked increase" occurred in the 1970s in the number of African-American suicides among both males and females. Chunn's data reveal that "the rate in 1981 for blacks is 24 per 100,000 persons, compared with 15 per 100,000 in 1973, nine per 100,000 in 1940, and 13 per 100,000 in 1932 and 1920."

Chunn identifies several factors that correlate with African-American suicide. They include chronic unemployment, loss of personal relationships (largely through migration), alienation, lack of opportunity for advancement, and alcohol and drug abuse.

You need to be alert to the suicidal ideas and/or plans that African-American clients may have. You may need to inquire actively about such thoughts when the client asks for help with depression or with problems that correlate with African-American suicide. Many blacks perceive suicidal thoughts as expressions of weakness and are likely to conceal them.

Cultural Attitudes Against Self-Disclosure

Like the notion concerning the "strength" of blacks, the cultural attitude against self-disclosure may exert prominent influences on the African-American client's relationship with a counselor. A general disposition shared by some blacks is that people should not discuss personal problems outside the family. This attitude may come into play at any time during counseling. Like many attributes of culture, it is likely to become apparent in earlier sessions, when the level of unfamiliarity is the greatest between the two participants.

Clients may express this attitude in a host of forms. These include guardedness, discussions of nonprivate matters, concealment of secrets, silence, stubbornness, and feelings such as guilt and hostility. One of the most common expressions is to avoid situations in which you may expect them to disclose personal matters.

Some case examples will add further clarity.

Ann is a 33-year-old, lower-middle-class African-American student at a junior college. Married and the mother of three young children, she works full-time with a flexible schedule. She seems extraordinarily ambitious and success-oriented. Her behavior and comments in the first counseling session are common among many blacks. Initially, she is silent and obviously hesitant to begin talking. Before discussing the problems for which she is seeking help, she explains that her mother had taught her to "Never tell your business to strangers" and that "Black people have to be careful about who they talk to in this world." Ann comments that she felt "bad" about coming to talk to a counselor. She adds that she just has to talk to someone who can help her. She says she feels as if she is "ready to blow up" because of marital, academic, and work pressures. Ann keeps every other appointment. She seems to feel guilty about discussing personal matters with the stranger-counselor. After missing three of six sessions, she terminates abruptly.

Teeya manifests another variation of the anti-self-disclosure attitude. A 21- year-old, middle-class African-American senior majoring in pre-med at a highly prestigious university, she asks her black peer counselor many questions. Do African-American students who use these counseling services "spill their guts"? She asks about her counselor's own attitudes concerning blacks "spilling their guts" in "these kind of places." Her counselor's impression is that Teeya is attempting to employ him to attenuate her feelings of guilt about the prospect of confiding in him.

When you question them, some blacks may have knee-jerk-like hostile reactions. Verbal responses may include statements such as:

"That's none of your business."

"That is personal."

"You don't have anything to do with that."

"You don't need to know that to help me."

"What do you want to know that for?"

While the anti–self-disclosure attitude constitutes and gives rise to resistance, it is likely to be culturally based and culturally formed. Its influences at times may be particularly evident. Of a 40-year-old African-American client who was hospitalized because of a suicide attempt, Hendin (1969) states, "The patient came close to losing his usual politeness when he warded off questions about his mother. 'How would I know? I mind my own business,' the patient defended." Hendin viewed this reaction as an indication of the patient's feelings that Hendin did not mind his own business.

Implications for Counseling

Peer counseling is a highly specialized helping method that works largely with the cognitive-intellectual realm of the personality. As such, it depends heavily on the client's active cooperation. You therefore need to adapt the process to the individual needs of each client.

When you observe the impact of the cultural anti–self-disclosure attitude on your counseling relationship with an African-American client, you may consider several possibilities. Perhaps first and foremost, you should avoid interpreting responses in a literal, concrete way. It helps to see reticence and/or hostility as signals of anxieties and styles of armor. To react defensively is to give legitimacy to the client's need for such protection. It may also inhibit the person from resolving any guilt that may arise in the session as he or she violates the cultural anti–self-disclosure attitude.

Second, you may want to work toward genuinely accepting your client's attitudes as part of that person's personality. If you achieve that understanding, you may choose to explain that the peer counseling process works best with the client's full cooperative participation. Sometimes, depending on your judgment, you may raise open-ended questions that encourage the African-American client to talk without feeling defensive. Sometimes it pays off to wait acceptingly until the person decides to disclose. But you should rarely resort to simple silence. Some blacks may perceive such a stance as a put-down and a needless show of superiority. As you may know, clients often observe and assign meanings to your behavior in session.

Cultural Attitudes of Distrustfulness

Closely paralleling the attitude of anti–self-disclosure is that of distrustfulness. A cultural trait of anticipating danger and hurt, this distrust is characterized by doubts regarding others' interest in and authenticity toward oneself. It also consists of vague thoughts concerning the potential deceptiveness of others, perceptions of anger in the environment, feelings of unsafeness, and vulnerabilities to humiliation. Grier and Cobbs (1968) portray the attitudes as an African-American norm and see them as adaptive. These psychiatrists explain that, because of their many years of painful experiences, blacks have developed "a suspiciousness of their environment which is necessary for survival. Black people, to a degree that approaches paranoia, must be ever alert to danger from their white fellow citizens. It is a cultural phenomenon peculiar to Black Americans."

Moore and Wagstaff (1974) conducted a study of African-American educators in white colleges and obtained data that coincide with the observations of Grier and Cobbs. Of their findings, they write:

> So general is the feeling of alienation, discrimination, unfairness, anger, and frustration among black educators that those who did not share unpleasant experiences and felt they were being treated fairly in their jobs also felt the need to apologize for their lack of suspicion and feelings of satisfaction.

The cultural attitude of distrustfulness is widespread, seemingly transcending class. Also dynamic, it tends to surface when blacks are in unfamiliar situations, such as white restaurants, white communities, and large institutions. Once they feel at ease in the situation, it tends to subside.

Implications for Counseling

In the office of the African-American or white counselor, distrustfulness may manifest in the client's reluctance to provide a phone number, home address, or other identification data. It may also be apparent in questions pertaining to confidentiality. Thus, it is often useful to explain with honesty the counseling agency's policies and practices regarding confidentiality. You should attempt to be faithful to the policies.

You may need to observe the signs of distrustfulness quite carefully. They may constitute as well as conceal serious disorders of paranoia, although they may appear as what seem like legitimate concerns about the realities of racism and other kinds of racial injustices in the United States. Do not immediately attempt to validate the person's manifested concerns. Nor should you feel guilty. Simply observe these concerns empathically. Distrustfulness is a dynamic attitude, and it tends to diminish once the individual is familiar with or has accurate information about the anxiety-evoking situation.

The persistence of suspicions, misinterpretations of activities in the environment, obviously erroneous ideas concerning abuses of confidentiality, and preoccupations with the dangers of whites may strongly suggest psychopathology. However, the dividing line between real-life experiences and manifestations of psychopathology may be extraordinarily thin in blacks. As a peer counselor, you do not typically make formal diagnoses, but you can be alert to the presence of problems that are best dealt with by other professionals. After a few meetings, if you sense that the client has emotional problems that may interfere with solving problems through peer counseling, you may refer the client to a psychotherapist.

Cultural Values Pertaining to Communication Skills

The desirability of "good" communication skills is an emotionally charged issue in the African-American culture. Some blacks have adopted a general standard of communication skills that the dominant culture deems acceptable. Using that standard as a basis for comparison, many blacks evaluate their own individual communication skills as bad and undesirable. These perceptions may stimulate considerable personal and group shame and other painful reactions.

Some blacks see good communication skills as the *sine qua non* for self-approval and authentic membership in the white world. The case of Mr. D is instructive, although it may not necessarily be typical. Almost in the middle of one of the many sentences he had difficulties verbalizing in the first counseling session, this 42-year-old African-American man stopped talking. With a sense of embarrassment, he said, "You see that I get this speech thing. I get mixed up. But I talk the way I am. I'm me—nobody else! I'm not suppose to talk like Sinatra or somebody like that. I'm different. Some people think you have to talk like white peoples to be somebody."

While complicated, the vignette illustrates many points. Mr. D has apparently observed the communication skills of the African-American counselor and is feeling ashamed and defensive about his own. Further, he appears to see Frank Sinatra as the embodiment of whites and of good communication—by which he judges himself. Also, through this preoccupation with and negative evaluation of his skills, he seemingly reveals a great sense of personal inferiority and of being in poor control of himself. One may speculate that he is saying in part that he would "be somebody" were he skilled in communicating verbally and were he white.

Shame, anger, and self and group devaluations are common responses for some African-American people who are self-conscious about speaking. Recent years have seen increasing scholarship about and respect for the concept of Black English as a legitimate dialect, with its own syntax and grammar. Still, this new cultural attitude now exists side by side with the old. African-Americans who associate mainstream verbal skills with intelligence and personal acceptability may "talk proper" and use pretentious words. They may apologize for "busting verbs" or for using words incorrectly. Some may avoid talking in situations in which they fear their skills will betray their intelligence.

Blacks' concept of good communication skills sometimes encourages particular patterns of interacting among blacks. They are prone to feel embarrassed and critical of African-American leaders who demonstrate unsatisfactory communication skills in public. They sometimes engage in verbal critiques of each other's manner of talking:

"You can't even talk."
"You ought to go somewhere and learn how to talk before you try to talk about me."
"You are trying to talk like the white people."

Some parents impress on their children concepts of good speech. Simultaneously, blacks may isolate or admire blacks who are natural in the employment of "good" communication skills. When an African-American person returns home to the South after a long stay on the East or West coast, friends and relatives may scrutinize his or her "style" of talking. If the returnee has a modified way of talking, people may think, "He's changed."

Essentially, large numbers of African-Americans are self-conscious about their communication skills and are prone to be ambivalent about "good" skills manifested by other blacks.

Implications for Counseling
Blacks' values regarding communication skills suggest several implications. One is that you need to be aware that some African-American clients may be feeling ashamed and humiliated by their communication skills while they are talking. You ought to become familiar with the specific types of signs that

point to people's emotions, although you may not work actively with these feelings. To humanize the relationship to a greater degree, allow yourself to experience silent compassion freely toward your client. An awareness of the person's emotions is invaluable for developing links between you, and it enhances the likelihood that the counseling will be effective.

Another implication is that the African-American client is likely to scrutinize your communication skills and compare them to his or her own. Of importance is that the person may have a variety of reactions to this evaluation, all of which you need to note mentally.

Maintain a natural style of communicating. Do not shift to more "polished" or "down to earth" skills. Interventions such as paraphrasing should reflect empathic listening and should be natural. If you alter your style, some African-American clients may see it as a put-down. Further, it is generally helpful to keep in mind that your manner of talking with an African-American client will inevitably reflect your attitudes concerning the client. It will also reflect your own momentary senses of personal insecurities or securities.

Finally, a specific risk exists that you may make value judgments about African-American clients based on their communication skills. As with these clients, you may associate verbal skills with degrees of intelligence and personal worth. You need to be aware of your own values in this area and to monitor their influence on any evaluations of people's communication skills.

Cultural Values Pertaining to Education

The African-American culture places great value on education. As with communication skills, a good education is seen as a passport into the world of professional, economic, and political power. Although it sometimes acquires the proportions of a cure-all for the personal and social problems of blacks, the African-American community always considers education an important qualification for self-determination. For example, in one of his weekly newspaper articles, "Racism: What Should You Do?," Dr. Charles Faulkner (1981) offers suggestions to blacks for coping. Among other things, he says: "Get as much education as you can—be prepared for what is to come."

Blacks' strong embrace of the cultural value appears in many aspects of African-American life. The importance of formal schooling is a recurring theme in African-American publications. Many black professional, social, political, and religious organizations have scholarship funds and/or education committees. African-American ministers preach sermons about the values of education, and parents admonish their children to "get a good education." Graduation ceremonies are particularly important for many blacks. Older African-Americans sometimes apologize for their lack of an education, guiltily pointing to some of the obstacles that were in their way. Some of the blacks who seek counseling report the urgency of their need to get an education.

Implications for Counseling

Culturally esteemed achievements and standards of education may be very dynamic forces. They may be the sources of realistic and unrealistic aspirations for African-American clients. Failure to attain such goals may prompt strivings for compensatory types of achievement, either deviant or socially sanctioned. Or failure to attain them may prompt defeatist attitudes, which are all too common among many blacks.

Clearly, an education is an esteemed African-American cultural value. As a peer counselor, you should become familiar with this value, largely because it may contribute to states of low self-esteem and discouragement in many blacks. It also lends itself easily to disguises of serious psychopathology.

Considerations Regarding Referring African-American Clients

Informal observations suggest that African-American clients are high-risk referral prospects, particularly after a client–

counselor relationship has been established. Most blacks terminate counseling when referred to another counselor. They
strongly prefer the rapport they have with the original counselor, black or white. They resist referrals by offering a variety
of obstacles—a lack of time, inconvenience, a scarcity of
money, a lack of need for further help, doubts about the usefulness of counseling, the prospective counselor's lack of knowledge about them, and feelings of being pushed around. Some
return to the original counselor later, if they follow through
with the referral; but most rarely follow through on a referral or
successfully become attached to another therapist.

One may offer a number of general speculations concerning blacks' tendency to terminate rather than accept referrals. In addition to being perceived as a personal abandonment
by you, the referral probably arouses fears of venturing into
another unfamiliar setting. Many African-Americans restrict
themselves to familiar locations and people. At the same time,
like counseling itself, the referral lacks cultural support and/or
sanctions.

You should therefore avoid referring the African-
American client to another counselor except when the person's
problems clearly indicate it. Should you determine that a referral is warranted or required after you have established rapport
with a client, you should generally avoid referring blacks to
group methods of counseling. The African-American culture
emphasizes individualistic attitudes, self-reliance, self-sufficien-
cy, and autonomy. It opposes the resolution of personal problems in the context of groups, and many blacks may perceive
group counseling as "white folk's stuff." Such a referral might
stimulate anxieties that discourage the person from pursuing
counseling altogether.

Summary

Comprising a variety of values, attitudes, beliefs, and habits, the African-American culture exerts strong moral-like directives for behavior and perceptions. It rewards compliance with and punishes opposition to cultural rules and expectations, thus exerting a major influence on the personality of blacks. This chapter has focused on the following aspects of that culture:

1. The belief that African-Americans are a strong people
2. Cultural strictures against self-disclosure
3. Cultural attitudes of distrustfulness
4. Cultural values pertaining to communication skills
5. Cultural values pertaining to education
6. Considerations regarding referring blacks

These factors inevitably affect the counseling relationship and African-Americans' decisions to seek counseling. They also suggest possible sensitivities of the client and some bases of his or her painful feelings. To enhance the effectiveness of counseling and to enable the African-American client to resolve feelings generated specifically by the culture, you must have an emotional and intellectual appreciation of black culture and its influence. Success in the counseling process rests on your ability to combine empathy, acceptance, and understanding with the application of various counseling techniques.

Counseling Chicanos: Some Considerations
by Alejandro Martinez

The goal of this section is to help you become aware of culture-specific aspects in the counseling process and in your particular counseling styles. You can then deal more skillfully with individuals of Mexican descent.*

   Mental health professionals have identified several significant issues in intracultural counseling. These issues have been most succinctly summarized into four themes by Draguns (1976):

1. The etic–emic distinction
2. Relationship versus technique
3. The mutuality of the client–counselor relationship
4. The autoplastic–alloplastic dilemma

It is hoped that counselors working with Chicanos will share and be sensitive to these concerns.

The Etic–Emic Distinction
The terms *etic* and *emic* represent two contrasting frames of reference for describing and analyzing behavior. An *etic* approach provides insight into the human universals of certain problems, while an *emic* approach clarifies the culturally unique elements of these problems. Recognizing the value of each orientation and understanding their complementarity is essential, because the concerns that Chicanos bring to a counseling situation are not necessarily uniquely Chicano problems. They often appear

---

*The word *Chicano* as used here refers to persons of Mexican descent. The reader should be aware, though, that this and other ethnic group labels (i.e., Mexican American, Latino, Mexicano, Hispanic, American of Mexican descent) can have ideological implications. Its use here does not represent a consensus of the way individuals of Mexican descent self-identify ethnically.

similar to or indistinguishable from those faced by any other individual (e.g., self-doubts, indecision about a career choice, interpersonal conflict, motivational problems). Interpreting such concerns solely in terms of their universal attributes may provide the Chicano client with an appropriate and well-intentioned intervention. However it ignores the problem's cultural characteristics and significance.

For example, counseling that focuses on individuation issues of a young Chicano outside the context of family and familiar values is less effective than counseling that also explores the impact of the process of individuation on the relationship with the person's family. It is often the case that family is relatively more important to Chicanos, and thus of greater significance when dealing with the emergence of independence in young Chicanos.

Relationship versus Technique

A second consideration for counselors is the relative importance of relationship and technique. Despite their great variety in theoretical orientation and methods, counselor training programs in the United States are based on certain assumptions and values that reflect a U.S. cultural viewpoint. The accompanying chart contrasts some of these assumptions and values with those that might prevail elsewhere.

The indiscriminant and uncritical use of counseling techniques that are rooted in the dominant culture lead to an unfulfilling undertaking for both the client and you. You must be prepared to adapt your techniques to your client's cultural background. When working with Chicanos, this might mean explicitly asking about language-related issues, nonverbal cues, and the different meanings that they may ascribe to various uses of personal space, eye contact, and conversational conventions.

When you meet an individual for the first time, you may not hear the real problem right away. The Chicano client may want to chat first or may present a problem that he or she con-

U.S. Assumption/Value	Contrasting Assumption/Value
1. People are isolable individuals.	1. People are integrally related with other people (in groups such as families).
2. Personal growth and change are valuable and desirable.	2. Conforming to time-tested ways of behavior is desirable.
3. Individuals have control over their life circumstances.	3. External forces (political, economic, social, natural) dictate one's life circumstances.
4. Personal problems are often soluble, through greater understanding of their origins and/or through remedial action.	4. Problems are fated to occur, and fate may or may not remove them.
5. "Professional" people can help other people solve their problems. a. People (counselors) can be genuinely interested in the welfare of strangers. b. People (counselors) can be dealt with as occupants of roles.	5. One's problems are beyond the control of other human beings. a. Only one's close friends and relatives can be trusted. b. Other people are dealt with as whole people.
6. Open discussion of one's problems can be beneficial.	6. It can be dangerous to reveal oneself to others.
7. Emotional disturbances have their roots in the individual's past.	7. Emotional disturbances have their roots in external forces or situations.
8. People are (more or less) equal.	8. A hierarchical ranking of people exists in society.
9. Males and females are (more or less) equal.	9. Males are superior.

Reprinted from Horner et al. (1981), *Learning Across Cultures*, by permission of the publisher, the National Association for Foreign Student Affairs (Washington, DC; pp. 37–38).

siders socially acceptable. You must be sensitive to each individual's self-disclosure style and attempt to provide an opening where clients can feel comfortable discussing the issues that really concern them. You may achieve this with such questions as:

How are things at home?
How is school going?
Are you finding enough time to be with friends?

You may also need to be relatively more active in the interaction, for aloofness may be interpreted as a lack of interest in the client's concerns.

In sum, you must be able to engage in supportive communication that promotes the development of trust, rapport, and ease in disclosing concerns or problems.

The Mutuality of the Client–Counselor Relationship

The counseling interaction is a reciprocal process, affecting both the counselor and the client. By working with Chicanos, you can learn a great deal about people of Mexican descent and their acculturation issues:

- Ethnic identity
- Family structure, roles, and role expectations
- Effects of racism, prejudice, poverty, and opportunities
- Attitudes toward the family, competition, marriage, sex, death, whites, blacks, religion, etc.
- Gender identity issues

You may learn about a host of culturally diverse and interesting aspects. While this is a legitimate and valuable avenue for learning the "subjective culture" of Chicanos, you should not indulge your own curiosity at the expense of the client's efforts and time. The client's concerns and goals must be paramount in the counseling relationship.

The Autoplastic–Alloplastic Dilemma

Should you help people adapt themselves to troublesome circumstances, or should you help them changes those circumstances? This is the *autoplastic–alloplastic dilemma*, a fourth concern for counselors working with Chicanos.

Historically, counseling has encouraged *autoplastic* behavior by helping people accommodate themselves to their social settings and structure. It was not until the 1960s, with the development of the Civil Rights movement, that people seriously questioned this approach to human problems. The community mental health movement offered exciting and innovative ways of approaching problems. Social situations were no longer assumed to be immutable, and people sought institutional and broader social change.

For Chicanos, this new approach was an extremely significant development. As a group, they have encountered major sociopolitical barriers to opportunities in education, employment, housing, cultural expression, and political participation. This new *alloplastic* orientation encouraged them to shape external realities to suit their needs.

People continue debating the appropriateness of each approach. As a peer counselor, you must examine your own values and attitudes about what constitutes an ethical intervention. What are the immediate and long-term political implications of either orientation? We may walk a tightrope between helping Chicanos learn to act on other people, objects, and situations, and helping them accommodate themselves to existing situations.

An example of this dilemma involves a Chicano student who begins to lose interest in school or becomes depressed and angry because he or she cannot find faculty who understand or even appreciate an academic interest in ethnically oriented topics. Does one help this person "see the reality" of the situation and adapt to what the school offers? Or does one work with this individual so that he or she changes the status quo?

All counselors who work with Chicano clients must confront these tough questions.

Counselor, Client, and Ethnicity

Who can best counsel Chicanos? Is the most appropriate counselor a bicultural-bilingual Chicano? A Chicano counselor who has assimilated the Anglo culture? A non-Chicano counselor?

Two positions seem predominant on this matter. One suggests that a counselor whose cultural background parallels that of the client can understand the client's personal experience and perspective much better than a counselor who has a different background. The shared experience may enhance rapport and promote the client's willingness to disclose material, and the common mode of communication may enhance the counseling process. It may help, too, if the person perceives the Chicano counselor as a potential change agent who is sensitive and responsive to the unique sociocultural attributes of Chicanos. Working with a Chicano counselor may help change a client's perception that counseling is only for the white middle class or that the "status quo" has no interest in Chicanos being able to maintain ethnic identity and self-pride.

The other position suggests that some clients may prefer a counselor whose background differs from their own, particularly if they want to deal with material that would be embarrassing to share with individuals of the same ethnic background. For example, it may be easier for the person to talk about not feeling a strong affiliation to Chicano culture and values if he or she is seeing a non-Chicano counselor. Or, someone dealing with constant antagonism by the white majority may best be helped by "confronting" a white counselor with his or her feelings of anger, helplessness, and anxiety.

Both positions have some merit. Each offers important benefits, yet each has potentially negative aspects. In the white counselor–Chicano client dyad, a significant language barrier may exist. White counselors tend to be English-speaking monolinguals, while some Chicanos speak only English, other speak only Spanish, and many speak both. Significant dissimilarities in values also tend to exist. Some are due primarily to differences in socioeconomic class, others to cultural differences (such as in self-disclosure styles, normative behaviors, family values, and customs). These differences can and often do contribute to mutual stereotyping or denial of cultural dissimilarities, resistance, transference, countertransference, misdirected diagnosis, patronization, and low expectations of success of counseling.

The barriers in the Chicano counselor–Chicano client dyad have received less attention but are equally important. A Chicano client may react with anger or jealousy when confronted by a Chicano counselor. The client may perceive the counselor as being overly identified with an Anglo-controlled institution. The client may resent the counselor for breaking out of an oppressive environment. Or the client may stereotype the counselor as a super-Chicano. Another concern is that the Chicano counselor may deny identification with the Chicano client. On the other hand, because the two are similar culturally, the counselor may over-identify with the client, make unjustified assumptions about shared feelings, or inappropriately project a self-image onto the client.

Counseling the Chicano Student

How Chicano students deal with higher education and its many intellectual, social, and personal challenges depends largely on the extent to which they identify with either the Anglo culture or the Mexican/Mexican-American culture. Those who strongly identify with one culture or who have a strong dual identity will probably not experience major problems with their identity or self-concept. Nonetheless, they may still find themselves in situations where others pressure them to choose one cultural identity over the other. In contrast, those who are deliberately attempting to replace one set of cultural values with another or those who may not identify with either culture often experience particularly powerful and debilitating stress.

The more you know about the cultural identity of a Chicano client, the more possible it becomes to counsel that person successfully. One client may be a bilingual student whose parents are immigrants from Mexico, who is a member of an extended Roman Catholic family, who prefers ethnic food, and who prefers being called Mexican. Another client may be an English-speaking, non-Catholic Chicano from a nuclear family who has no preferences for the diet or clothing of his or her ethnic group and who prefers being called American.

Your peer counseling process with these two clients is likely to be very different. Both of these clients may present concerns about self-concept and ethnic identity, for example, yet the issues will probably vary dramatically. The first person may be concerned about the pressures of acculturation toward the U.S. culture and is likely to be more sensitive to culture-specific pressures (such as obligations to parents). The other may be more concerned with external pressures to be Mexican. Or, as is the case with students who "rediscover" their ethnic heritage in college, some people may be struggling to integrate something that has always been theirs and the accompanying feelings of mourning, sadness, anger, and excitement.

Certain stresses affect most Chicano students regardless of cultural preferences. Historically, Chicanos as a group have been subjected to prejudice and discrimination. They generally have lower personal and family incomes, have fewer years of education, are over-represented in low-paying occupations, are under-represented in higher education institutions, and are victims of the cycle of poverty. Negative consequences for the Chicano community include a reduced quality of life and denied opportunities for advancement. For the individual, negative consequences may include an impaired self-image, defensive attitudes of denial, withdrawal, passivity, self-depreciation, dissimulation, and identification with the aggressor.

The cost of breaking new ground in academia is another source of stress. The historical under-representation of Chicanos in higher educational institutions tends to present unique challenges to the Chicano student's sense of individual, familial, community, and cultural identity and continuity. While an educational experience can provide many majority-culture students with a means to integrate themselves in the community and dominant society, for Chicanos it frequently represents a distinct break with family and community. The dearth of role-model Chicanos who have achieved success through continued education or training often intensifies and further complicates the stresses of this transition. The Chicano student can see what he or she is "leaving" but does not know where the educational experience will lead.

A Chicano in higher education, therefore, faces many questions that, because of cultural background, are of particular significance.

Will participation in higher education mean alienation from my family and community?

How will my family and community perceive personal changes that stem from my educational experience?

Will I be able to retain the capacity for intimacy with my family and community?

What responsibility do I have toward my community and family?

How much education should I strive for when my parents may have less than a grammar-school education?

How will I deal with the pressure of giving my family its first real opportunity to escape the poverty cycle?

Chicanos in universities also have to address some difficult self-concept and interpersonal questions. These include how well they can maintain their ethnic identity within the university and still participate fully in an Anglo-dominated educational experience, and why they were admitted into institutions that in the recent past rarely accepted Chicanos in any significant proportions. What is the personal significance to Chicanos of affirmative action in higher education? How do they deal with the insensitivity of the institution to Chicanos' needs? How do they deal with overt and covert prejudice and racism? How do they deal with genuine feelings of acceptance and concern by Anglo students, staff, and faculty? What kinds of relationships do they want and what types of relationships can they have with other Chicanos? How about with non-Chicanos? Whom can they date? Whom should they date? Should they only date other Chicanos? What does it mean when they date non-Chicanos?

Summary

When providing peer counseling services to Chicanos, you should be aware of at least six issues:

1. Counseling has two basic levels of analysis: one provides insight into the human universal of certain problems, while the other clarifies their culturally particular elements. You need to consider both levels when counseling Chicanos.

2. Despite their great variety in orientation and methods, counselor training theories in the United States share certain assumptions and values that reflect the viewpoint of the majority culture. If you counsel minority-culture clients, you must adapt your techniques to the cultural background of each individual. With Chicanos, this means explicitly checking out language-related issues, nonverbal cues, and different meanings that they may ascribe to the use of personal space, eye contact, and conversational conventions.

3. The counseling experience is a reciprocal learning process that affects both you and your client. It is a particularly meaningful way to learn about Chicanos, yet you should not indulge your curiosity at the expense of your client's effort and time.

4. Given the often oppressive situation of Chicanos, you must address the ethical and political issue of how much to help the person adapt to a given reality and how much to encourage him or her to work at changing that situation.

5. Counselors must recognize the unique demands of intraethnic and interethnic counseling. Both of these counseling dyads offer important therapeutic benefits as well as potentially significant limitations. The client's needs determine whether a Chicano or a non-Chicano counselor will be most appropriate and effective.

6. You need to be sensitive to and aware of the sources of stress that most affect Chicano students: prejudice, discriminatory practices, socioeconomic conditions, and the unique social and psychological demands on Chicanos in academic settings. You also need to be aware of how each person's cultural preferences or degree of acculturation to the majority Anglo culture may mediate these stresses.

HISTORICAL AND CULTURAL CONSIDERATIONS IN COUNSELING ASIAN/PACIFIC AMERICANS
by Karen Huang, Jane Pao, and Franklin Matsumoto

The Asian/Pacific American (A/PA) population in the United States has more than doubled since 1980 and is projected to continue growing. According to the 1990 U.S. census, Asian/Pacific Americans numbered 7.3 million—outnumbering African Americans in ten states, and Latinos in three states.

Although they account for only three percent of the U.S. population, they are highly visible in some areas:

State	Number of Asian/Pacific Americans	Percentage of State Population
California	2,845,659	9.6
New York	693,760	3.9
Hawaii	685,236	62.0
Washington	210,958	4.6

Thirty-nine percent of all Asian/Pacific Americans live in California. Due to a combination of overall population growth and the continue influx of foreign students from Asian countries, college campuses will continue to see rising numbers of A/PA students.

Asian/Pacific Americans as College Students

Asian/Pacific Americans are setting the educational pace for the rest of America and cutting a dazzling figure at the country's finest schools.

—*Time*, 1987

Many writers as well as the popular press have focused on the educational attainments of Asian/Pacific Americans, usually to the neglect of other aspects of their lives as students. Peng

A/PA Enrollment in U.S. Colleges

Over the past two decades, the number of minorities enrolled in U.S. colleges has risen from 15.4 percent in 1976 to 21.8 percent in 1992. Unlike African-American enrollment rates, which have not changed during this period, A/PA enrollment has more than doubled, from 1.8 percent in 1976 to 5 percent in 1992 (U.S. Department of Education, 1993).

Enrollment of foreign students at U.S. colleges and universities has also been on the rise after leveling off during most of the 1980s. In 1992–93, foreign student enrollment reached a new high of 438,618 students. Of these, 59.4 percent were A/PA nationals. According to the Institute of International Education (1993), nine of the ten largest sending nations were in Asia:

	Sending Nation	Number of Students
1	China	45,130
2	Japan	42,840
3	Taiwan	37,430
4	India	35,950
5	South Korea	28,520
6	Canada	20,970
7	Hong Kong	14,020
8	Malaysia	12,660
9	Indonesia	10,920
10	Thailand	8,030

A/PA foreign students have different rates of graduate and undergraduate enrollment. East Asian foreign students are primarily graduate students: 80.5 percent of Chinese, 65.5 percent of Taiwanese, and 52.2 percent of South Korean foreign students are graduate students. By contrast, only 16.3 percent of students from Japan and 21.2 percent of those from Hong Kong are in graduate programs. Among South and Central Asian students, the majority (66.9 percent) are graduate students, due to the high rate (79.4 percent) of graduate enrollment among Indian nationals; most other South Asian students are undergraduates. Finally, for Southeast Asians, the pattern is mixed. Most (64.1 percent) are undergraduates, while 79.4 percent of Singaporeans and 57.2 percent of Thais are graduate students.

(1988) reported that 86 percent of A/PA students are found in higher education programs two years after graduating from high school, as compared to 64 percent of whites. According to the Bureau of the Census (1990), A/PAS exceed the national average for graduating from high school and college.

On the other hand, the U.S. Department of Education (1994) found that among adults over the age of 25, whites and A/PAS have the same rates (77.9 and 77.5 percent, respectively) of graduating from high school. However, A/PAS have a higher rate than whites (36.6 versus 21.5 percent) of graduating from college.

Studies and data about A/PA attainment often obfuscate the fact that Native Hawaiians are poorly educated. For instance, only 4.65 percent of all adult Hawaiians over 25 years of age have completed college (Native Hawaiian Study Commission, 1988).

The A/PA Sociohistorical Context

Both in the counseling encounter and out, many mainstream individuals have noted that Asian/Pacific Americans appear relatively more deferential or obedient to authority than individuals from other backgrounds. A/PA culture certainly plays a role in encouraging overt behavior that can be interpreted as personality traits of humility, reticence, and deference. Another major influence on behavior has been the sociohistorical context in which Asian/Pacific Americans live in the United States. Racist discrimination and other forms of violence have been visited upon many Asian/Pacific Americans—sometimes personally, sometimes through familial relationships. For instance, an A/PA adult who suffers discrimination in the workplace is likely to transmit his or her emotional reactions to his or her children.

Recent Violence Against Asian/Pacific Americans

In the first national audit of violence against Asian/Pacific Americans, the National Asian Pacific American Legal

Consortium (1993) wrote that violence against people of color is a national problem, and that hate crimes against Asian/Pacific Americans are on the rise. Of all the nationally reported hate crimes in 1992, 3.4 percent were against Asian/Pacific Americans (who represent only 3 percent of the total U.S. population). The report also noted that intimidation was the most frequent type of hate crime in the United States in 1992, but that assault was the most common type of hate crime against Asian/Pacific Americans.

The number of hate crimes reported is a mere fraction of the number committed. There are two primary reasons for this. First, local and state agencies report hate crimes to the Federal Bureau of Investigation on a voluntary basis. Because this reporting is not mandatory, those agencies often do not keep detailed, standardized statistics of the ethnicity of victims. So many cases are not included in the national statistics. Second, many cases are not classified as hate crimes because the FBI uses a narrow definition of hate crimes (NAPALC, 1993). For example, an Asian Indian graduate student attending the University of Nevada at Las Vegas was killed by two men who, according to another student, "threw a liquid at him, and while they were lighting him on fire, told him that there were too many of his kind at the University" (NAPALC, 1993, p. 12). This was not categorized as a hate crime because the coroner's report and the arson investigation contradicted the student's statement.

From 1989 to 1990 in Los Angeles County, reported hate crimes increased by 46 percent. Reported hate crimes against Asian/Pacific Americans increased by 157 percent that year, and another 48 percent from 1991 to 1992 (NAPALC, 1993). The NAPALC noted that the pattern was similar in other metropolitan areas with large A/PA populations. In New York City, reported hate crimes against Asian/Pacific Americans rose more sharply than those against other ethnic minorities. In New Jersey in 1991, over half the ethnic-bias incidents were against Asian/Pacific Americans.

Violence against Asian/Pacific Americans is not restricted to large urban centers. It has also occurred on college campuses nationwide. At Pomona College, a private southern California campus, a three-foot-high banner that read "Asian Pacific American Studies Now!" was vandalized to read "Asian Pacific Americans Die Now!" In Seattle, an Asian American university student managed to fight off an attack by six "angry white men wielding tire irons and baseball bats." They approached him in a parking lot and began calling him names like "gook, Chink, Jap" (Ohnuma, 1990). According to a news report, none of the 15 or so onlookers called the police. In fact, two or three encouraged the attackers by yelling, "Brain the gook!" And in Coral Springs, Florida, a pre-med Vietnamese undergraduate was beaten to death on August 1, 1992 by a "mob of white youths who called out, 'chink,' 'Vietcong,' 'sayonara,' and other racist slurs" (NAPALC, 1993, p. 8).

Historical Violence Against Asian/Pacific Americans

Violence toward Asian/Pacific Americans has occurred since their original landing on U.S. soil (see Toupin, 1980, for a brief review). While some of the violence has been perpetrated by individuals, other forms appear to have been socially sanctioned. For instance, the widespread scapegoating of Chinese Americans during the economic downturn of the late 1890s led to blatantly discriminatory laws. These include the Sidewalk Ordinance of 1870 which forbade persons from walking on the streets while using poles to carry goods, a common Chinese practice at the time (NAPALC, 1993, p. 7).

Historically, anti-Asian sentiment appears to have swept the United States in waves, responding to the immigration and economic conditions at the time. On the west coast in the 1880s, the first Chinese immigrants (who were imported and exploited for cheap labor) were subjected to a variety of violence. This not only made them feel unwelcome by the white mainstream but also led to their physical segregation. Only three generations ago, Chinese were forced to live within the confines of this country's Chinatown ghettos. They were targeted for special taxes, not allowed to marry whites, excluded from immigration, exploited as workers, and sometimes lynched by angry mobs (see Chang, 1991, and Takaki, 1989, for further history).

One of the most financially and psychologically devastating acts of violence was the World War II internment of all Japanese Americans residing in the western region of the United States. Two-thirds of these people were U.S. citizens. War hysteria forced them to lose their homes, livelihoods, dignity, and families.

Most of these citizens were Nisei, or second-generation Japanese Americans (children of immigrants). In the camps, they were exploited at wages of six dollars per month. The impact of this camp experience has also deeply affected the Sansei (third generation), who have recently come of age.

Meanwhile, from the start of the 19th century, U.S. merchants and missionaries arrived in the Hawaiian Islands to "civilize" a society that they viewed as culturally inferior to their own. By the end of the 1800s, two thousand Westerners had taken over most of the land in Hawaii. In 1887, armed U.S. merchants forcibly overthrew the Hawaiian monarchy; and in 1898 the United States annexed the islands as a U.S. territory. The "Big Five"—family-owned corporations whose directors included a large number of sons of missionaries—took over Hawaii's economic system and exploited native workers. Not until almost a century later, in 1974, did the U.S. government recognize native Hawaiians as Native Americans—a title shared with only two other groups: the American Indians and Alaskan natives.

Several waves of Filipino immigrants, like other waves of A/PA immigrants before them, were largely employed as a source of cheap agricultural labor in California. Although Filipinos were U.S. nationals who had easy entry into the States, they too have experienced anti-Asian hostilities. In fact, when the Philippines declared independence in 1934, the United States restricted immigration to 50 Filipinos per year. This was a dramatic curtailment compared to the immigration flow in the decade just prior, from 1920 to 1930, when more than 27,000 Filipinos had entered the States (Ong & Azores, 1991).

In recent history, Korean Americans were affected by the U.S. war effort in their native country in the 1940s and 1950s. Similarly, the Vietnam war has had a direct or generational effect on many Southeast Asian Americans. In the United States, many Koreans and Southeast Asians have been further targeted for attack. For instance, much of the violence during the Los Angeles Rodney King riots of 1992 was aimed at Korean American owners of small businesses. Similarly, Southeast Asian tenants of San Francisco housing projects have been targeted for "name-calling, physical and emotional intimidation, threats, assaults, and even beatings and killings" (NAPALC, 1993, p. 11).

Asian/Pacific Americans as Clients

Researchers have repeatedly noted that A/PA clients have a 50 percent dropout rate from counseling. Much of this is the result of frustrating first encounters that stem from different perceptions regarding the best approach to treating the presenting problems and the client's expectations of therapy. Cheung and Snowden (1990) note that Asian/Pacific Americans underutilize services compared to Blacks, Hispanics, Native Americans, and Alaskans. Asian/Pacific Americans are less likely than Caucasian Americans to rank mental health professionals as a first choice for assistance with serious interpersonal or emotional problems (Suan & Tyler, 1990).

Seeking to uncover reasons for the high dropout rate and continued underutilization of psychotherapy among Asian/Pacific Americans, researchers have focused on four factors:

- General acceptance of counseling as an intervention
- Preferences for particular types of treatment
- Preferences for therapists of A/PA ethnicity
- Interpersonal dynamics during the counseling session

Acceptance of counseling may correlate with acculturation: the more acculturated the person, the more accepting he or she is of counseling services. Atkinson and Gim (1989) found that the most acculturated students were most likely to recognize personal need for professional psychological help, and most open to discussing their problems with a psychologist. Gim et al. (1990) found that A/PA women expressed greater willingness than A/PA men to see a counselor, but that low–medium acculturation students were more willing to see a counselor than high-acculturation students. They speculate that this might be the result of high-acculturation students having fewer stressors and thus less need for counseling, compared to the low–medium acculturation students.

With regard to preferences for a particular type of counseling, recent findings have been mixed. One study found that Asian/Pacific Americans have no preference between problem-solving and client-centered approaches (Yau et al., 1992). Others have noted that psychotherapy and its focus on affective exploration and insight may run directly counter to the traditional Asian values regarding appropriate responses to problems. For instance, Asian cultures generally believe that rumination makes things worse and that a person should respond to stressors with patience. The Japanese say, "*Shigata ga nai*" ("It can't be helped") or "*Gaman*" ("Persevere"). Koreans recommend *cha ma*, and Japanese urge *enryo*; both mean "Be patient, be hesitant, hold back"—highly valued traits in these cultures. With such values, some A/PA clients would prefer a solution-oriented psychotherapy approach to a psychodynamic exploration approach. Any counselor working with A/PA clients must inquire as to the client's view of these approaches.

In terms of expectations for a type of treatment provider, the research consistently shows that Asian/Pacific Americans prefer to be treated by A/PA psychotherapists. In a study by Atkinson and Matsushita (1991), Japanese American subjects rated the credibility and attractiveness of counselors presented in tape recordings of simulated counseling sessions.

Subjects were the most willing to see a directive Japanese American counselor. Similarly, another study (Atkinson et al., 1978) found that A/PA university students rated A/PA counselors as more credible and approachable than Caucasian counselors. More recently, Sue et al. (1991) also found that ethnic matching related to the length of treatment for A/PA clients.

The finding that A/PA clients consistently prefer A/PA counselors may be partially explained by the history of racism, violence, and discrimination. Based on the sociohistorical context in which most Asian/Pacific Americans live in the United States, many such clients enter the treatment session, if they arrive at all, with a negative expectation. They are often silently wondering, "Is this counselor an ally or an 'outsider' who will not understand, respect, and empathize with me?"

At the same time that an A/PA client is testing your responsiveness, he or she is also likely to accord you high levels of authority and respect because of the cultural tradition to revere caregivers (e.g., physicians and psychotherapists). To show respect to the counselor, A/PA clients often behave in an overtly deferential way and avoid making any complaints or comments about their reservations or dissatisfactions regarding counseling.

As a peer counselor, you need to be alert to these considerations but also recognize that Asian culture teaches individuals to feel ashamed of their suffering and not to speak up. Self-expression is thought to bring on more shame to both themselves and the therapist.

Research indicates that the need to save face, and to avoid the shame that results from loss of face, can have a critical role in the counseling process. Confucian-based cultures (e.g., Chinese, Japanese, and Korean) teach people to worry constantly about how others will react to something they say or do. The aim is to make certain to behave in a manner that will maintain face for both parties. According to Pye (1968),

face cannot be translated or defined. It is like honor and yet not honor. It cannot be purchased with money. It gives a man or a woman material pride. It is hollow and what men fight for and what women die for. It is invisible yet by definition exists by being shown to the public. It exists in ether and yet can be heard and is solid. It is amenable not to reason but to social convention. It protects lawsuits, breaks up family fortunes, causes murders and suicides, and yet often has made a man out of a renegade who has been insulted by his fellow townsmen. It is prized above all earthly possessions. It is more powerful than fate or favor, and more respected than the constitution. It often decided a military victory or defeat. It can demolish a whole government ministry. It is this hollow thing which men in China live by.

Because face is of utmost importance, loss of face is felt acutely. Loss of face entails both social condemnation and the loss of confidence in the ego's character. This loss is a very real dread that frequently has a greater impact on the psychology of an Asian/Pacific American than physical fear (Hu, 1975, p. 452).

The influential role of maintaining face results in a pattern of socialization that emphasizes a responsiveness to very subtle nonverbal signals in any interpersonal encounter. This world view is diametrically opposed to the individualism that characterizes the U.S. mainstream culture. For Asian/Pacific Americans, the answers for questions about behavior come from the social outside, not the psychological inside. Adults constantly admonish children with sayings such as "Have you no eyes?"—meaning, "Can't you see and meet the needs of others without being asked?" As a result, many A/PA clients carry a permanent fear of being caught behaving without insight, which would then expose them to the experience of shame, failure, and/or criticism. Exposing oneself to shame is further distressing because it places the other person in the uncomfortable position of causing or noticing the embarrassment.

The power of the need to avoid shame and loss of face is dramatically illustrated in the tale of Princess Tegona:

Tegona was renowned for her beauty and had a great num-
ber of suitors. Among them, two men in particular contend-
ed violently for her love. Confronted with their heated
competition, however, Tegona felt increasingly uneasy about
her marriage and finally ended her own life without saying
which one of them she would choose. The two suitors, as if
still vying with each other, both hurried to take their own
lives.

According to the traditional Japanese interpretation offered by
Doi (1986), Tegona committed suicide not out of indecision,
but out of modesty. It would have been shameful for her to
proudly choose a suitor.

Certain behavioral consequences may arise during the
counseling process as a result of the Asian emphasis on face
saving. Counselors have noted that Asian clients are frequently
reluctant to express their pain openly or to describe their problems in great detail. One of the reasons is that this sort of disclosure leaves the person feeling vulnerable to the therapist's
shaming him or her for having such problems.

Also, many Asian/Pacific Americans appear to nod in
agreement, not to say, "Yes, I agree," but "Yes, I hear you." This
is partly rooted in the view that directly disagreeing with a superior—in this case, the counselor—would cause the counselor to
lose face for having said something incorrect. As a result, A/PA
clients sometimes appear disingenuous during the session.

Asian/Pacific Americans with traditional cultural values
would also tend to pick up nonverbal cues from you and hold
them in an internal dialogue, meanwhile talking about those
issues that they feel you would like to hear. You must be
attuned to nonverbal signals that may indicate that clients are
responding to their own perceptions of your needs.

Unless you intervene accordingly, a client may eventually become angry at you for accepting these discussions as his
or her innermost concerns. Eventually, the frustrated client will

realize that you have not picked up on the nonverbal cues that indicate otherwise. Rather than complain, which would cause you to lose face for doing a poor job, the a/pa client will probably end treatment abruptly or with a face-saving excuse.

Cultural Considerations

This section examines some culture-related problems that Asian Americans face. As mentioned, the term *Asian American* covers a diverse group of Asians that includes Chinese, Filipinos, Hawaiians, Samoans, Japanese, Koreans, other Pacific Islanders, and Southeast Asians. Each ethnic group possesses its own distinct characteristics and culture. In counseling Asian Americans, knowledge and familiarity with the historical, political, and cultural factors behind the Asian American identity is crucial for effective interaction.

In this section, when we speak of Asian Americans, we are referring primarily to Chinese and Japanese Americans, since these two groups are the largest and oldest Asian groups in the United States. However, the guidelines discussed here can be adapted to helping members of other Asian cultures. It is our hope that you will develop an awareness and sensitivity to the Asian American and that this section will stimulate further discussion on cultural issues.

Image of the Asian American

Despite a long history of racial discrimination, abuse, harassment, economic exploitation, and prejudice, Asian Americans have managed to function reasonably well in U.S. society. The public's image of Asian Americans has shifted from one of "Yellow Peril" to that of a successful "model minority." Asian Americans are generally believed to have a large degree of upward educational, occupational, and economic mobility. People generally perceive them as quiet, law-abiding, hard-working, and nonthreatening— and as good students. These images of success attained by some Asian Americans are reinforced by visible signs of affluence, acculturation, and assimilation into the community.

The question is whether Asian Americans today accept these stereotypes and conform to them. And if so, to what extent? How does this affect the Asian American self-concept and psychological well-being? In some instances, failure to adhere to these expectations may add to the discontent and frustrations of Asian Americans. For example, people expect Asian Americans to perform well academically. When students are unable to met the demands of scholastic achievement, they face a dual stress. They feel they have failed personally, and they feel some degree of shame and disgrace for not living up to an expected image. In another sense, when an Asian student's behavior is contrary to the stereotype of the passive, industrious, quiet student in class, the teacher may comment, "I didn't expect that from you."

Asian Americans often do not express these dilemmas and others because the cultural value is to resolve personal conflicts and problems independently. It is not unusual to hear the statement, "I prefer to work out my own problems rather than burden others with them." Most Asian Americans are reluctant to seek outside help. They are more likely to seek assistance within their own family. Social and emotional problems of youth and the elderly—such as juvenile delinquency, poverty, and unemployment—are therefore well hidden from the public. It is not surprising, then, that many people believe Asian Americans experience few problems. This misconception, unfortunately, is reinforced by studies that consistently reveal low utilization of mental health facilities by Asians (Kitano, 1973; Sue & Kirk, 1975; Sue & McKinney, 1975).

One possible reason for this underutilizaton could be that cultural factors inhibit self-referral. These factors may include pride, shame, and disgrace of admitting to adjustment or emotional problems. Those Asians who come forth often express their problems as somatic complaints (Sue & Sue, 1974). Or, as Bourne (1975) observed, they tend to suffer "major adaptive failures or have conflicts of considerably greater magnitude than Caucasian students."

The existence of these myths and stereotypes makes it doubly important for you to keep in mind the beliefs of students seeking help. It is especially important to examine your own culture-bound values and assumptions when you interact with students who experience difficulties related to their cultural background.

Traditional Cultural Values

For generations, the family has been the nucleus of Asian culture. It is the primary institution from which is woven the social fabric of life for the individual. The structure of the family has been patriarchal; sons are desirable over daughters because they can ensure the family line and provide support for the aged. Filial piety is of prime importance. Respect and obedience to elderly authority figures is expected.

Adults condition children to restrain any expression of emotions that might disrupt the family's balance and solidarity. To control their children's behavior, parents tend to instill guilt and shame as part of their disciplinary action. Families expect their members to behave appropriately and not engage in acts that will bring dishonor to the family. Conflicts and disagreements between children and parents arouse anxiety and guilt. To express feelings openly is difficult and often not encouraged. Individuals are expected to exercise self-restraint, endure hardships, and not to disclose weaknesses.

However, this traditional family model is changing gradually. Younger generations identify with the western practice of asserting independence and are attempting to modify the family tradition and structure.

The emphasis on filial piety and family responsibility can at times create internal stress for the individual:

N is away at college when his father becomes seriously ill. Being the eldest son, N feels a responsibility to return home to help the family. He becomes depressed while caught between the family's desire for him to pursue uninterrupted schooling and his own feelings of filial obligation to help out at home.

In such cases, you need to be cognizant of, and empathic about, the profound obligation N feels toward his family. It is necessary to understand the feelings of guilt and obligation that accompany the conflict. You could gently encourage exploration of feelings only if you have already established a working relationship of trust and rapport.

Cultural Conflicts

The term *cultural conflict* refers to the "personal discomfort or dilemma of individuals exposed to different cultures" (Sue & Kitano, 1975, p. 7). Assimilation and acculturation challenge Asian values, and this causes various kinds of cultural conflict. Sue and Sue (1971) offer a conceptual framework for understanding these conflicts. Their model describes three types of stereotypical characters: the traditionalist, the marginal person, and the Asian American.

The *traditionalists* wish to hold strongly to their traditional Asian values. Conflict occurs when the person finds it hard to maintain allegiance to the traditional family expectations. Examples include conflicts between family obligation and desires for individual freedom, and independence over career choice and interpersonal relationships. An Asian American student describes his feelings:

> *It's important that my parents are happy with me. They want me to become a doctor and have financial security. All their lives, they have self-sacrificed and saved so that I could get a good education. In a way, I feel obligated to repay them for what they've done for me. You see, I was once a pre-med. Now, I'm more interested in art. I'm afraid to even let my parents know. They'd be so disappointed in me. I've let them down, but why can't I do my own thing?*

Another Asian American student related the following:

> I went with a white boy for three years. I could tell you how bad it was for my family. The most important thing to me was my personal feelings for the boy. The way my folks were behaving implied what I was feeling was wrong. That was a big conflict. Being Japanese is just as important to me. Not that interracial dating threatened it at all. My parents kept saying that I could lose something.

The *marginal* persons—the second type of characters described by Sue and Sue—want to reject the family tradition. They deal with cultural conflicts by attempting to dissociate themselves from their Asian heritage to the extent of repudiating it and Asians. When they cannot identify substantially with either culture, they experience an identity crisis. This may express itself in low self-esteem, self-hatred, insecurity, isolation, and ambivalence. Examples of this often manifest in dating attitudes and social relationships. The following vignette shows that rejection and hostility toward oneself may be a transitional phase which could turn into a positive experience.

> I remember when I was age 15. I was an anomaly at school. I didn't have any real dates. I used to pray to God to make me blond and blue-eyed. I hated myself and the way I was. When my prayers weren't answered, I knew I was left with two alternatives. One, I would be miserable for the rest of my life, wishing that I could be someone else I couldn't be. Or two, I could become a fighter for Asian American pride.

A new Asian American identity emerges as individuals strive to seek a balance between the two cultures. To promote their ethnic pride, these individuals have collectively sought to raise consciousness among other Asians about (1) their Asian culture and (2) society's unfair treatment of them as a minority group. Some have adopted a militant approach to express their views on racism and stereotypes. In extreme cases, individuals may become so obsessed with oppression that they become bitter and angry toward others who do not think or feel the way they do. Some feel that if they express themselves as Asian Americans, it may appear that they are engaging in "reverse discrimination." Perhaps this new identity can best be generalized by a statement that Sommers (1960, p. 644) made about two individuals who were experiencing cultural conflict:

> They can now enjoy a new-found sense of belonging—a belonging with their own family and their (Asian) heritage, as well as belonging to the country of their birth and their Western culture. Through this fusion of both cultures . . . they are gaining something unique and valuable for themselves and society that they could not have done previously by their torn allegiances.

The level of cultural conflict experienced obviously varies from one individual to another. Reactions depend largely on people's degree of ethnic identification and acceptance of their own culture. The impact of cultural values on a person's identity certainly covers a much wider range of behaviors. For most individuals, having problems related to cultural conflicts does not necessarily indicate clinical maladjustment. Young people may merely be coping with youth's search for identity. It should be acknowledged that such stress-points in life do place additional pressures on Asian Americans.

Thus, in dealing with the concerns of Asian Americans, it helps to be aware of and knowledgeable about the experiences that have shaped their behavior. It is also important to be sensitive to people's level of ethnic identification, and to some who may have inhibitions about self-disclosure and reflection of feelings. Some studies suggest that Asians prefer structured counseling situations as opposed to nondirective counseling approaches that deal with affect and reflections (Sue & Kirk, 1973; Atkinson et al., 1978). Finally, as a peer counselor, you need to be continually alert to your own cultural and class-bound values and assumptions. so that you do not impose them on your clients.

Summary

In working with Asian Americans, it is helpful to:

- Be knowledgeable about the Asian American experience—recognizing the overt racism and oppression encountered by Asians during settlement, and the subtle forms of racism that may still prevail.

- Be tuned in to your own cultural values and assumptions about others.

- Be aware of the level of ethnic identification that your client brings into the counseling situation.

- Be sensitive to the inhibitions some Asian Americans may have concerning self-disclosure and expression of feelings.

- Be sensitive to some Asian American clients who may be more receptive to structured, direct approaches in interactions, as opposed to ambiguous ones.

EXERCISES

The following vignettes involve problems that clients can present in peer counseling. We hope these examples will generate thought and discussion. In each case, ask yourself how you might handle the problem. As a peer counselor, what skills could you use to establish rapport and help the culturally different individual clarify his or her problems?

1. "I've been dating this Caucasian girl for some time, and I want to spend more time with her. But my parents are giving me a hard time lately about using the family car, coming home late, etc. . . . They weren't like this before."

2. "My parents are very pleased that I'm pursuing a pre-med program. I'm doing fine with the science courses, but I'm finding literature fascinating and more interesting. I've always been told to enter a practical field like science, engineering, or computer sciences—I'm afraid my parents will cut off the financial aid if I switch."

3. "I just couldn't believe my mother when she actually took the yearbook out and went through every single Asian's picture and asked me about them."

4. "I'm so different from the rest of the Asians here. In Hawaii, there's no such thing as discrimination, and I've never heard the term Asian American before. I don't see why there's such a big fuss about it."

5. "I wanted to get involved in Asian American activities, but my Caucasian friends told me that I was alienating them, so I didn't get involved."

SEXUAL ORIENTATION:
NEW PERSPECTIVES FOR PEER COUNSELORS

by Nadja B. Gould

During the past decade, dramatic changes have occurred in the United States in both popular thinking and clinical theories regarding sexual orientation. In 1973 the American Psychiatric Association removed homosexuality as a diagnostic category, and the therapeutic community began listening to what was already emerging in the culture: the increasingly public voices of gay, lesbian, and bisexual people. Many gays and lesbians viewed mental health professionals as oppressors rather than healers, as perpetrators of unjustifiable and outmoded views of homosexuality fueled not by scientific knowledge or by compassion but by prejudice and homophobia.

Peer counselors, their clients, and many of their supervisors have grown into adulthood during this era. It is a time characterized by the post-Stonewall exuberance of the Gay Liberation Movement, annual gay pride marches in cities across the United States, bookstores with well-stocked shelves of gay and lesbian fiction and nonfiction, openly gay film and sports stars, gay members of the U.S. Congress, the appearance of gay-identified health and counseling centers and, beginning the early 1980s, the tragic explosion of the epidemic of Acquired Immune Deficiency Syndrome (AIDS).

This chapter focuses on contemporary views of sexual orientation, including the variety of concerns that bring young people to counseling. It addresses:

- Identity formation and the assessment of sexual orientation

- Special developmental issues for gay, lesbian, and bisexual adolescents

- Disclosure (coming out to self and others)

- Characteristics of membership in an invisible minority

- Effects of growing up with a stigmatized identity

- Dilemmas of the straight counselor–gay client or gay counselor–gay client dyad, with a view to both pitfalls and opportunities

- Supportive counseling to persons with AIDS

The chapter ends with some practical suggestions for peer counselors, enabling you to feel more connected to the people, activities, and ideas in the gay, lesbian, and bisexual communities around you.

IDENTITY FORMATION

In the United States today, at least 10 percent of the population are thought to be exclusively homosexual. In large urban areas and on many college campuses, the percentage may be significantly higher. Also, many people who think of themselves as heterosexual have had occasional same-sex sexual experiences, either as adolescents or as adults. As a peer counselor, you are likely to encounter numerous questions about sexual identity, such as the following:

"How can someone know for sure if he is gay?"

"If my roommate just met the right man, she would get over being a lesbian, right?"

"I fooled around with my best friend when we were twelve, and now he tells me he's bisexual. He thinks maybe I am too, but he's crazy! Don't you think so?"

"When I came out to my parents, they freaked out because they are positive they must have done something wrong. What can I tell them?"

The most important point to remember about identity formation is that no one *really* knows what causes heterosexuality, homosexuality, or bisexuality. As far back as 1948, the researcher Alfred Kinsey described a seven-point scale (with 0 being exclusive heterosexuality and 6 being exclusive homosexuality). Most people fell between the two extremes. Bell and Weinberg, in a 1981 study with nearly 1,500 respondents, found that sexual preference is likely to be determined by the time boys and girls reach adolescence, even if they have not yet become sexually active. *Feelings* rather than particular sexual behaviors, were crucial in the formation of heterosexual, homosexual, or bisexual identities. Thus, listening and attending to the feelings of a client are the most important foundations of good peer counseling, as earlier chapters discuss.

The Bell and Weinberg study made two other interesting observations:

1. Among both men and women, a strong connection appeared to exist between gender nonconformity in youth and the development of homosexuality.

2. Identification with the opposite- or same-sex parent did not significantly affect the child's subsequent sexual orientation.

They concluded that "homosexuality may arise from a biological precursor" but "cannot be traced back to a single social or psychological root" (Bell et al., 1981; p. 192).

Supported by the majority of informed mental health professionals, these conclusions go a long way to refute several myths. As peer counselors, you will confront some of the following myths in your clients, and perhaps in yourself.

- Gay men are effeminate, limp-wristed men who like to cross-dress in women's clothes.

- Gay men have grown up in families with absent ineffectual fathers and overbearing mothers.

- Lesbians hate men, like to look and dress tough, and tend to ride motorcycles.

- Both lesbians and gay men are born that way, have different biochemical and hormonal systems, and can never change.

- Gay people could change if they really wanted to, and they just haven't tried hard enough (or met the right man/woman).

These and other myths are still prevalent in our society. (For a more complete discussion of myths and facts, see Appendix E.) For a young person coming out or trying to come to terms with a same-sex attraction, it is often confusing and difficult to differentiate fact from myth. Homophobic myths that stereotype or stigmatize gays and lesbians can do severe damage to a young person's self-esteem. Since gay and straight youth grow up in similar cultural climates and are exposed to the same distortions, both may benefit from counseling in which they can explore and debunk the myths.

If peer counselors are to work effectively with gay students, their training should include presentations and workshops led by "out" students as well as older "out" adults in the community. The experience of being gay in a college setting may be strikingly different from that in an urban neighborhood or rural community. Counseling needs to help people explore the transition into as well as out of college.

COMING OUT WHILE GROWING UP

Coming out is the developmental process through which people recognize their gay, lesbian, or bisexual preferences and choose to integrate this new identity into their personal and social lives. It is probably the single most frequent concern of such callers and drop-in clients at peer counseling centers. This is partly because coming out does not occur just once, but rather is a lengthy process that continues to varying degrees throughout life.

Coming out is multidimensional: experienced on cognitive, affective, and behavioral levels, and often occurring in stages. These stages are called "coming out to self" and "coming out to others" such as family, roommates, or coworkers. Sometimes a caller or client comes right to the point about a coming-out issue. More often, the opening statements may seem vague because the person is testing the waters. Some examples of both:

Male: *Hi . . . I've been thinking all summer about coming out to my roommate, but I just don't know how to get started.*

Helpful response: *Well, I guess that's a big step but an important one, too.*

Or: *What kind of things would you really like your roommate to know about you?*

Unhelpful response: *Maybe he already suspects that you're gay.*

Or: *Why do you need to tell him? That's pretty risky.*

Female: *I'm planning to take my best friend home for Christmas, but she's nervous about meeting my parents.*

Helpful response: *Well, could you tell me a little more about your friend?*

Or: *Hmm, are you a little nervous as well?*

Or: *Could you say more about why she is nervous?*

Or: *Well, what are your parents like?*

Unhelpful: *Why, is there something about your relationship that is weird or something?*

Or: *You probably just need to reassure her that your parents are great, and not to worry!*

The adolescent who struggles with coming out while growing up is beset by enormous hurdles at an early age. These include dealing with all the physical changes of puberty, emerging sexual feelings, peer pressure, striving for independence from parents, job demands, or academic expectations. Gay, lesbian, and bisexual young people are often aware of "being different" at an age when most teenagers find it virtually impossible to talk about their feelings. Boys may be aware of same-sex attractions by age 13, often younger, and first act on these feelings at an average age of 15. The corresponding ages for girls are slightly later: awareness at 14 to 16, and acting on the feelings at an average age of 20 (Troiden, 1989; pp. 54–55). So college peer counselors may encounter students who have struggled in isolation with their sense of emerging identity. In that struggle, they may have felt guilt in relation to their families, shame about their secret, and depression—sometimes to the point of suicidal behavior.

A final point about coming out. Young people in racial minority groups (e.g., African-American, Hispanic, Asian-American) are likely to find acceptance and help from their families about feeling secure in their racial identity. But because most gay and lesbian children grow up in heterosexual families and are an "invisible minority," it is within their own families that gay children often feel the most isolated.

> *The denial of sexuality in children and the denial of homosexuality as well, makes homosexuality virtually invisible in childhood. In this regard, the experience of gays is different from that of other minorities. Whereas with other minorities the experience of difference may be negative and yet unavoidably present while growing up, with gays the experience of being different is not supposed to have existed in childhood. Therefore, gays may have a susceptibility to invalidation, different from that of ethnic minorities, for example, because of the former's pervasive invisibility.*
> —deMonteflores, 1986; p. 88

How can one be sensitive to and avoid invalidating a minority group that is "invisible"? The most basic advice is also the simplest: never make assumptions about someone's sexual orientation. (In the 1970s, a popular button read, "How dare you presume that I'm heterosexual?") Certainly, we see evidence on college campuses today that some gay and lesbian students are comfortable being quite visible. Some wear styles of clothing, T-shirts proclaiming just about everything, pink triangles, and so forth. Yet as many other gay or bisexual students are invisible and may remain so throughout their lives.

BISEXUALITY

Psychologists now believe that we are all born with components of bisexuality and that for unknown reasons, both biological and environmental, some of us become heterosexual and others homosexual. Many people who later in their adult life self-define as heterosexual have had one or several same-sex experiences or attractions. Some young people, especially in high school or college, label themselves bisexual during a transitional stage in the coming-out process. On the other hand, there are those for whom bisexuality remains a lifetime identity involving strong emotional and sexual relationships with both sexes.

Straight Counselor–Gay Client . . . Gay Counselor–Gay Client

A gay client seeking peer counseling is looking for a special kind of help: acceptance and validation, which he or she may feel is unattainable from friends and family. Even so, the client is likely to see the peer counselor as an authority figure, a representative of the mainstream culture, and a potential source of disapproval. Unless the peer counseling center specifically designates itself as gay-identified, or the counselor feels comfortable about self-identifying as gay, the client will probably assume that the counselor is heterosexual.

The challenge for each counselor, gay or straight, is to convey an open, nonjudgmental acceptance and to listen carefully to the client's story. The pitfall is imposing your own attitudes, fears, or beliefs, even when such statements are well meaning. For example, a straight counselor, wanting to reassure a gay client, may underestimate the obstacles the client faces in coming out to family and friends. Sometimes a counselor's own unconscious fears or discomfort or even homophobia may make it hard to listen to similar fears coming from the client. Supervision groups led by professional counselors can provide a safe place to discuss such situations and come to understand and modify one's own unconscious responses.

Likewise, a gay, lesbian, or bisexual peer counselor may provide a much needed role model for a client on the brink of coming out. But be wary of subtle pressures toward self-disclosure until the client is ready. A person's first disclosure of sexual identity is a profoundly personal and emotional moment. It deserves to be treated with great care and respect. Again, professionally led supervision groups can help gay, lesbian, and bisexual peer counselors who are struggling with their own coming-out issues to focus their personal concerns within the group.

Ongoing training and supervision by mental health professionals is an absolute must for a successful peer counseling program, both to assure quality of care for the clients and to provide support for the counselors' morale. Supervision should include guidelines about when to refer clients for professional counseling, including referrals to gay-affirmative or gay-identified professionals.

A Word About Labels

Labels are indispensable. Some people cherish them, some shun them, many fear them. In addition, labels are as changeable as the weather in New England. For some gay, lesbian, or bisexual people, labels are the rungs of the ladder leading them out of confusion and shame into self-acceptance and pride. Labels can help these young men and women feel identified as members of a group, just at a time when they feel most isolated and rejected by the world around them.

We need to recognize the psychological meaning of labels as a vital part of identity development, to hear them in their ever-shifting meanings, and to have the courage to ask clients gently for more explanation if we do not understand them. For example, three undergraduates described themselves to me as follows:

> "Last year I was straight . . . this fall, I'm straight and questioning."

> "I'm attracted to other guys, but I'm not gay . . . I'm not sure exactly what I am."

> "I'm a lesbian, but mostly I'm a dyke."

THE IMPACT OF AIDS

Acquired Immune Deficiency Syndrome, which the Centers for Disease Control first described in 1981, has had a devastating effect on many lives. These include any person with AIDS (PWA), those who have tested positive for the human immuno virus (HIV) but are not yet symptomatic, and those who test negative or have not been tested. As a peer counselor, you may find yourself dealing for the first time with young people facing life-threatening illness and death. AIDS forces us to look directly at two areas that are taboo in our society—sex and death—and to understand the ways in which they are linked.

Persons with HIV disease need an outlet for their anger, guilt, and shame ("I must have deserved this"). They also need support in dealing with potential social rejection from family and the community. Many cities now offer "buddy programs" designed specifically as peer counseling and support for persons with AIDS. Because AIDS forces us all to face our own mortality, counselors dealing with PWAS should have special training in understanding the medical, psychological, and spiritual process-es of death and dying, anticipatory grief reactions, and their own feelings of impotence in the face of another's death.

As a peer counselor, you may also encounter other situations:

- "The worried well"—those fearful of AIDS who may or may not have engaged in unsafe sex

- Questions about specific sexual practices with which you may be unfamiliar (This illustrates the importance of using descriptive language rather than euphemisms when discussing sexual behavior!)

- Assessment of risk factors and other issues about HIV antibody testing (Who should be tested? Who should not? Who decides?)

PRACTICAL SUGGESTIONS

How can you, as a peer counselor, become even more sensitive to your gay, lesbian, and bisexual clients (regardless of your own sexual orientation)? Here are a few suggestions, not only to give you practical information about the gay community in your area but to help you become a more empathic listener. (If you like, team up with another peer counselor for support in any of these ventures.)

- Browse through the gay/lesbian/bisexual section in your local bookstore. Check the library as well. Borrow or buy a novel that has a gay theme. Read it and discuss it with your friends.

- Find and buy the local gay newspaper and go to a concert or movie that is advertised in it.

- If you know someone who is gay, lesbian, or bisexual, ask him or her to talk with you about what it was like growing up, in school, as an adolescent, in the family, and so on.

- Have some books in your peer counseling office that are affirming of gay, lesbian, and bisexual relationships. Get a gay "yellow pages" directory if one exists in your area, so you know about and can refer to health clinics, gay religious groups, anonymous HIV test sites, recreational groups, and so on.

- Obtain information on Parents and Friends of Lesbians and Gays (PFLAG), a national organization that helps gays and their families, has pamphlets, and runs support groups.

Finally, remember that you do not have to be gay, lesbian, or bisexual to be a good counselor to others who are or may be so. Empathic listening is the key.

8

PEER COUNSELING IN COLLEGES AND UNIVERSITIES:
A DEVELOPMENTAL VIEWPOINT*

by Vincent J. D'Andrea

The Community Mental Health Act of 1961 was a powerful set of national legislative acts which provided the impetus for the development of the concept of community mental health centers providing a variety of services in defined population areas and relying heavily on the notion of local and community responsibility for health care as well as social services. The notions of the "indigenous nonprofessional" and "paraprofessional" gained steady impetus in the development of community action and community mental health programs in the early 1960s. Many such programs addressed themselves to the broad issues of newer approaches to mental health treatment for labor and lower income groups. A general notion developed that the use of indigenous nonprofessionals could span the gap between professional worker and people in the urban community. Neighborhood health centers and Head Start programs developed as a result of Office of Economic Opportunity activities in the late '60s.

By providing the need, there developed as a direct consequence an increasing demand for counseling services and a

*Reprinted with permission of The Haworth Press, Inc., from Journal of College Student Psychotherapy, 1(3), Spring 1987.

shortage of professionally trained personnel to provide needed assistance.

In the medical area, two noteworthy programs were those of Smith and associates (1971) in the development of the so-called "Medex" program, in which individuals were given intensive training to work with general practitioners in rural areas; the Smith group also proposed training and placement of psychiatric paraprofessionals termed "Pinels," who would work in emergency services in relationship to a psychiatrist. The Physician's Assistant Program at Duke University also gained momentum at that time.

The exact wording of one of the recommendations of the Joint Commission on Mental Illness and Health is interesting:

> Non-medical mental health workers with aptitudes in training, practical experience and demonstrable competence should be permitted to do general short-term psychotherapy—namely, the treating of persons by objective, permissive, non-directive techniques of listening to their troubles and helping them resolve those troubles in individual and insightfully useful ways.

A number of studies were undertaken to test the hypothesis that there were people who could be trained to do psychotherapy under limited conditions. A noteworthy study was undertaken by Rioch et al. in 1963. In that program, 80 forty-year-old married women with children were trained in a practical program sharply focused on teaching therapy. As therapists, it was felt they all performed useful services to patients, doing useful work in various agencies. The study was influential for raising the question of whether there was a need and space for new professions in the field of mental health. Later, Kubie proposed a new profession, a doctorate in medical psychology (Rioch et al., 1963).

A parallel track following the 1961 enabling legislation was exploration of ways to extend the usefulness and expertise of the psychiatrist in application of emerging principles of mental health systems consultation in a variety of public and institutional settings (Caplan & Killilea, 1976).

Beginning in the mid '60s, the successful use of paraprofessionals in a wide range of counseling roles was reported with increasing frequency. A number of evaluation studies documented the effectiveness of paraprofessional counselors in community and anti-poverty programs, in mental hospitals and outpatient clinics, and on school and college campuses.

Brown (1976) noted that professional reaction to the paraprofessional movement took two principal directions: one reported the meaningful contributions made by selected paraprofessionals and stressed the unique advantages of using them in almost all aspects of the counseling process.

Another warned about the practical and legal dangers of lowering professional standards and recommended that "paraprofessionals be restricted to routine duties that would free professionals from clerical and other menial tasks." There were powerful forces aligned arguing against the use of such personnel in any manner that would replace the professional counselor in the counseling role itself (Brown, 1976).

As increasingly positive outcomes of paraprofessional employment were reported from numerous studies, the American Personnel and Guidance Association adopted a more receptive position toward the role of paraprofessionals. Since that time, the use of nonprofessionals in counseling roles has a reasonable, systematic research history in the psychological literature. Generally, minimally trained nonprofessional counselors were rated by clients as no less effective than their professional counterparts.

However, there was little research in the actual implementation of nonprofessional programs, although there were some interesting descriptions. Brown, in his review of the literature of the previous 15 years, noted numerous positive reports on the effective use of paraprofessional counselors. However, he stated most of the studies were plagued with design inadequacies that "characterized most of the research published up to that time." He noted that fewer than 25 percent of the reports compared experimental with control samples, used both pre- and post-assessment measures, or employed objective rather than subjective criteria. He also noted that only a few of the studies attempted to isolate independent variables through matching experimental and controlled conditions or to collect adequate follow-up data to check on the possibility of the Hawthorne effect.

Despite these shortcomings, Brown concluded that the number and variety of studies reported collectively provided compelling evidence as to the effectiveness of paraprofessional counseling. Specifically, research directed by Carkhuff and his associates (1969), and Brown and associates (1974) in academic settings, demonstrated the effectiveness of paraprofessionals in programs designed for specific counseling objectives.

Brown cites Carkhuff and Truax in drawing the following conclusions: (a) lengthy professional training is not a necessary prerequisite for effective functioning as a therapist; (b) individuals possessing such personal characteristics as nonpossessive warmth, interpersonal sensitivity, empathic understanding and overt genuineness can rapidly develop therapeutic skills; and (c) paraprofessionals receiving limited training can be just as effective as professionals in facilitating constructive client change over relatively short periods of time (Brown, 1974).

In 1974, Ivey and associates published work in *microcounseling*, an innovation in interviewing skills training. Subsequently, Ivey et al. developed various training modules designed to provide specific skills training to selected populations using role-playing and videotape feedback and discrete learning of separate skills as the core of the program.

By 1974, a considerable body of work around training programs and evaluations had developed in the literature. In a special issue of the *Personnel and Guidance Journal*, Delworth, the guest editor, defined *paraprofessional* as follows:

The term paraprofessional has become as difficult to define as the term professional. In this special issue we are defining paraprofessionals as persons who are selected, trained and given responsibility for performing functions generally performed by professionals. They do not possess the requisite education or credentials to be considered professionals in the field in which they are working, but they do perform tasks central to the function of the agency, for instance, counseling, group work, etc. They are usually paid for their work but they may participate in volunteer programs if they meet the other criteria of this definition.

That issue of the journal attempted to present an accurate picture of the "state of the art," giving an overview of viable programs in counseling and human services and addressing training issues (Delworth, 1974).

By the mid to late 1970s, the term *paraprofessional* had been gradually supplanted by the term *peer counselor*. One can conclude from the literature that the evolution was from the term *indigenous nonprofessional* to *paraprofessional* to *peer counselor*. Reading in the literature indicates that the term *paraprofessional* has continued in use in community action and community mental health programs, paralegal, rape crisis, and suicide hotline structures. The term *peer counseling* came into its own in the late '70s. Indeed, D'Andrea and Salovey in 1983 noted over 5,000 references to peer counseling theory, training, and programming in an exhaustive review of the literature at that time.

They defined *peer counseling* as "the use of active listening and problem-solving skills together with knowledge about human growth and mental health by students in order to help advise and counsel other students." They further stated the basic premise underlying peer counseling as "students are often capable of solving their own problems of daily living if given a chance," and "the peer counselor assists other students to find their own solutions by clarifying thoughts and feelings and by exploring various options and alternatives" (D'Andrea & Salovey, 1983). Giddan and Austin (1982) also reported extensively on peer counseling and self-help groups on college campuses and noted over 5,000 references in the literature.

The concerns of professionals about peer counselors and paraprofessionals were already prominent in the literature in the late 1960s. Some writers suggested that professionals should move to establish the kinds of controls over paraprofessionals that were necessary to ensure the effectiveness of services provided. Others were advised that "professionals maintain a flexible attitude and recognize that they were not exempt from feelings of jealousy and insecurity" (Rioch, 1963). Gruver (1971) warned that

> *unsophisticated paraprofessionals, while intending no harm, could easily project their own difficulties onto their clients, burden clients with their own personal problems, "play" at psychotherapy with clients, or exploit their relationship with clients, all with potentially disastrous consequences for the client's welfare.*

Undoubtedly, these cautions continue to be of concern to any responsible professional who is in relationship to a peer counseling program and certainly to mental health professionals in general.

Along this line, Brown (1974) cites Carkhuff (1969) in speculating that the methods employed in selecting paraprofessionals "attempted to select individuals who exhibit capacity for empathy, warmth and sensitivity and that by contrast the selection process for professionals is typically predominated by intellectual indices, primarily grade point averages and performances on the graduate record examination." Carkhuff speculates that the two approaches differ meaningfully in that "paraprofessional programs select psychologically healthy persons while professional programs emphasize selection on intellectual factors that may or may not correlate with effective interpersonal functioning" (Carkhuff, 1969).

The matter is further compounded by the well-known observation that often peer counselors in specific areas such as rape crisis, suicide counseling, child abuse, and abuse of women have often themselves been victims. This underscores an imperative for a training program, namely, that an understanding of one's self should be a prerequisite or should be a process as important as gaining knowledge of helping skills and application of those skills. (The issue of training will be addressed later in this chapter.)

It must also be kept in mind that much of the theoretical underpinning and development of methods of training of peer counselors in counseling skills comes from the tradition of counseling psychology and more specifically, from the theories and practice of Carl Rogers. That body of knowledge is perhaps more consistent with the notion of the student development model than that of the psychodynamic model with its emphasis on the influence of early experiences on the development of mechanisms of defense and character structure.

In terms of college counseling, one can use the analogy of a doughnut, in which the student development counselor would see the doughnut whereas the psychodynamically trained person might be focused on the hole. The student development model assumes more health than pathology. The student development model is more interested in ways in which the learning environment of the university in its totality—i.e., in the communal living situations and the social interactions of students—can provide learning opportunities in which students learn and appreciate differences in values and the importance of interdependence.

The psychodynamic model—in particular, the Eriksonian, as well as ego psychology models—focus on developmental tasks, particularly those having to do with separation and individuation, and entering the adult world of work, in the context of increased autonomy and working out satisfactory relationships with others. Or, as Lyons (1983) puts it,

> it is important that students know they are assuming respon-sibility for their own affairs. Most students learn they can be independent of home, family and adolescent structures. In fact, they probably would develop independence (maybe even more) if they did not attend college; but independence is not enough. The real challenge is to develop interdepen-dence—the webs of social and personal relationships—and learn how to give and receive the help and support of friends and peers. Peer counseling programs provide the opportunity to learn, practice, and appreciate interdependence.

And again,

> what is learned can be transferred to life after college; the experience of being part of a helping group might well lead to an increased awareness of needs in the community where those graduates live and work.

These statements by an educator and an expert in the values of the college student community represent an eloquent expres-sion of the student development model in action.

Those institutions which, in their counseling and mental health services, are dominated by clinicians who are dynamical-ly trained may find it strange to be faced with the question of the selection, training, and supervision of students who might be involved in counseling other students. Some psychiatrists and psychologists trained in social psychiatry or psychology and systems consultation would find it less strange, particularly if they are consulting with the student program as clinicians and teachers and serving as role models for student who are inter-ested in the helping professions.

But it is within the context of the educational commu-nity that peer counseling comes into its own. The educational mission of a college or university is expressed in the work of peer counselors at all levels—in residential counseling, personal counseling, academic advising, residential advising, career planning, etc. In this context, peer counselors are less paraprofessionals and more students working through developmental issues in the context of a defined community [that is] giving them an opportunity for service, role trial, and the "interdependence" that Lyons refers to above.

It is perhaps at this point that peer counseling programs in colleges and universities diverge from the model of cooperative and communal clinics and centers devoted to dealing with specific health problems or crisis issues in human life. In the latter, although the individuals involved are often peers in relationship to the people they serve, they are more often regarded as paraprofessionals working side by side with lawyers, physicians, nurses, and other professional crisis workers. . . .

When a number of student groups came to the Counseling Service at Stanford with an interest in peer counselor training, . . . what was familiar was the already existing energy and attention being paid to the selection, orientation, and training of residential staff, the facilitation of interactions of professionals from the counseling staff with the residential staff, liaison, teaching, and consultation services provided in the dormitories. Since there was already substantial commitment by the service in consultation roles of various sorts, the development of a peer counselor training and consultation program was consistent with the mission and function of the Counseling Service.

Twelve years earlier, the question of how professionals might relate to paraprofessionals was being highly debated. As Danish and Brock (1974) said then:

> As the use of paraprofessionals has accelerated, considerable attention has been directed towards the problems associated with their use: what to call them, how much independence to give them, what they should do and how to resolve relationships between them and the professional community.

Presumably, in the intervening years, as a result of the community mental health act legislation, a body of experience and knowledge accumulated; and certainly in social psychology, counseling psychology, and social psychiatry, those principles were well known. Even so, the issue needs to be approached thoughtfully and carefully; it is probably still the case that there is considerable apprehension on the part of professionals in working with students who are in helping roles. When the question of how to relate to peer counselors of various sorts is no longer the primary focus of concern, the emphasis can turn to how to train such people and what kinds of skills they need to do their work effectively.

[At Stanford,] three existing training models were turned to: those of Carkhuff, Ivey, and Kagan. Carkhuff (1969) identified a series of several qualities present in established helping relationships; those qualities were derived from the conditions put forth by Rogers, namely, the necessary and sufficient conditions of empathy, unconditional positive regard, and genuineness. The Carkhuff program is built around the process of teaching people to make responses at those specific levels.

Ivey (1974) defined verbal behaviors in terms of specific response categories, added the dimension of nonverbal attending behavior, developed a training model termed "microcounseling" as a means of implementing the training. It is characterized by a focus on single skills taught in sequence, utilizing extensive videotape modeling and feedback to the trainee.

Kagan (1972) focused his efforts on a different approach to the training of helping relationship skills. Also using a videotape feedback model, he expanded it into the "interpersonal process recall" procedure, focusing less on teaching discrete skills than on assisting the trainee to understand the interaction between a helper and a helpee by recognizing the impact that each has on the other. Both models also include the competence of fostering an understanding of one's self, as well as knowledge of helping skills and experience in applying those skills.

The underlying educational principle is that of skills learning, a model which assumes that having knowledge about skills is not enough and that effective learning involves acquiring a conceptual understanding of the components of the skill, viewing models of others using the skill effectively, and having an opportunity to use the skill in practice. How the application of these methods has fared is of interest.

In a 1984 survey of 200 college counseling centers, 57 reported using no particular model, and 43 reported using microcounseling, client-centered, eclectic, and Kagan models. A minority [reported] using models based on student development, cognitive behavioral approaches, and interpersonal process recall. It does appear that the majority of college counseling centers are using established models to train peer counselors (Salovey & D'Andrea, 1984).

What other learning takes place in such training? Earlier, allusion was made to themes developing out of consideration of the programs at Stanford. Lyons' foregoing remarks certainly serve as a statement of the educational social value of student-to-student service. At a more individual level, the following themes and issues can be identified:

Altruism. Altruism has been referred to as a healthy mechanism of defense and coping skill. This is often the underlying theme for service.

Affiliation. The coming together of a group of people for a common highly held purpose is positive to the individual for the emotional support, esteem of one's peers, and strength through numbers of a group. Through affiliation comes support, heightened confidence, a lessening of the sense of individual deviancy, information sharing, and collective action.

Heightened Self-Definition. Commonly reported by students who are involved themselves in such programs has been a clearer sense of self and a heightening of self-esteem. Through mechanisms of openness and self-disclosure, the ongoing support of the group, and fulfilling of a valued role in the group, many students have found the experience, either in the training or in the work as peer counselors, to be important in the shaping or reinforcing of identity formation in the transition from youth to adulthood.

Role Trial. Our society, with its prolonged preparation for adult roles, has not offered many experiences for the younger person in "meaningful roles." A large difference between the role of youth and adults is in the responsibility for others; the adult is expected to assume such responsibility and the youth, in general, is not. The peer counseling experience offers a role trial for those interested in professions such as teaching, counseling, mental health, medicine, and others where there is a measured responsibility for another person.

Social Skill Learning and Broadened Interpersonal Competence. Students wishing to heighten their sills in working with other people regard the training as a form of "intimacy training" which might be important in personal life; for others, it can be social skill learning which could be useful in work roles. Through their training and interaction, students wish to achieve a better understanding of individual psychology (perhaps their own), of group processes, and ways of facilitating communication and interaction. In our complex society, many of the adult economic roles are in groups, organizations, and institutions. Competence in working with people becomes a sought-after skill in the instrumental sense.

Learning Adaptive Coping Interpersonal Skills from Others. These coping skills involve cognitive, intrapsychic mechanisms and behaviors to deal with environmental situations and feeling and maturation states in individuals. This learning of coping skills goes on in all peer relationships and broadly in human relationships. One learns from others by observation, by identification, by precept, by example, and by coaching. In the peer counselor training, there is a heightening of this normal process (Dorosin, 1977).

This can be regarded as a constructive opportunity for mental health workers on a college campus; the interaction of the student with the counseling center can be viewed as a way of facilitating processes which are part of normal personality development and opportunities for education for personal competence. Additionally, such activities can enhance the supportive aspects of the social environment of the campus as well as contributing to the personal development of those student who involve themselves in the training and the work of service to other students.

In 1984, Salovey and D'Andrea undertook a study to document peer counseling activities at colleges and universities in the United States and Canada. Particular attention was paid to the roles ascribed to peer counselors, the typical problems with which they are confronted, the training that they receive, and the institutional enablers and constraints, i.e., financial issues and the availability of professional liaisons under which peer counselors work.

Directors of counseling services in 200 colleges and universities were asked to complete a questionnaire. One hundred fifty-six responses were received. One hundred twenty-two indicated ongoing peer counselor activities in a wide variety of settings at the respective campuses. Most common were residence hall counseling and advising, academic tutoring, academic problem solving, services for minority students, services for women, career guidance services, suicide and crisis intervention, general psychological counseling, contraceptive and abortion counseling, gay and lesbian counseling, rape and battered women counseling, freshmen orientation, draft registration, alcohol and drug counseling, and health and wellness counseling.

The number of peer counselors was reported as ranging from 2 to 450, with an average of 107. If the figures are representative, this survey reflected about 12,000 active peer counselor nationally. On the average campus, approximately one-fourth of the student body made use of the peer counselor in the typical academic year and there were approximately 3 peer counselors per 100 students.

The most common kinds of concerns confronted by peer counselors involved academic difficulties and issues and relationships with friends and lovers; career anxieties, monetary problems, and difficulties with parents were also listed as common issues. Other problems mentioned but not scaled were alcohol and other drug abuse, roommate difficulties, eating disorders, religious and values conflict, competency and self-esteem difficulties, role conflicts, independence issues, anxiety and stress, and study skills. It is noted that student-organized self-help groups for drug abuse, common in the past decade, were reported infrequently.

More serious or sensitive problem areas, such as suicidal thinking or sexual dysfunction, were typically not presented to peer counselors, although the presentation of depression was relatively common.

In the same study, the nature and duration of training was noted. The training programs varied widely, from brief workshops of less than ten hours to long classes of more than ten hours; in-service training provided the bulk of preparation for service.

According to the survey, professional counseling center staff and staff from other specific campus settings were involved in the training. The models have been mentioned already— generally speaking, skill-based models as developed by Ivey, Carkhuff, and Kagan. Nonetheless, the survey revealed that only 36 percent of peer counselors received substantial training prior to doing their work, and there were few carefully designed studies evaluating the relative effectiveness of these various training models.

As for funding support, program funding sources varied widely but were generally from on-campus resources, e.g., federal grant or work study money, Dean's Office money, student government or student fee money, and health service and counseling service funding. Two programs generated their own income.

When one considers the variety of colleges and universities in this country and the differing bureaucratic structures and mixes of residential and nonresidential students, one is not surprised at the reports of different structures of programs, sources of funding, training, resources, and kinds of problems addressed. It is a temptation for those who have worked in programs to develop notions which might cut across the variety of structural situations in colleges and universities. However, it appears that rather than using a cookie-cutter approach, colleges and universities are employing a cut-and-paste method; that is to say, they are using pieces and components in common, but they are arranged differently. Quite clearly, this must be the case; a program developed in a large and largely residential university would have little directly in common with programs developed at the large or small commuter college.

But what other generalizations can be made about programs and those programs which work best? Following are some ideas and suggestions gleaned from the literature and from the same survey.

1. Those programs work best which are relatively autonomous of university administration (e.g., they are student organizations with faculty or staff advisors training, through credit courses, in association with the counseling center staff as trainers and consultants.

2. Those programs which work best provide listening skills and problem-solving skills with a specific content appropriate to the task of the peer counseling group.

3. Those programs work best which have a defined role and a defined population to serve.

4. Those programs work best which provide some mechanism for the continuity of the program, policies and practices; a mixture of students of different levels of education, different majors and interests, and whose program provides for outreach activities by the students.

5. Those programs work best on campuses where there is networking with other student peer counseling and advising interest groups; the networking may be in training, may be in consultation, may be in fund-raising and cross-referrals.

6. Those programs work best which have good working and consultation relationships with counseling and mental health staff as trainers, teachers, and consultants. (See the next section, "Note.")

It appears further that the peer counselors are not being used as "paraprofessionals" in the sense that they are not, with some exceptions (academic and career advising) working in the same space as the professionals.

The issue of having a defined role and defined population to service is an important one; those programs which are entirely volunteer and which depend upon personal persuasion or simply the fact that they are "different" from professionals seem to flounder. Situations in which the training and evaluation of the work is provided through an academic course legitimize the learning process and at the same time lead into a practicum for the students. The settings in which the students work are student-run organizations or groups sponsored by a university office or professional staff.

This approach places programs squarely in the tradition of the student development model. In this model, students performing peer counseling functions are not junior staff, nor are they vulnerable to being utilized as staff extenders by desperate administrators facing budget and billet cuts. Flowing with the educational enterprise of the institution protects the student from exploitation.

Further, an orientation toward a proactive, developmental model of counseling services enables the service to legitimize consultation and outreach services, joint programming with academic departments, and more sensitive focal responses to particular needs of students or student groups, deemed at risk through needs assessments.

One such student-focused model, a proposal by Harman and Baron (1982), places peer counselors in an array of services organized at levels of crisis, remediation, and development. the peer counselor as resident assistant or walk-in counselor is viewed as a front-line resource in a network of supportive services at the three levels. Emphasis is placed on the developmental level of intervention with this model as well as the crisis and remedial functions.

A three-tiered approach is proposed within the crisis, remediation, and development interventions for assisting the developmental process:

1. At *the student environment level:* through workshops, presentations, academic coursework, seminars, media, etc.

2. At *the staff, faculty, peer counselor level:* through providing training and consultation, workshops presentations.

3. At *the social system level:* through research, consultation, committee work, and environmental design; these are aimed at identifying and helping to alleviate barriers in the system to student development and broadly to enhance the support for students in their growth process (Harman & Baron, 1982).

Staff, faculty, student leaders, peer counselors, and others who work with students would be active in each level of intervention.

We can trace peer counseling, originally a paraprofessional form of self-help, from the time of the 1960s through the often anti-intellectual period of the '70s. Many valid self-help groups continue to evolve through perceived social needs (e.g., in the areas of rape, child abuse, alcoholism, drug abuse, eating disorders).

Peer counseling is distinguished by its place within the educational mission of colleges and universities. Legitimized within a student-development model of helping services, it provides an opportunity for students, faculty, and staff to join together in a cooperative venture, reducing the separation between education and individual development.

Note

It is interesting to compare these findings with suggestions made by Delworth in 1974, who identified the following features of successful campus programs:

1. Assessment in terms of program needs with administrative support, resources and benefits to the school, the program, and the students.

2. Planning and organization involving specific and clear work for the students, sufficient backup and funding.

3. Selection of students with recruitment procedures established and qualifications for work set forth.

4. Selection of professionals: Professionals working with peer counselors should be interested, secure in their roles as teachers. Skills learning based on modeling should necessarily be able to demonstrate the various aspects of the skills.

5. Training: It is recommended that there be both core and specific training components. This is echoed in the recommendations above; it seems to be a general observation: general skills are required as well as skills specific to the particular task.

6. Evaluation: This important component provides feedback to the program that goals are being met and may, secondarily, provide data according credibility to the program in terms of justification for funding from various offices of the college or university.

It is often the case that while program descriptions (cookie cutters) may seem reasonable, trainers may experience difficulties in implementing programs designed by others and thus, it seems imperative that the trainers themselves be trained and that the delivery of the training programs be tailored to the situation of the particular college or university.

9

RESIDENT ADVISORS*

by Alice Supton, Matthew Wolf,
and Jan P. Boswinkel

On many college campuses, resident advisors working in dormitories and other forms of student housing constitute the single largest group of peer counselors. Unfortunately, resident advisors (RAs) often receive minimal training in peer counseling skills. The purpose of this chapter's first section, then, is to explore issues and problems that are particularly common in student residences and to provide the RA with a framework for dealing with such problems. The second section discusses when and how to refer peers for professional counseling.

RAs AND PEER COUNSELING

One of the things that resident advisors do is counseling, which we can broadly define as a process of assisting people in using resources they already have, or directing them to other resources they can use to reach their desired goal. It includes giving people information or advice, helping them sort out

*This section is reprinted in part from *The RA's Role in Counseling*, a training booklet for Stanford University's residence staff. It was written by Alice Supton and the staff of Stanford's Counseling and Psychological Services. Matt Wolfe and Vince D'Andrea wrote an earlier version of some of the incidents reprinted here, which was distributed at Stanford as *How To Be There When You're There.*

alternatives with the information already available to them, steering them to some resource that might be an appropriate aid in solving problems they face, and so forth.

Much of the success in counseling lies in knowing the resources available to both you and the person you are counseling. A knowledge of the bureaucratic, academic, and personal resources will be helpful to you in many situations. The act of counseling helps define any problem for both the counselor and the client. It also helps sort out alternatives and define resources needed in solving the problem.

Although RAs are not trained counselors, they are in a position to be very effective helpers for students with problems. Because they share the same residence, RAs know the individual students, and most residents feel comfortable talking with RAs.

Showing You Care

To be helpful counselors to students in their house, RAs need to be accessible and approachable. You should be visible around the residence, present at mealtimes, and available in your room (perhaps with your door open) a fair amount of time. The way you organize your room and interact with students on a day-to-day basis can either invite or discourage their visits.

Being approachable also means showing interest in and concern for others. By sitting at dinner with a student who doesn't seem to have many friends, you communicate concern, present the student with an opportunity to talk, and establish the basis for future contacts.

Be alert to how students in the house are feeling. Although you have a large role in recognizing and helping residents cope with problems, you can also share their joys and successes. You can show interest in and compliment students when they have performed well, contributed to dorm life, or otherwise acted in a constructive way.

You also need to be sensitive to students' moods and watchful for signs of unhappiness or stress. Because you live in the dorm, you may notice changes in people's normal living patterns. Usually, students who haven't been eating or sleeping properly and who don't appear to be taking care of themselves in other ways are sending out messages that all is not well and that they need help. When you find yourself remarking on a student's changed habits or appearance, you should report your observations to the Senior Resident Advisor* and talk with the student. As in this example, when roommates or other students report that someone is upset or anxious, RAs should follow up by talking with that resident.

> One Friday night a student came to me and told me about a woman who was knocking back straight shots of vodka on the patio. She had told the student to go away, and he came to me. I did not know the woman.
>
> I went out onto the patio and sat down next to her. I asked if she wanted to talk, and she said it didn't matter, because nobody cared. I told her that I cared and that I approached her because I cared. I took her hand in mine and she thanked me for my concern. She said that she wanted to talk with me about the problem the next day, and she stayed on the patio.
>
> I went inside and got a close friend of hers to go outside and get the drinking woman inside and to bed. I saw her the next day. She thanked me for my concern and related the difficulties of an interpersonal relationship. She had good reason to be upset.
>
> I handled the situation in a good way. I let the woman know verbally and nonverbally that I was concerned. I called upon her existing social supports to get her to stop drinking and go to bed. I gave her the freedom to refuse my help. I followed up on the incident as I had promised I would; from my actions, she learned to trust me.

---

*Among campuses, the titles for senior staff in residences vary widely. We are using "Senior RA" to describe the person most responsible for administering the residential program and maintaining the residents' quality of life.

Students really appreciate it when an RA notices how they are feeling. Just knowing that the RA is aware of a problem and cares can be helpful to a student facing a difficult time.

> Around Thanksgiving one woman in our dorm was upset with the approaching anniversary of her mother's death. I talked to her about her feelings, directed her to sources of professional counseling, suggested various plans of activity for the Thanksgiving weekend. She survived the holiday well, and we've talked about family problems several times. She seemed to benefit from knowing there was someone near who knew how she was feeling but kept things confidential. Also, we have developed a friendship beyond her family problems.

Often, opening up to the RA can enable the student to talk to others.

> This quarter I've kind of taken two guys in my hall under my wing. Both of them have been programmed to be the "macho male" and never talk to anyone about any problems or thoughts going on in their heads. By some long talks and just spending time together, they've opened up to me and I feel really good about it because I think it's really healthy for them. The last couple of weeks one of them has started opening up with someone else in the dorm, and it really excites me to see him talking to people in this way when he never had before.

Some RAs find that talking with a student away from the dorm gives the person some perspective on the problem.

> One woman in our house was feeling maladjusted, insecure, homesick, and lonely. Her roommate, on the other hand, was feeling just the opposite (which made this woman feel even worse). After one unforgettable 3 A.M. scene in my room—replete with tears and general hysteria—I took her

out for lunch . . . [and] we just had a heart-to-heart talk. As it turned out, she concluded that her expectations of herself were too high and unrealistic, and that she would be happier if she relaxed more and studied less. While her formula might have been dangerous for others, I'm pleased to report a happy ending—she's more at home and she even scored a 4.0! I think taking her off-campus was good because we had more privacy, and being physically removed from the scene of her anxieties afforded her a special and well-needed objectivity. All I had to do is listen, be sincerely sympathetic, and promise support. This was a rewarding experience.

What Is the Problem?

Students may come to you with a clear idea of what is bothering them. A student may think she's pregnant. Another may have failed a midterm in calculus. Another may be upset because his family member is sick. Someone may be fighting with a roommate over the volume of the stereo. A dorm romance may break up and leave the couple uncertain about how to relate to one another. A student may be considering taking a leave of absence from school.

Each year, RAs in the houses with first-year students report that many of those newcomers think someone somehow made a mistake in deciding to admit them. Everyone else appears incredibly smart, athletic, attractive, talented. They feel themselves somehow at the bottom of the heap, whereas in high school they were valedictorians, class presidents, yearbook editors. Lowered self-esteem and worries about whether they'll make it in college are feelings common to new students.

Upper-class students tend to be concerned about what will happen to them after they graduate. Often, in addition to worries about career or graduate school, students experience feelings of anxiety related to becoming independent from their families and striking out on their own. Friendships and romantic relationships are the source of many counseling concerns, as are feelings of loneliness and alienation.

Sometimes people aren't exactly sure what is bothering them. They may have general feelings of anxiety, depression, or ennui. This "depressed for no particular reason" syndrome, as one RA described it, might show up as poor appetite, failure to go to class, or lack of interest in house activities. RAs can encourage students who seem depressed to talk about how they are feeling. When students are distressed because they feel depressed and don't know why, it is particularly important to free them from the need to provide explanations—for themselves or for you—of why they feel the way they do. By showing concern and listening, you can help depressed students air their feelings, which is the first step in helping them get in touch with what is troubling them. Homesickness, death or divorce of parents, unexpressed anger, and unresolved questions of identity often occasion feelings of depression among college-age students.

It helps to be familiar with the problems that appear most frequently in the work in residences. As this RA points out, however, each problem is different and unique.

> I try not to label any one-to-one interaction with students as "my counseling them" on roommate or emotional/romantic problems or whatever. I try not to categorize other people's problems. I can then avoid treating a person as "just another homesick freshman"; and my listening skills improve, so that I can pick out the key personal details. Nonetheless, I have spent a great deal of time counseling students about their academic needs/goals/expectations; helping with many types of male/female communication problems; pointing out personal biases and personal strengths; smoothing roommate situations; encouraging a workable balance between home and college. More than anything else, I want people to know that it is not wrong or a great failing to admit personal defeat or confusion . . . we are only human.

Whose Problem Is It?

Regularly, students come to RAs wanting to switch roommates. They complain that one roommate is a slob. They protest the roommate's sexual activity in the room. They say the person is inconsiderate and selfish. Often they want you to tell the roommate to behave differently—to clean up the room, to entertain elsewhere, to stop playing the stereo at 10 P.M. You may need to examine who has or "owns" the problem and to help the complaining student do the same. Is it the offending roommate or the complaining student?

When RAs ask, "Have you spoken with your roommate about this?" the answer is often no. The person is afraid that the roommate will be angry or resentful. People often need help being assertive. You can encourage them to tell their roommates how they feel about certain behaviors. Also, you can give them some practice in voicing their complaints by role-playing a discussion between the student and the roommate.

It is often helpful to encourage students to verbalize their ideas of the worst possible reactions from the roommate. One effective technique is as follows.

1. Have the student play the role of the roommate (or any person they want to confront). You play the student's role and enact the confrontation.

2. Reverse roles, so that the student plays him- or herself and you take the part of the roommate.

This kind of practice can allay anxieties about real-life encounters. By helping people practice assertive behavior, you enable them to solve their immediate problems and gain confidence in their ability to handle future problems on their own.

You may often find that roommates can settle things between themselves without your becoming an actor in their conflict.

A student came to talk about her roommate, who spent all her time with a boyfriend in the room the two women shared. The student would often leave her room angry, unable to study or sleep. My perception of the situation was that both women were extremely nice and liked each other a great deal. Yet the arrangement of the roommate and her boyfriend was creating tension.

I had to convince the student of her right to use her room, too. She didn't want to intrude on her roommate's relationship. I also convinced her that she had done nothing to resolve the situation. The roommate didn't know this woman was uncomfortable and was beginning to resent her. What I suggested to the woman was that she have a talk with the roommate, for I felt the problem would escalate as the year progressed.

My evaluation of the result was this: (1) The student saw herself as being part of the room. She had a responsibility as well as a right to correct the situation. (2) The roommate became aware of this woman's feelings, and the initial conversation has helped the two of them become closer and enjoy each other more. (3) The roommates have a satisfactory living arrangement without any harsh feelings. I was right: the roommate didn't know the woman was upset and wasn't intentionally hogging the room. (4) I think the situation showed the woman she doesn't have to avoid conflict, and that her feelings are important. (5) The problem was solved before it became too difficult.

When you do get involved in a roommate dispute, it is often in the role of diplomatic negotiator. Usually you should not take sides. Rather, provide encouragement to both roommates and help them hear each other and agree on some compromise solution to their differences. RAs have sometimes learned the hard way that, if they are going to have a role in resolving a roommate or other dorm conflict, they need to make sure they have heard from everyone affected by the problem. They cannot rely simply on what one roommate reports. In roommate switches, for example, it is essential to speak to all four parties, not just the two roommates desiring the switch.

If attempts to deal with roommate conflicts or other problems meet with limited success, you may want to involve the Senior RA. In fact, it is a good idea to keep the Senior RA informed of problems, even if they seem to have resolved.

> One woman in my dorm—"M"—was not getting along with her roommate. She couldn't bring herself to talk to her roommate and express what was bothering her. She wanted me to tell her roommate not to sleep with her boyfriend while M was there, to turn off the light when M was trying to sleep, etc. Most of her complaints seemed legitimate, but I told her that I would only mediate between her and her roommate, to encourage some interaction. She had to face her difficulties and try to solve them.
>
> Well, she tried to talk to her roommate, who flew off the handle and reacted with verbal abuse. This happened repeatedly. I made some attempts to talk to the roommate but was either ignored or verbally insulted. I talked to the Senior RA, who agreed to talk to the roommate. I set up an appointment—they talked. A roommate switch was made.
>
> Although the results may seem a disaster, I think we all learned quite a bit. I learned when I couldn't handle a situation alone. The roommates found out how necessary it is to communicate with others to prevent misunderstanding from growing to overwhelming proportions.

Sometimes, no matter how skilled the RA or the Senior RA is in negotiating, the conflict cannot be resolved easily. As in the last example, one of the persons involved may be unwilling to cooperate with the problem-solving process. Or the problem may not have an "answer." You cannot offer a "remedy" to a student who is grieving over the death of a parent. You need not feel helpless at times like these, however. You can help troubled people by noticing how they feel, by expressing concern, and by offering to spend time together. One very important way you can communicate support and caring is through good listening skills. You can also direct students to campus offices or organizations with professional staffs trained to deal with students' problems.

Listening and Referral Skills

In your counseling role as an RA, you need two basic kinds of skills:

Listening Skills

To listen effectively means that you help students express their thoughts and feelings. Do not offer advice or assume responsibility for solving people's problems. Instead, you can help students clarify the problem and identify appropriate responses to it.

Referral Skills

You need to know appropriate campus resources to which you can refer certain counseling problems, and you need to know how to make an effective referral. You can assist the student to follow through on the recommendation and, when necessary, you can take an active role in setting up a meeting between the student and the appropriate office or service.

Most of you already possess an intuitive ability to listen well, to indicate to others that you are attentive and responsive to what they are saying, and to offer your advice and opinions only when it is appropriate to do so. Even though you may already possess the following skills, we think it helpful to review some of the components of good listening.

As you read, please remember that we are not urging anyone to acquire mechanical and artificial techniques. On the contrary, we are convinced that these skills, adapted to and interwoven with your own personal style, lead to more natural and more effective counseling experiences for all concerned.

Identifying Alternative Solutions

You can use open questions to help people identify and evaluate possible solutions to their dilemmas.

"What have you already tried?"

"How did that work?"

"What would you like to happen now?"

By asking people to focus on coping strategies, you express confidence in their ability to solve their own problems.

We all like to come up with our own solutions to problems. Although you might think you have perfect remedies in mind, you have to decide if and when it is appropriate to offer suggestions or to direct students to other resources. No matter how apt your advice may be, it gives the message that you think they can't handle the problem themselves. What you want to do is help them take responsibility for their own problems and gain confidence in their ability to work out their own solutions. So, before offering suggestions, you need to find out what the person has tried and how those coping strategies have worked. By assessing why a problem-solving approach was or was not successful, students often arrive at effective solutions on their own.

After people have talked about what they have tried and how the various attempted solutions worked, you may think it appropriate to offer suggestions. If so, you can say gently, "Well, I have some ideas that may or may not work," or "There are some people I might suggest you talk to." If students are responsive, you can help them anticipate how they will act on these suggestions or approach the resources. By helping them create a "game plan," you enable people both to do something to improve the situation and to act on their own behalf.

If students seem hesitant to pursue their own ideas or your suggestions, you might say, "You seem apprehensive about this. What feels uncomfortable to you?" By inviting students to explore their fears ahead of time, you help reduce their anxiety about acting to solve their own problems.

Putting Away Personal Values

Inevitably, some alternatives a student considers to resolve the problem will conflict with your own personal values. You might or might not approve of abortion. You might be an advocate or opponent of gay rights. You might have strong, definite religious beliefs. Your role as an RA is to help students clarify their opinions, beliefs, and values. Try to be conscious of situations in which your own moral views may influence your interactions with a student, and be honest about your feelings.

For example, you might feel strongly that abortion is not an acceptable way to deal with an unwanted pregnancy. Therefore, you might say, "I want you to know that my upbringing influences me a great deal in responding to your problem. I can suggest another person to talk to about what you want to do. What I can do is help you know what all your options are. The choice is yours."

Sometimes people will ask, and it may be appropriate for you to tell, what you would be inclined to do in a particular situation. When you can, turn the questions around so that the person is deciding which course of action seems right ('If I were in that position, I'd want to look at all my options before deciding. What options do you see?"). What you might do probably isn't relevant to the student's choice. People need to decide which alternative is best for them.

Making the Techniques Your Own

Effective listeners are relaxed, open, and natural in their counseling style. They practice the traits of good listening in their own personal way. Knowing a repertoire of possible responses and techniques lets you choose the most appropriate way of handling a situation. But you need to fit the techniques to your own personality and to the situation. After a while, techniques don't feel foreign or awkward. Try out these skills in various situations and find what feels comfortable to you. Personalizing the techniques and integrating the skills with your own style of relating to others will enhance your counseling effectiveness.

EXERCISES

The following vignettes or "critical incidents" illustrate the need for learning about resources and cooperating with fellow staff members in using these resources. It is our hope that reading and discussing these incidents will achieve the following goals.

1. To expose you to the range of problems that may occur, so that few or no surprises arise later

2. To provide an opportunity for discussion of problem-solving alternatives based on what others have done in the past

3. To teach you some helpful responses through discussion, group problem-solving, and peer feedback

4. To open avenues of communication among house/residence staff members

5. To suggest the possibility of consultation with staff members of student services, including the dean's office, health service, counseling and psychological services, and so on

How To Use This Section

Our experience is that the problems presented here are fairly typical of those you may expect to encounter. We suggest that the senior house associate lead a discussion about one or more of these incidents, exploring your group's knowledge of the range of resources and approaches to solving particular problems. The best way to learn about what is available is to work with a specific problem and then find out what can be done about it. Unfortunately, many staff members don't learn the necessary information until after they handle a given problem. *It is our hope, then, that house staff members will use these incidents in small group discussions as a dry run for working with real-life problems in the residences.* In this way, you can broaden your knowledge of the kinds of resources available to students.

In using the incidents, we encourage you to be creative in teaching each other how to perform in your roles as residence staff members. You may find it helpful to use techniques other than simple discussion, such as role playing in pairs of "students" and "RAs." Or you can use other ways to simulate the real-life situation. Sharing information and approaches constructively also structures part of your time together as staff members while you focus on common and often problematic areas of concern.

We have provided a background sketch for each incident, including characteristics of the student(s) involved, the situation in which the problem is presented, and the important issues involved in solving the problem. In your discussions, you may wish to ask the following questions:

- What are the important issues of the problem presented? (Be certain to consider the effects of an individual's behavior in a dorm situation.)

- What are some helpful responses? Why?

- What responses would be least helpful? Why?

- To which student services could you appropriately refer the student, if need be?

- How would you follow up to determine whether your help was effective?

At the end of this section, we provide a brief account of what the RAs actually did in each situation. After discussion (and knowing that some problems do not present easy solutions), decide whether the RA involved took a constructive course of action.

INCIDENTS

1. You are a woman staff member in a coed, all-freshman dorm. A freshman male comes to your room, wanting to talk, in the middle of fall quarter. He says he was very "experienced" sexually in high school but can't seem to find a girlfriend in the dorm. He announces somewhat arrogantly that he wants to get "back into the swing" of things and that he has been "noticing" you around for some time now. He then states that you are a "most likely candidate" for him.

   What do you say? How do you feel? How might he respond to what you say? Why?

2. As a male RA in an all-freshman dorm, you gradually become aware that T, a male student on your floor, is not getting along well with people in the dorm. Although he is vaguely aware that something is wrong, he is not aware that his bearing and manner are offensive to nearly everyone in the dorm. Consequently, he has made no close friends. People avoid him because in social situations he frequently acts inappropriately. You and others are uncomfortable with him, but he seems insensitive to these signals from other people.

   How do you talk to him about his "problem" without putting him down? How could you help him to improve his relationships, even though he might not be aware that they need improvement? How would you feel about talking to this person about how other people see him?

3. You are a female RA on an all-women's floor in an upper-class coed dorm. You first learn of two roommates having

problems when roommate A tells you early in fall quarter that "something is wrong with my roommate—she is very quiet." Roommate A, who now has a boyfriend and is having academic problems, returns in winter quarter with the same story. The conflict grows, and you next hear of it when roommate A goes to the infirmary and refuses to return to the dorm until B leaves her room. In the meantime, B has developed an eating problem, seems depressed, and is losing weight. You soon discover that no one is willing to room with A.

How would you intervene? To whom would you talk? Who could help you in determining a course of action?

4. You are an RA in a coed dorm and learn that a junior male has been selling drugs for quite some time. Lots of unknown people are coming to the dorm, and the student is beginning to have some regrets about selling. You have not talked to the student directly but know of the situation from other students who have bought drugs from him.

What would you do?

5. You are a female RA in an all-freshman dorm. Freshmen women repeatedly approach you about their difficulties with adjusting to the university's intense academic and intellectual pressures. One talks to you several times about her feelings of inadequacy during intellectual conversations in groups, particularly with men. She is considering leaving school because of her feelings.

How would you approach the problem? What are her needs in this situation?

6. A freshman student comes to you, worried and upset after receiving a notice of academic probation. He is considering dropping out of school because he lacks confidence in his ability to succeed academically. He fears he may flunk out. Previously, you have noticed that he has

irregular sleeping habits, and other students tell you that he has poor study habits.

How do you help him stay in school?

7. As a female RA, you continually hear complaints of wronged parties in love affairs between RAs and other students. You also hear repeated stories of one RA seeking (and failing to achieve) a relationship with another. All of this convinces you of the difficulties of relationships between residence staff members and students. In one incident, a freshman woman tells you that a male RA in your house is searching for "the perfect lover" among the freshmen woman and repeatedly throwing over his rejects. After finding the "perfect" freshman mate, the male RA withdraws from involvement with the rest of the dorm students.

What can you do to help the women who have been rejected? How would you approach the male RA about his behavior?

8. Roommate J knocks on your door at 2 A.M. on Saturday night and tells you that he is very concerned about K, who is tripping on LSD and seems to be having trouble. J informs you that K has had upsets before while tripping, but none so serious as this one.

How do you handle this?

9. You and other staff members gradually become aware that a certain male staff member is not performing his job up to par. He is rarely in the dorm, and you suspect that he is exploiting some students. Rumors are that he is also having problems in a personal relationship outside the dorm.

How do you confront the sensitive issue of inappropriate or incompetent actions on the part of another RA?

10. On the first day of fall quarter, you receive a phone call from the infirmary. A nurse informs you that L, a male

student on your corridor, was found passed out drunk the night before and is now in the infirmary. The nurse asks you to visit him and provide company. You see L several times during the next few weeks and gradually realize that drinking is a serious problem for him.

What can you do?

11. A sophomore woman on your hall, Q, begins acting in a bizarre manner. She laughs inappropriately and runs through hallways, bumping into walls and shrieking. By the third week of fall quarter, her roommate indicates that Q has stopped attending classes. Q comes to your room repeatedly, talking for several hours at a time and insisting that people are watching her. She says that because people keep staring at her in class, she can no longer attend lectures. Finding out that she has a disease resembling hemophilia, you refer her to the health center. After two visits, she refuses to continue going there and claims that the doctors "know too much about me." One evening you arrive in the dorm to discover that she has taken a bottle of aspirin and may be in serious danger from stomach bleeding.

How do you respond? Whom do you call?

12. You are an RA in an all-male freshman dorm. Two roommates, both African-American students, have trouble getting along because of differences in lifestyles. You learn of their conflict as each comes to you individually, complaining of the other's actions. They argue quite frequently over petty issues and soon request to change rooms. However, the policy in your freshman dorms is to switch roommates only as a last resort. In addition, interracial tensions exist in your dorm. So you encourage these roommates to try communicating differently. Despite your sensible advice on how to get along with the

conflict, it continues to the point where some action must be taken.

What do you do?

13. You are a male RA in a coed freshman dorm. One male student, S, is somewhat immature and becomes known for his aggressiveness in "hustling" women. Other dorm residents ridicule him, and as the quarter progresses, S gets more and more lonely and isolated from the rest of the people in the dorm.

What can you do?

14. A sophomore woman, W, comes to your room and tells you that she seriously considering dropping out of school. As you talk, you discover that she feels out of place, feels that she does not really "belong" on campus. She has been unable to decide on a major, has gotten only mediocre grades in recent quarters, and doesn't really know why she is in college at all. Furthermore, she is not very satisfied socially, has made only a few friends, and does not really feel comfortable with people in the dorm.

What do you do?

15. A freshman male comes to your room late one night in a panic. He explains that he has an important exam the following morning, but is too anxious to study. In talking, you discover that he has had this problem before. On several occasions his mind has "gone blank" during exams, even though he had adequately prepared. Over the last few weeks, he says his study habits have deteriorated greatly. He puts off work until the last minute and then attempts to cram before tests.

How can you help him for tonight? What can you suggest for the future?

16. The roommate of L informs you that he thinks L is a homosexual. The roommate is extremely uncomfortable sharing a room with him. A few days later, L comes to you and states that he is worried about "sexual matters."

    How do you respond to each student? Would you refer L to someone?

17. You notice that C, a female student on your floor, has been spending a great deal of time in her room and has frequently missed meals and classes. C's roommate tells you that C seems very distracted and withdrawn, but won't talk about what is bothering her. C's roommate finally requests a roommate change because of C's behavior.

    What can you do to help?

18. You become aware that interracial friction is growing between the students in your house. In the lounge, they tend to congregate in color-exclusive groups. A white student complains to you that he can no longer live with his two African-American roommates because of subtle pressures he feels from them.

    How can you ease the situation? Who could help you?

19. A freshman woman tells you that she thinks she may be pregnant and doesn't know how it could have happened.

    How do you respond to her?

20. A senior tells you that he's received rejection letters from all 15 of the medical schools to which he applied. He is now very confused about his future.

    How can you help him sort it out?

Responses to Incidents

1. The RA responded by telling him she was flattered, but it wouldn't work because of her position as a staff member in the dorm, among other reasons. Because his ego was involved, he felt rejected. Awkward feelings arose between them for the rest of the year. He eventually found a partner to "satisfy his needs."

2. The staff met to discuss T and enlisted the advice of persons trained in counseling. One staff member approached T and asked general questions about how he was doing in school, how he was feeling, and so on. The conversation then focused on how he felt about his lack of friends. The staff member confronted him with the perception that T was unhappy and perhaps lonely. The staff member suggested T might talk with someone at the peer counseling center to learn how to relate to others more effectively. The student was unwilling to seek help, however, and his "problem" continued during the year.

3. The RA consulted other staff members, and they decided to hold a floor meeting. After a long discussion in which people aired many feelings, the staff arranged several roommate switches. They also referred A to a psychiatrist, and she eventually decided to leave school temporarily. B also sought professional help and decided to leave school.

4. The RA approached the dealer and advised him on the possible consequences of his behavior, including legal repercussions, potential harm to drug users, and the possibility of thefts in the dorm.

5. The RA tried to get the student to focus on her strengths and to understand that she couldn't compete equally well in all situations. She also assured the woman that

upperclassmen weren't perfect either, and that the RA also had some of the same feelings.

6. The RA took these steps to help the student:
   a. Clarified the meaning of *probation* (which was not very serious, as it turned out), explained the alternatives to the student, and pointed out that he was not the only one on probation
   b. Suggested "easy" courses to help bolster his grade-point average
   c. Referred him to a learning assistance center to improve his study habits

7. The RA discussed these issues with the Senior RA and then decided to talk with some of the women who had been rejected, to help them understand what was going on. In addition, the female RA and the Senior RA both discussed their concerns with the male RA about not performing his job adequately.

8. The RA talked to roommate K, carefully avoiding judgmental remarks about K's drug-taking behavior. The student and the RA decided to go to the peer counseling center, where they talked with a peer drug counselor. After a few hours, K calmed down and decided to spend the night at the infirmary. The RA visited K the next day, and K decided to seek professional help in working through some of his personal concerns.

9. Two RAs discussed the matter and decided to take up the issue with the Senior RA. The three called a staff meeting (which the RA in question failed to attend) and discussed the problem. The person who knew him best ("Y") approached the RA and discussed the concerns of the other staff members. He and Y conferred with the Senior RA, and the male RA admitted that he was having personal difficulties. He decided to withdraw from the staff at the end of the quarter.

10. Over the course of the year, the RA slowly developed a relationship with L by eating with him and paying attention to him frequently. The RA gained L's trust by not pressuring him to talk, and L eventually began confiding about his drinking problem. It turned out that most of his friends also drank heavily. The RA introduced him to a new group of people who did not drink so heavily, and L was able to make some new friends. By the year's end, he was doing a lot better and had reduced his drinking.

11. The RA had been in touch with the woman's roommate and with the Senior RA for several weeks regarding Q's behavior. Taking a bottle of aspirin was tantamount to an act of suicide for her, because of her preexisting bleeding condition. The RA acted quickly to get medical attention for Q and also made certain that the incident was not disruptive to the other members of the floor. Eventually, this case involved the Dean of Student Affairs office and both the medical and psychological units of the health service. The RA regrets that he did not respond sooner by pressing the woman to get professional help or to contact her parents.

12. The RA eventually had to make a roommate change. Before doing so, he consulted with the Senior RA and the associate dean and his staff because of the various tensions in the dorm. Making a compatible roommate exchange required much time and effort in meeting with the students involved.

13. The RA approached S to talk over the situation. In this and subsequent discussions, the RA learned that S was not the only male in the dorm who felt badly about not finding a good relationship with women in the dorm. Many freshmen males in this dorm had decided to stop pursuing such relationships. Withdrawing from the

"competition" and harboring resentments about their failure to establish relationships, several of the men felt the same as S but were not as demonstrative of their feelings. After several talks with the RA, S was able to relax more and participate in dorm life more actively.

14. After getting to know W through several more talks, the RA discovered that W was under a great deal of pressure from her parents to stay in school. She would have preferred to take some time off. To help her work through her dilemma, the RA suggested that W might wish to see someone at the university's counseling center. W eventually decided to take some time off and to work. She later returned to school with a better idea of what she wanted to do.

15. The RA encouraged the student to go to sleep, miss the exam, and then talk to the instructor afterward to explain his problem and to request a make-up assignment. The RA also referred him to the nearby learning assistance center, where he worked on developing better study skills and habits. That center referred him to the counseling center, where he was able to reduce his acute test anxiety.

To stimulate your discussion, we are not including the actual responses to incidents 16 through 20.

Keeping Your Balance
To be helpful to students in your house or dorm, you need to take care of yourself. Make time for yourself, see your friends, and maintain a balance between your RA responsibilities and the rest of your life. When you think it would help, talk over your feelings about the job with friends, other RAs, or your senior RA. By attending to your own needs, you can maintain a healthy perspective on yourself as an RA and on students' problems.

Referrals for Psychotherapy*

As a Resident Assistant, you can play a crucial role in providing mental health services on a college campus. You are exposed to the students daily and can identify problem situations before they turn into crises. In addition to providing counseling yourselfself, you may want to refer certain students to psychological services or mental health professionals on campus.† This section deals with the process of such referrals. . . .

Many students with serious emotional problems are reluctant to approach a professional therapist for help. They don't recognize their problems as treatable, resist treatment or are scared off by the stigma associated with psychotherapy. Too often, their problems go unrecognized and untreated until a serious crisis occurs. The dual role of the RA is as both a peer who interacts with students daily and as a counselor with connections to the professional care available on campus. This gives you a unique opportunity to help the troubled student who is reluctant to see a psychotherapist. . . . You should be able to provide peer counseling services for the students on the dormitory hall and to refer students to other services when necessary.

Your role in providing counseling services on a college campus is by its nature ambiguous. On one hand, you are a peer to the students on the hall you supervise; on the other, you are the counselor (and college "official") with whom students deal most frequently. This ambiguity is both a problem and an asset. Because of your daily interaction with them, you may get very involved in the problems of students on your hall. That "distance" which characterizes the professional who sees the student once a week is something you may have to make a

---

*This section was written by Jan P. Boswinkel (1986) and was first published as "The College Resident Assistant and the Fine Art of Referral for Psychotherapy." Part of that article is adapted and reprinted here with permission from the *Journal of College Student Psychotherapy*, 1(1), (c) 1987 by The Haworth Press, Inc.

†For convenience, I use *psychological services* to refer to any mental health or counseling service.

conscious effort to acquire. And you will have to figure out what role you are playing at any given time.

However, this dual role has an inherent flexibility that puts you in a unique position to help provide psychological services . . .. Being in close touch with students, you are likely to be able to identify problems before they develop into crisis situations. You may become concerned when you see a student who remains very depressed for long periods of time. A friend or roommate of a student on the hall may tell you of concern about a student. Sometimes you will suddenly find yourself discussing a broken relationship with a student who just came in for a Band-Aid.

For you to be able to fulfill this role, your relationship with the people on the hall has to be good enough for them to feel comfortable to come and talk with you. The way to establish such relationships is to spend a great deal of time with students on the hall, especially early in the school year. In your dual role, you will have to establish a relationship that is casual enough to make a relaxed conversation possible, but "professional" enough to allow for counseling when necessary. The RA who only wants to help with "real problems" all the time is as likely to fail as the one who is not interested at all. To be effective, you have to use your flexibility creatively.

You will be able to deal with many problems yourself. In many cases, however, you will feel that the problem itself, your level of training, or time constraints make it impossible for you to deal with students' problems. Quite frequently, you will suddenly find yourself in a position where someone asks you to deal with a problem that is clearly beyond your competence. You should regard these cases as occasions for cultivating the fine art of referral to a professional therapist.

The Fine Art of Referral

While you may have been able to identify a problem as serious and to decide that additional help is needed, making a referral to the professional is often the most challenging part of the process. This is especially true in cases in which no immediate crisis makes the need for referral self-evident to the student. As an RA, you are likely to run into a number of cases every year in which professional help would be beneficial without there being any kind of immediate crisis. In many of these cases, students are reluctant to seek help . . ..

Now the advantage becomes clear of spending considerable time and effort early in the year to developing a counseling/advising relationship with students. Some basis of trust is essential for a referral to "take." Early in the year, you may have felt that a certain student needed professional help, but you should recognize that an actual referral can only be effected much later. Meanwhile, you may have to spend a few weeks getting to know the student and establishing a counseling relationship. This helps create an initial trust and awareness of issues that need to be presented in psychotherapy. This process should not destroy your peer relationship with the student. When every interaction with you is a serious counseling session, the student struggling with resistance is likely to withdraw from you.

Having determined a need for professional help and having established a strong enough basis of trust in the counseling relationship, you can test the water for possibilities of a referral. When you first introduce the idea, you can usually get a good idea about the student's attitude toward psychotherapy and readiness to deal with the issues at hand. This initial introduction should be casual and noncommittal. Point out the possible benefits of therapy, but avoid presenting the referral as a "big deal."

You may have to counter the notion that psychotherapy is for "nut cases" with its utility for self-development, especially since the stigma attached to seeing a psychotherapist is substantial for most students. Many students think you have to be "pretty crazy to see a shrink." Providing good information about the process and a realistic assessment of the benefits is crucial in the referral conversation. Very often the mentioning of the term psychotherapy evokes images of German-speaking, bearded men who put you on a couch and discuss your toilet training. If it is not so threatening to the client, it may be useful to point out that people who go to psychologists do so because they want to improve. If you have seen a psychotherapist, you may be able to note that experience without insisting that "what has worked for me will work for you." Whenever the student is not receptive to the referral, it is necessary to introduce the notion more slowly.

In addition to recoiling from the stigma attached to seeing a professional psychotherapist, the student may feel rejected by you. This is especially true, ironically, if the student values his or her relationship with you. Thus, it is important to introduce the professional as an *additional* source of help and to emphasize that the present counseling relationship can continue.

Many students are very eager to obtain the best help they can get and quite rightly see psychological services as an additional resource for self-development at college. In most cases, however, you will have to deal with strong resistance to the notion of seeking help. RAs generally consider referral when they come up against a problem they are not trained to handle. In the referral conversation, it is important to discuss this fact as well as the utility of consulting more qualified and experienced people. You should do this without impressing on the student a feeling of "it must be really bad with me if my RA can't help me." The referral conversation is in general the time when resistance will first come out and have to be addressed. This will also give you an indication of how much additional help and support you will have to give to increase the odds that psychotherapy will be successful.

In some cases there are immediate indications of the referral and psychotherapy difficulties you can expect. Any behavior that indicates the student's unwillingness to take responsibility for his or her actions also warns you of difficulties ahead. This is what seems to make referring people with drinking problems often especially problematic. The very notion of taking responsibility for one's life and actions may threaten the person who is "acting up" or "acting out." Thus, the nature of the problem itself may be an additional obstacle to a successful referral.

You should be familiar with the specifics of available services. Before referring someone, it helps if you have used (or at least visited) the service(s) and know the people who work there. Your referral should be as specific as possible, which may require contacting the service beforehand to find out which psychotherapist will have time available. It definitely means knowing the available psychotherapists as well as the student so that you can help create a good therapist–student match. Although this match is clearly very important, it is almost impossible to develop general rules. It is definitely helpful, however, if you know something about the personalities and working styles of various available psychotherapists and keep this information in mind when suggesting specific people to the student.

The most obvious referral variable in client–counselor relationships is gender. One often hears that it is generally better to refer men to men and women to women. I have not found this to be the case. You should keep the specifics of the problem and the personality of the client and available psychotherapists in mind when trying to make a match. For example, the woman who has problems dealing with older men because of a problematic relationship with her father is not necessarily better off in the long run with a female therapist. Referral to an older male therapist, who is likely because of gender and age to remind her of her father, is both risky and ambitious. During the initial stages especially, the development of the therapeutic relationship can be quite difficult. You should then be prepared to provide the additional support the student is likely to need to continue therapy. If successful, however, this ambitious match-up can provide a good model for dealing with the underlying problems.

Similarly, the male student who has difficulty relating to women might do best with a woman therapist. On the other hand, if therapy must be brief and referral is especially difficult, a less ambitious match-up may be most feasible. Often you can get a good sense of which of the available therapists may be "right" by discussing them to some extent with the student.

When you have identified one psychotherapist (or more) who you think is likely to work well with the student, check on that person's availability. Then you should provide the student with specific information about the therapist's availability. Writing down the name and number for the student and explaining how to make an appointment may be enough. If the need is particularly urgent, it may be good to let the psychological services know that this student will be calling and will need an appointment soon.

Although the aim of the referral process is to have the student decide for him- or herself to seek help, in some cases additional assistance may be necessary. In certain instances, it may be necessary for you to make the appointment and even walk with the student to the appointment. Do this only with the student's consent, of course, and not if the student doesn't need it.

After referring a student, you should check with that person to see if an appointment was made and kept, and how it went. Frequently, students describe the experience as negative. It is then your role to try to figure out if this is the result of a basic incompatibility of therapist and client or some other unrelated reason. If the former seems to be the case, a change of therapists may be required. In some cases, students may see two or even more therapists before finding one they can work with or getting used to the idea of being in psychotherapy. You will have to deal here with the feelings of discouragement and increased resistance the client is likely to feel.

Creating realistic expectations is important. Far too often people are disappointed after one or two visits to a psychotherapist because they are "not getting anything out of it." This can be avoided to some extent if you emphasize that the process can be slow and that one or two sessions will not resolve everything.

If you are not quite sure about the reasons why the referral didn't work out, you may consider asking the student to return at least one more time "if only to say you aren't going to go again." Sometimes it may just be necessary to deal further with some of the issues already mentioned (stigma, lack of quick results, and other forms of "resistance"). Be careful here not to become so identified with the notion of referral that the student cuts off ties with you in order to avoid dealing with a difficult and sometimes painful process. If you are anxious to help, it can be tempting to engage in conversations in which you constantly stress the need for referral, and the student constantly denies it. The only result of such talks will be reinforcing the student's resistance to seeking help. In these instances, you may have to back off for a while. Some patience may be required. During this period, you may have to emphasize the peer aspect of the relationship.

The process described so far can be very slow. Although some students are very receptive to the idea of seeing a psychotherapist, you are likely to run into cases in which it takes a long time to develop an awareness of the problem and deal with resistances. Although you have the advantage of easy access to the student you are concerned about, the lack of emotional distance inherent in living close to that person can become a serious concern if the referral is slow and the problems at hand are serious. Be careful to balance your role and not to be perceived by the student as the final and sole source of salvation.

Confidentiality

As an RA, you are free to ask some general advice from the therapist on how to proceed with a student. And given the student's consent, further contact between you and the professional may be beneficial. The ambiguity of your role is likely to be especially problematic here. Except in life-threatening situations, the psychotherapist is not able to convey information about the student's therapy to you. This can be frustrating to you. You are concerned about a student's progress in therapy and may have difficulty feeling sure that the professional therapist will take appropriate action (including contacting you if necessary in life-threatening situations). Of course, you can make your own observations and contacts with the student to determine the person's progress.

As a peer counselor, you also have an obligation to maintain as much confidentiality as possible given the need to find help in life-threatening situations. However, since it is likely that you made the referral because the student's problems were beyond your competence, it may be necessary for you to discuss the student with the professional. If you wish further contact with the therapist, you should establish an understanding with the student that permits such contacts. This can make contact an asset rather than a source of mistrust in the referral process. Thus, the student should be made aware of these contacts and consent to them. The person should understand the one-way nature of the conversations and know that you will minimize disclosure of specifics on your part whenever possible.

There are non–life-threatening situations in which feedback to the therapist from a person who interacts with the student daily is very helpful. In this process, you are a peer to the student, and feedback can definitely be appropriate. (To others, of course, confidentiality should be maintained.) Quite frequently, this feedback can take the form of relating behavior by the student which you have observed on the hall. Since this information is clearly in the public domain, disclosure to the therapist is less problematic. These contacts are only appropriate, though, if there is a clear understanding in your relationship with the student about the nature of these contacts and their benefit to the therapeutic process. They should not be at the expense of your peer relationship with the student.

If used judiciously, these contacts can be very beneficial to the therapeutic process. In some cases, experiences in the daily life of the student will create unexpected emergencies which make crucial some form of cooperation between you and the professional. For example, a student whom I had referred to a therapist a month earlier suddenly seemed very upset one day.

His behavior worried me. When I talked to him, I found out that a friend of his had gone through an experience that day which was similar to the one he was dealing with in therapy. After we had worked through his feelings about this for a while, I asked him if he would like to talk to his therapist that evening. When he declined, I asked his consent to my consulting the therapist, since I wasn't sure how to proceed. The therapist and I discussed the situation on the phone and formulated a response. We then both discussed this conversation with the student.

This was a case where communication between professional and RA was absolutely crucial for providing the care that the student needed. The situation had begun to develop into an emergency, which was averted. In addition, the coordinated response actually helped the therapeutic process. As a peer, I was around when the emergency began to occur; and as a counselor, I was able to support him and call upon the resources necessary to make this an experience that was actually beneficial for the referral.

Although in non-emergencies some contact between RA and therapist may be appropriate, different considerations are in order in emergency situations. Both the RA and the therapist have a clear obligation to communicate about life-threatening situations. In these cases, divulging details may be inevitable and actually crucial. It is important in these cases for neither party to hesitate to contact the other.

In general, you should be aware that the referral doesn't end when the client starts seeing a professional psychologist. After the referral has been made and seems initially successful, reverting back to more of a peer role can put you in a good position for monitoring progress. You have the opportunity to check every now and then with the student on how therapy is going. To the extent the student feels comfortable discussing it (and you should make no attempt to force this), you can provide additional support as a nonprofessional. The person may need support in dealing with resistances and day-to-day situations as they relate to the therapy. Specifically, the student may be more likely to discuss hesitations about the therapeutic process with you than with the therapist. You can then help the student deal with these hesitations or encourage him or her to discuss them with the therapist.

Conclusion

To be able to play the necessary active role in the referral process, you have to be equipped with basic interpersonal and counseling skills and a good knowledge of the available psychological services on the college campus. Your relationship with the students is by its nature ambiguous. While this can be troublesome at times, it can be an asset in making referrals. If you succeed in balancing your dual role as peer and counselor, you can play an important role in the referral process.

Because of your daily interactions with students, you can identify problems before they turn into crises and refer students to psychotherapists when their problems are beyond your competence. Your dual role allows for greater flexibility in response to a student's problems and for active participation in the referral process. This process can be slow and difficult, but you can influence it in important ways by providing information, dealing with problems and resistances, and helping the therapeutic process after it has started. Here the ambiguity inherent in your role will actually be an advantage.

PART IV

SPECIFIC ISSUES

Introduction to Part IV

In keeping with our intention to offer material useful for training peer counselors in a variety of applications, this new section provides specific, practical information. Since our first edition, the issues of sexual assault and HIV testing have shaped a new set of challenges for peer counselors. Today, the AIDS epidemic affects approximately one in five hundred college students and has brought about radical changes in dating and sexual practices.

So the next two new chapters address these issues. The chapter on sexual assualt on campus between friends and acquaintances, "Date Rape," has particular relevance for students, as more and more studies report. Current data yields dismaying prevalence figures for date or acquaintance rape, ranging from 15 to 44 percent of college women. Studies also indicate a similar risk range for gay and lesbian students. Chapter 10 details the background, presents data, and offers sound advice and information for peer educators and counselors, RAs, and other students who are working in educational, preventive, and counseling programs around the country. Correlations between date rape and drug use, particuarly alcohol use, are also important to address.

Chapter 11 is on HIV peer counseling. It reflects the invaluable experience of a peer counseling program devised by and for students. (The same student authors wrote about the genesis and implementation of that program in Appendix F.) Growing out of student needs, campus surveys, and student urgings, the program was devised to provide an anonymous alternative to students who were unwilling to go to a physician for testing and thereby "be public" about their fear of having been exposed to the virus. Again, that chapter offers a specific, practical perspective on training for and implementing such a program.

10

DATE RAPE:
"FRIENDS" RAPING FRIENDS*

*by Jean O'Gorman Hughes
and Bernice Resnick Sandler*

When you hear the word *rape*, what do you think of? If you imagine a stranger jumping out of the bushes on a dark night and attacking someone, you are only partly right—because most rapes are not committed by strangers but by men who know their victims, who often have gone out with them previously and are supposedly their friends. This phenomenon is called *acquaintance* or *date rape*.

Acquaintance rape is forced, unwanted intercourse with a person you know. It is a violation of your body and your trust. It is an act of violence. It can be with someone you have just met, or dated a few times, or even with someone to whom you are engaged. The force involved can come from threats or tone

---

*This chapter is reprinted by permission of the publisher. Copyright 1987 by the Project on the Status and Education of Women, Association of American Colleges. Copyright 1991 by the Center for Women Policy Studies (2000 P Street N.W., Suite 508, Washington, DC 20036).

This material, although intended to help prevent acquaintance rape or to alleviate its effects, is furnished as a service only. Acquaintance rape is not always avoidable and its aftereffects may vary from person to person in ways that we cannot foresee. Therefore, no one can guarantee that our suggestions will be appropriate for or successful in every situation. The Project on the Status and Education of Women, the Association of American Colleges, and the Center for Women Policy Studies shall not be liable for any damages arising from the information presented in this chapter.

of voice, as well as from physical force or weapons. Experts estimate that as many as 90 percent of all rapes are never reported;
in those that are reported, about 60 percent of the victims
know their assailants.* Of these, women 15 to 25 years old are
the majority of victims (McDermott, 1979).

In 1985 Mary Koss, a professor at Kent State University,
surveyed approximately 7,000 students on 32 campuses on
behalf of Ms. magazine and found that one in eight women were
the victims of rape. One in every twelve men admitted to having forced a woman to have intercourse or tried to force a
woman to have intercourse through physical force or coercion;
that is, admitted to raping or attempting to rape a woman.
Virtually none of these men, however, identified themselves as
rapists. Similarly, only 57 percent of the women who had been
raped labeled their experience as rape; the other 43 percent had
not even acknowledged to themselves that they had been raped
(Sweet, 1985).

Date rape occurs on virtually all campuses, small or
large, private or public, rural or urban. Unfortunately, it cannot
always be prevented. The more you know about it, however,
the more likely it is that you can avoid being put in a situation
where it could occur. You can learn the early warning signs and
how to react to them. The majority of men are not rapists but
some are. We hope to show you what to watch out for, why it
occurs, and what to do should it happen to you or a friend.
Thinking and talking about acquaintance rape and what you
might do if you find yourself in a bad situation can increase
your chances of avoiding rape.

Because the overwhelming majority of rapes are committed by men, we will refer throughout this [chapter] to the
rapist as he and the victim as she. We will use acquaintance rape
and date rape interchangeably.

---

*In one study by the National Center for the Prevention and Control of
Rape, 92 percent of adolescent rape victims said they were acquainted with
their attackers. Reported in Newsweek, April 9, 1984.

Bob and Patty: A Study Date Gone Awry

Bob:

Patty and I were in the same statistics class together. She usually sat near me and was always very friendly. I liked her and thought maybe she liked me, too. Last Thursday I decided to find out. After class I suggested that she come to my place to study for midterms together. She agreed immediately, which was a good sign. That night everything seemed to go perfectly. We studied for a while and then took a break. I could tell that she liked me, and I was attracted to her. I was getting excited. I started kissing her. I could tell that she really liked it. We started touching each other and it felt really good. All of a sudden she pulled away and said "Stop." I figured she didn't want me to think that she was "easy" or "loose." A lot of girls think they have to say "no" at first. I knew once I showed her what a good time she could have, and that I would respect her in the morning, it would be okay. I just ignored her protests and eventually she stopped struggling. I think she liked it, but afterwards she acted bummed out and cold. Who knows what her problem was?

Patty:

I knew Bob from my statistics class. He's cute and we are both good at statistics, so when a tough midterm was scheduled, I was glad that he suggested we study together. It never occurred to me that it was anything except a study date. That night everything went fine at first. We got a lot of studying done in a short amount of time, so when he suggested we take a break. I thought we deserved it. Well, all of a sudden he started acting really romantic and started kissing me. I liked the kissing but then he started touching me below the waist. I pulled away and tried to stop him but he didn't listen. After a while I stopped struggling; he was hurting me and I was scared. He was so much bigger and stronger than me. I couldn't believe it was happening to me. I didn't know what to do. He actually forced me to have sex with him. I guess looking back on it I should have screamed or done something besides trying to reason with him, but it was so unexpected. I couldn't believe it was happening. I still can't believe it did.

How Does Date Rape Usually Occur?

Date rapes typically occur when a woman is alone with a man. If you go to a man's room or apartment or even get into his car alone, you are vulnerable. Date rapes can occur when others are relatively close by; for example, they can take place in an upstairs bedroom while 50 people are attending a party on the first floor.

Alcohol and drugs are sometimes a significant factor in date rape. Many victims may say later that they drank too much or took too many drugs to realize what was going on; by the time they realized their predicament, it was too late. Sometimes a woman passes out and awakens to find a man having sex with her. On the other hand, some date rapes occur when alcohol is not involved or when the victim has had little or nothing to drink but the man has been drinking and becomes sexually aggressive.

Mixed signals are another element in date rape. The woman acts in a friendly manner; the man interprets this friendliness as an invitation to have sex. "No" is heard as "maybe" and even a strong protest can be ignored under the delusion that women say "no" when they mean "yes." Some men find it sexually exciting to have a woman struggle. If the woman protests only mildly, the man may think he is merely "persuading" her, not forcing her to have sex. (He may think the same, however, even if she protests vigorously.) Sometimes a woman is not clear in her own mind about what she wants or she may think she will make up her mind as she goes along. If she changes her mind at some point and decides not to have sex, the man can feel cheated, rejected, and angry. He may be interpreting her nonverbal messages, such as her enjoyment of kissing and caressing, as meaning that she wants to have sex with him. At this point he may decide he has been teased or misled and "deserves" to get some satisfaction, regardless of the woman's wishes. The result can be rape.

Although acquaintance rape is often a spontaneous act, many are planned, some days in advance; others in the preceding hour(s). Sometimes men plan to have sex with a woman even if they have to force the issue. These men have typically forced sex before and gotten away with it. They usually look for victims who are unassertive; perhaps [women who are] not very popular and would be flattered to go on a date with [them]. Needless to say, these men do not see themselves as repeat rapists; they are merely "out to have a good time."

CAUSES OF DATE RAPE

There is no one direct cause of date rape. Although there are usually three key elements involved—socialization, miscommunication, and/or changing sexual mores—one major reason for date rape is a lack of consideration for a woman's rights and wishes.

In a general sense, traditional male and female roles in society are part of the problem. Men are taught at a very early age to be aggressors; they participate in aggressive team sports, are encouraged to be competitive, not to give up, to keep on trying. They are encouraged to have strong sexual feelings and to experiment with their sexual satisfaction as a part of their masculinity. This environment which encourages men to be competitive and get what they want often leads to a belief in the "right to have sex." Women on the other hand are socialized to be more passive, dependent, to be peacemakers, to avoid scenes, to be "lady-like." They are discouraged from experimenting with their sexuality: "Good girls don't fool around." The double standard allows men to have sexual feelings and act on them; in contrast, a woman is allowed to be sexual primarily when she becomes "carried away" with emotion.

Communication between men and women is often problematical, especially in the realm of sex. Especially in a first sexual encounter with someone, some women may say "no" when they mean "maybe" or even "yes," and men have been taught to try to turn that no/maybe into a yes. Thus, it is sometimes hard for men to know when "no" really does mean "no." Women, on the other hand, don't want to agree to sex too readily for fear they will be seen as "loose" or "easy." Misperceptions abound; a woman thinks she is merely being friendly, but her date thinks she's signaling willingness to have sex. Furthermore, stereotypes about women as passive and submissive can also foster a climate for sexual assaults.

The last few decades have seen a general loosening of sexual standards. With the advent of the birth control pill, many people are sexually active at younger ages than previously, including many college-age women and men. Thus, many college-age men may expect sex as a given after they have gone out with someone a few times. Sometimes the woman shares this expectation, but sometimes she does not. Some men believe they are entitled to sex when the have spent money on a date. Others may believe that if a woman is sexually active, she will willingly have sex with anyone, including him.

Acquaintance rape, however, is not simply a crime of passion, or merely a result of miscommunication. It is, instead, often an attempt to assert power and anger. Some men are sexually aggressive because they are basically insecure. Forcing sex on another person makes them feel strong because it makes someone else feel weak. Rape is violence against a woman. It is an issue that strikes at the heart of the personal relationship between a man and a woman, how they treat each other, and how they respect each other's wishes. People who respect others do not coerce others to do things they do not want to do.

Seduction vs. *Rape*

One of the key questions in the issue of date rape is the difference between seduction and rape: the man feels he has merely seduced a woman, the woman feels that she was raped. A useful distinction to keep in mind is that seduction involves no force, implied or otherwise. Seduction occurs when a woman is manipulated or cajoled into agreeing to have sex; the key word is *agreeing*. Acquaintance rape often occurs when seduction fails and the man goes ahead and has sex with the woman anyway, despite any protests and without her agreement.

AVOIDING DATE RAPE

You can't always avoid date rape. Nevertheless, there are some things you can do to minimize your chances of being raped.

- *Examine your feelings about sex.* Many women have been socialized to believe that sex means that they will be swept away with the emotion of the moment or that they can "make out" and then decide whether to say "yes" or "no" to sex later. The problem with this kind of thinking is that it gives too much control to the other person.

- *Set sexual limits.* It is your body, and no one has the right to force you to do anything you do not want to do. If you do not want someone to touch you or kiss you, for example, you can say, "Take your hands off me," or "Don't touch me," or "If you don't respect my wishes right now, I'm leaving." Stopping sexual activity doesn't mean that anything is wrong with you, or that you're not a "real" woman.

- *Decide early if you would like to have sex.* The sooner you communicate firmly and clearly your sexual intentions, the easier it will be for your partner to hear and accept your decision.

- *Do not give mixed messages; be clear.* Say "yes" when you mean "yes" and say "no" when you mean "no." (The ability to be assertive can be developed by training and practice.)

- *Be alert to other unconscious messages you may be giving.* Men may interpret your behavior differently from what you intended. Often women and men send strong nonverbal signs of willingness to enter a sexual relationship and unintentional signals that might conflict with their words, and thereby contribute to sexual assault. Be aware of signals you send with your posture, clothing, tone of voice gestures, and eye contact.

- *Be forceful and firm.* Do not worry about not being "polite." Often men interpret passivity as permission; they may ignore or misunderstand "nice" or "polite" approaches. Say something like "Stop this. I'm not enjoying it," or "Your behavior is not encouraging an open relationship between us." If a woman ignores sexual activity she does not like, a man is likely to interpret that as tacit approval for him to continue. Men are not mind readers.

- *Be independent and aware on your dates.* Do not be totally passive. Do have opinions on where to go. Do think about appropriate places to meet (not necessarily at your room or his), and, if possible, pay your own way or suggest activities that do not cost any money.

- *Do not do anything you do not want to just to avoid a scene or unpleasantness.* Women have been socialized to be polite.

In an effort to be nice, they may be reluctant to yell or run away or escape being attacked. Do not be raped because you were too polite to get out of a dangerous situation. If you are worried about hurting his feelings, remember, he is ignoring your feelings. Be aware of how stereotypes about women may affect your behavior. Accepting beliefs that "women shouldn't express themselves strongly" or that "anger is unfeminine" make women more vulnerable.

- *Be aware of specific situations in which you do not feel relaxed and in charge.* Unwillingness to acknowledge a situation as potentially dangerous and reluctance to appear oversensitive often hold women back from responding in the interest of their own safety. For example, avoid attending or staying late at parties when men greatly outnumber women. Don't be afraid to leave early because it might seem rude. Situations where there are few women around can quickly get out of hand.

- *If things start to get out of hand, be loud in protesting, leave, go for help.* Do not wait for someone else to rescue you or for things to get better. If it feels uncomfortable, leave quickly.

- *Trust your gut-level feelings.* If you feel you are being pressured, you probably are, and you need to respond. If a situation feels bad, or you start to get nervous about the way your date is acting, confront the person immediately or leave the situation as quickly as possible.

- *Be aware that alcohol and drugs are often related to acquaintance rape.* They compromise your ability (and that of your date) to make responsible decisions. If you choose to drink alcohol, drink responsibly. Be able to get yourself home and do not rely on others to "take care" of you.

- *Avoid falling for such lines as "You would if you loved me."* If he loves you, he will respect your feelings and will wait until you are ready.

- *If you are unsure of a new acquaintance, go on a group or double date.* If this is not possible, meet him in a public place and have your own transportation home.

- *Have your own transportation, if possible, or taxi fare.* At least for the first few dates, this establishes your independence and makes you appear to be a less vulnerable target.

- *Avoid secluded places where you are in a vulnerable position.* This is especially critical at the beginning of a relationship. Establish a pattern of going where there are other people, where you feel comfortable and safe. This will give you a chance to get to know your date better and decide if you wish to continue dating him.

- *Be careful when you invite someone to your home or you are invited to his home.* These are the most likely places where acquaintance rapes occur.

- *Examine your attitudes about money and power.* If he pays for the date, does that influence your ability to say "no"? If so, then pay your own way or suggest dates that do not involve money.

- *Think about the pros and cons of dating much older men.* Although they may be sophisticated and have the money to treat you well, they may also be more sexually experienced and may therefore expect more sooner.

- *Socialize with people who share your values.* If you go out with people who are more sexually permissive than you are, you may be perceived as sharing those values.

Remember . . .

It is possible to be aware without being afraid; to take responsibility for your own behavior without being a prude, to request that others not violate your space and your privacy without putting them down.

—*When "No" Is Not Enough:*
Date Rape on the College Campus (pamphlet),
Auburn University, AL

Danger Signals

Unfortunately, a nice, normal man can turn into a date rapist. However, there are some men who are more likely to be sexually aggressive than others. Watch out for:

- Men who do not listen to you, ignore what you say, talk over you or pretend not to hear you. Such men generally have little respect for women and would be more likely to hear "no" as meaning "convince me."

- Men who ignore your personal space boundaries.

- Men who express anger or aggression toward women as individuals or in general. Hostile feelings can easily be translated into hostile acts. Such men often get hostile when a woman says "no."

- Men who do what they want regardless of what you want. If a man does this in little ways—for example, if he makes all the decisions about what to do and where to go without asking your opinion—then he may also be likely to make the decision about whether you are ready to have sex with him.

Real Men Don't Rape

Real men accept the responsibility not to harm another person.

- It is *never* okay to force yourself on a woman, even if
    She teases you
    She dresses provocatively or leads you on
    She says "no" and you think she means "yes"
    You've had sex before with her
    You've paid for her dinner or given her expensive gifts
    You think women enjoy being forced to have sex or want
        to be persuaded
    She is under the influence of alcohol or drugs
- Rape is a crime of violence. It is motivated primarily by desire to control and dominate, rather than by sex. It is illegal.
- If you are getting a double message from a woman, speak up and clarify what she wants. If you find yourself in a situation with a woman who is unsure about having sex or is saying "no," back off. Suggest talking about it.
- Do not assume you know what your partner wants; check out your assumptions.
- Be sensitive to women who are unsure whether they want to have sex. If you put pressure on them, you may be forcing them.
- Do not assume you both want the same degree of intimacy. She may be interested in some sexual contact other than intercourse. There may be several kinds of sexual activity you might mutually agree to share.
- Stay in touch with your sexual desires. Ask yourself if you are really hearing what she wants. Do not let your desires control your actions.
- Communicate your sexual desires honestly and as early as possible.

- If you have *any* doubts about what your partner wants, STOP. ASK. CLARIFY.
- Your *desires* may be beyond your control, but your *actions* are within your control. Sexual excitement does not justify forced sex.
- Do not assume her desire for affection is the same as a desire for intercourse.
- Not having sex or not "scoring" does not mean you are not a "real man." It is okay not to "score."
- A woman who turns you down for sex is not necessarily rejecting you as a person. She is expressing her decision not to participate in a single act at that time.
- No one asks to be raped. No matter how a woman behaves, she does not deserve to have her body used in ways she does not want.
- "No" means no. If you do not accept a woman's "no," you might risk raping someone who you thought meant "yes."
- Taking sexual advantage of a person who is mentally or physically incapable of giving consent (for example, is drunk) is rape. If a woman has had too much to drink and has passed out, or is not in control of herself, having sex with her is rape.
- The fact that you were intoxicated is not a legal defense to rape. You are responsible for your actions, whether you are sober or not.
- Be aware that a man's size and physical presence can be intimidating to a woman. Many victims report that the fear they felt based on the man's size and presence was the reason why they did not fight back or struggle.

Note: Men can be victims of rape and have the same rights to counseling and legal action as women do.

- Men who try to make you feel guilty, or accuse you of being "uptight" if you resist their sexual overtures.

- Men who act excessively jealous or possessive.

- Men who have wrong or unrealistic ideas about women (for example, "women are meant to serve men"). Such men are not likely to take your objections to sex seriously.

- Men who drink heavily. A "mean drunk" can often get sexually aggressive, angry, or violent if he is rejected.

What Should You Do If Someone Tries to Force Sexual Activity on You?

- Stay calm and think. Figure out what your options are and how safe it is to resist.

- Say "no" strongly. Do not smile; do not act friendly or polite.

- Say something like "Stop it. This is rape." This might shock the rapist into stopping.

- Assess the situation. Figure out how you can escape.

- Are there any other people around?

- Look for an escape route. If you can figure out a way to distract him, you can sometimes escape.

- Act quickly, if possible. The longer you stay in the situation, the fewer your options.

- Ask yourself if it is safe to resist. This is a critical question. Women who fight back initially, who hit and scream, have a much higher chance of avoiding the successful completion of an assault than women who plead or try to talk their way out of the situation. Nevertheless, resistance will depend on one main question: is he armed?

- If the man is UNARMED, then you have many options, including:
  - Fight back physically—punch him in the Adam's apple, poke your finger in his eye, hit him with a lamp or other item, or kick him.
  - Fight so that you can escape, as it is difficult for most women to incapacitate a man. Resistance may discourage the man or convince him that it is too much trouble to continue. Resist only as long as it is safe to do so. If resistance is dangerous, stop.
  - Run away. There is no shame in escaping a dangerous situation.
  - Say you have to use the bathroom, and then leave.
  - Shout "Fire." If you shout "Help," some people will tend not to want to be involved in someone else's problem. "Fire" concerns them and they are more likely to respond.
  - Use passive resistance (pretend to faint, throw up).
  - Use intimidation (lie; tell him your male roommate is on the way home; tell him you have herpes or a venereal disease).
  - Try to talk him out of it—try to appeal to his humanity, his sense of decency.
  - Gain his confidence so that he might let his guard down and you can escape.
  - Try to get him to see you as an individual person. Make him aware of the effect he is having on you. Tell him that he is hurting you.

- If the man is ARMED, then:
  - Try to talk him out of it.
  - Try passive resistance.

Your options are obviously a lot more limited when the man is armed with a weapon. In those situations, you are taking your life in your hands if you decide to fight back. It may be possible to run away, if he is distracted, but only do this if you are reasonably sure you can get away.

WHAT TO DO IF YOU ARE RAPED

1. *Go to a friend's.* This is not the time to be alone. At the very least, you need emotional support. If there is no one to go to, then call someone you can talk to, no matter how late it is.

2. *Get medical attention.* Do not shower or clean yourself first. As soon as possible, go to a hospital or school health center to be examined and treated for possible venereal disease. You may have internal injuries that you are not aware of. If you decide to press charges, physical specimens collected soon after the rape will be valuable evidence.

3. *Report the attack to police and university or college officials,* whether or not you plan to file charges. (Reporting a rape does not commit you to filing charges. You can make that decision later.) Have someone go with you. You can go the next day, but the sooner the better. Rarely do date rapists attack one woman only; they get away with it and so they continue to do it. If you turn him in, you may break that pattern and save someone else from being attacked.

4. *Consider whether you want to file charges with the police* and/or with the campus authorities if the man is a student [see the "Legal Implications" section that follows]. If you do decide to press charges, the chances of conviction with acquaintance rape are low, although police, judges, and schools are increasingly more sympathetic than in the

past. Some states now have rape shield laws, so that the past sexual behavior of a woman cannot be brought up.

5. *Get help and support, such as counseling.* At the very least, call a rape or crisis hotline. Many schools and communities have them. Your school counseling center, student health center, or local sexual assault center also may be of help. You have been through a trauma and need help to deal with the situation and with your feelings. Women who get counseling get over their experiences faster and with fewer lasting effects than those who get no help.

6. *Write a letter to the rapist.* There is a particular kind of letter* that victims of sexual harassment have often used to stop harassment [which] can be used by a rape victim who knows her attacker. The letter consists of three parts:

   a. Part I is a *factual* account of what has happened *without any evaluation*, as seen by the writer. (People usually agree with the facts but disagree with the interpretation.) It should be as detailed as possible with dates, places, and a description of the incident.

   b. Part II describes how the writer feels about the events described in part I, such as shame, misery, distrust, anger, fear, and revulsion, such as "I feel humiliated," or "I feel I was exploited."

   c. Part III consists of what the writer wants to happen next.

---

*Based on M. P. Rowe (1981, May–June), Dealing with sexual harassment. *Harvard Business Review.* Subsequently developed by B. R. Sandler, Writing a letter to the sexual harasser: Another way of dealing with the problem. Project on the Status and Education of Women, Association of American Colleges.

The letter is delivered by registered or certified mail. Copies are not sent to anyone else.

A sample letter, which can be of any length: "Dear John, On November 23rd you and I went to the movies and afterwards you invited me to your room to see your softball trophies. When you kissed me, I enjoyed it but then you started undressing me and when I asked you to stop, you didn't. Then you forced me to have sex with you. I trusted you and you betrayed me. You ignored my protests and used me. I was so upset that I wasn't able to go to class the next day. I cried a lot, and I'm also having trouble sleeping. I think you are disgusting. I don't ever want to go out with you again or even talk with you and I hope you never do this to anyone else."

Writing the letter can give the victim a sense of doing something constructive abut the situation. It can also give the man a new perception of how his behavior is viewed by others.

8. *Do not blame yourself.* Many people assume that the man is *expected* to ask for sex and the woman is responsible for giving *permission* for sex. Thus the woman may feel it is her fault for not having said "no" more clearly or for having trusted the man in the first place. Some men and women may also blame the victim and offer little or no sympathy. Men may believe you must have somehow "led on" the rapist; some women may suggest you either used poor judgment or have a bad reputation, so it is your own fault. In both cases, they are trying to distance themselves from what happened. If you find that you are being blamed for what happened, it is helpful to go to a counseling center, a rape crisis center, or call a hotline. You need to be reassured that you are not to blame; the rapist is. Even if your body responded sexually to the rapist, it does not mean you "enjoyed" the experience or that it is

your fault. Even if you believe you were naive, not cautious, or even foolish, it is not your fault. Your behavior did not *cause* the rape; the rapist caused the rape.

EFFECTS OF DATE RAPE

Different people react to stress and trauma differently. However, most rape victims go through definable stages of rape trauma syndrome. This syndrome is composed of three parts: trauma, denial, and resolution.

Trauma

- *Fear of being alone.* This may be especially acute shortly after the rape but can also continue for a while afterwards.

- *Fear of men.* Some women may be fearful and angry at all men. Counseling can be especially helpful in preventing this from becoming a long-lasting problem. Victims of date rape, especially, are left doubting their choice of partners and wondering how they can ever again date safely and if they will be able to trust themselves and others.

- *Sexual problems.* For some people, these may continue for a long time since the sexual act now has been associated with so many negative feelings. Again, counseling can often be helpful in overcoming these problems.

- *Depression.* This can sometimes come and go over a long period of time Generally, the more a survivor can talk about her situation, the less severe the depression.

- *Fear of retaliation.* Unfortunately, this may be a legitimate fear, especially if charges are pressed. However, such retaliation is in itself illegal, and can result in additional charges. Any threat of retaliation should be reported immediately to the institution and/or the police. If this is not sufficient, a lawyer should be contacted to help obtain a restraining order and explore additional options.

- *Afraid to trust.* This may manifest itself long after the actual rape has occurred when the survivor begins to date again and wonders if it will happen once more.

- *Concern over reactions from family/friends.* It is not always necessary for a survivor to tell her family and/or all of her friends if she is very sure that they will not support her and will react badly. However, family and close friends may be more supportive than the victim anticipates.

- *Physical problems.* These include venereal disease, as well as physical symptoms of stress, such as stomachaches, headaches, back problems, inability to sleep, or diminished appetite.

- *Feelings of anger, helplessness, guilt, pain, embarrassment, or anxiety.* These are all typical reactions and generally disappear with time. In any case, keep in mind that whatever happened and however it happened, rape is the fault of the rapist, not the victim.

Denial
[This stage of the rape trauma syndrome involves] *Not wanting to talk about it.* There is a sense of wanting to get on with life and put the experience in the past. This may, in fact, last for months.

Resolution

1. *Dealing with fears and feelings.* The primary way to work through these feelings is to talk to someone, be it a friend, member of the clergy, hotline, or counselor.

2. *Regaining a sense of control over life.* This will happen usually only after a victim has dealt with her fears and

feelings. At this point, she will be ready to put the experience behind her and get on with her life; she is ready to be in charge again.

Family and Friends: How To Help

After a rape, survivors may be openly upset, even hysterical, or they may be numb and seemingly calm. The victim needs to:

- *Obtain medical assistance.*
- *Feel safe.* Rape is a traumatic violation of a person. Especially in the beginning, it is often difficult for victims to be alone.
- *Be believed.* With date rape especially, victims need to be believed that what occurred was, in fact, a rape.
- *Know it was not her fault.* Most rape victims feel guilty and feel that the attack was somehow their fault.
- *Take control of her life.* When a person is raped, she may feel completely out of control of what is happening to her. A significant step on the road to recovery is to regain a sense of control in little, as well as big, things.

THINGS YOU CAN DO TO HELP

- *Listen; do not judge.* It is not your place to play prosecutor and make her prove her story. Accept her version of the facts and be supportive. You may have to deal with your feelings separately if you feel that it was somehow her fault. Many rape counseling services can be helpful to friends and relatives of women who have been victims.
- *Offer shelter.* If it is at all possible, stay with her at her place or let her at least spend one night at your place. This is not the time for her to be alone.
- *Be available.* She may need to talk at odd hours, or a great deal at the beginning. She may not have a lot of people she can talk to and she may over-rely on one person. Be there as much as you can and encourage her to either call a hotline or go for counseling.
- *Give comfort.* She has been badly treated. She needs to be nurtured.
- *Let her know she is not to blame.* This is crucial. Many rape victims blame themselves. She needs to be reassured that the rapist is to blame; she is not.
- *Be patient and understanding.* Everyone has her own timetable for recovering from a rape. Do not impose one on the victim.
- *Encourage action*—for example, suggest she call a hotline, go to a hospital or health center, and/or call the police. Respect her decision if she decides not to file charges.
- *Do not be overly protective;* encourage her to make her own decisions. She needs to feel in control of her life [which] will not be possible if you do everything for her.
- *Accept her choice of solution to the rape*—even if you disagree with what she is doing. It is more important that she make decisions and have them respected than it is for you to impose what you think is the "right" decision.
- *Put aside your feelings, and deal with them somewhere else.* Although it is supportive for a rape survivor to know that others are equally upset with what happened, it does her no good if on top of her feelings, she also has to deal with, for example, your feelings of rage and anger. If you have strong feelings, talk to another friend or to a local hotline.

Legal Implications

Women who have been raped by an acquaintance have the same options as those raped by strangers. They can press criminal and/or civil charges against the man who raped them. In general, date rapes are often difficult to prove. A gun or knife is rarely used and so it is harder for a woman to prove that she was forced to have sex. It is almost always his word against hers. The man's attorney may argue that the woman "wanted" to have sex with [the defendant], did so, and then thought better of it and so charged rape. The woman has to prove that she did not want sex, resisted, and was overpowered.

Unfortunately, date rapists rarely rape only once. If a woman does go ahead and press charges, there is a chance that she will be able to stop the rapist from hurting other people. Pressing charges also helps many rape victims regain a sense of control over their lives; they are taking some positive action. A pamphlet from Stanford University, *Working Against Rape*, describes the dilemma:

> *The decision to press charges is difficult and important. As more women force their courts and communities to deal with rape, awareness about rape increases. By pressing charges, women claim the right to have the crime taken seriously. Legal proceedings may help prevent other women from suffering a rape. . . . Conviction rates have increased . . . in recent years. Some women press charges to demonstrate that they will not be passive when they are threatened. When women fight back—both literally and through the courts— men might not rape as easily. A woman who presses charges can decide for any reason, at any time, to drop them.*
>
> *On the other hand, some women decide not to press charges because they don't want their personal lives and rape experiences aired publicly. Sometimes women's anger and desire to act are limited by the time and stamina needed for a court case, and there are often educational or economic barriers to pursuing a case. Often women protest the fact that*

the man's and victim's race and class unfairly determine how they are treated in court. Some women don't want to jail rapists as a response to rape. And some avoid pressing charges because they fear retaliation, although even in cases when a rapist threatens to return if he is reported, repeat rapes are uncommon.

In some cases a woman's legal counsel will advise against pressing charges. It is difficult to get a trial, let alone a conviction, when the victim is raped by a husband or boyfriend, is hitchhiking, or is under the influence of alcohol or drugs at the time of the rape.

In addition to—or apart from—bringing criminal charges, a woman may also have the option of suing the individual man who raped her. Laws of evidence are less strict for civil suits so even if she does not file a criminal suit, or if she loses a criminal suit, it is still possible in some instances to collect damages. Some victims have filed suit against an institution or fraternity (if the rape took place at a fraternity function). If the perpetrator is a minor, the victim may be able to sue his parents. A woman should discuss these options with a knowledgeable attorney. Again, since date rape is so difficult to prove, a woman might spend a great deal of money in attorney's fees and lose the case.

Additionally, in some colleges and universities, it is possible to file a charge against a student who has violated the institution's rules. A woman can choose to file charges in her institution regardless of what she does in relation to criminal and civil charges. In some instances, the rapist has been suspended from school.

PHIL AND CINDY:
THE SAME STORY BUT TWO DIFFERENT POINTS OF VIEW

Phil:
I still don't understand what happened. Cindy and I had been dating for about two months and while we had not slept together yet, I had certainly made it clear that I was very attracted to her and eventually expected to have sex with her. We were supposed to go to a party and when she showed up in this sexy low-cut dress, I thought maybe this was her way of saying she was ready. At the party we drank some beer, which made her sort of sleepy and sensual. When she said she wanted to go lie down and have me come snuggle with her, what was I supposed to think? Of course I thought she wanted to have sex. Granted, she did grumble a little when I started to undress her but I just figured she wanted to be persuaded. Lots of women feel a little funny about being forward and want men to take responsibility for sex. I don't know. We had sex and it was fine. I took her home from the party and thought everything was okay. But ever since then she refuses to talk to me or go out with me. I thought she really liked me. What happened?

Cindy:
I'll never forget that night as long as I live. Phil and I had been dating a while and he had always acted like a perfect gentleman—well, we had done our share of kissing, but he never gave me any reason not to trust him. The night of the party I wore this gorgeous dress that I borrowed from my roommate. It was a little flashier than I normally wear, but I thought it was very flattering. At the party I had some beer and it made me really tired, so I wanted to lie down. Maybe I shouldn't have suggested we both lie down together, but it felt weird to just go upstairs by myself and leave Phil all alone. The next thing I know he was all over me, forcing me to have sex with him. It was horrible. I didn't want to scream and make a fool of myself with all those other people in the next room, but I tried to fight him off. I guess I was just too wiped out to be very effective. Needless to say, I never want to see Phil again. He seemed like such a nice guy. What happened?

Conclusion

All rape is traumatic but there is something particularly traumatic about a woman being raped by someone she knows and previously had liked and trusted. Although only a small percentage of men commit date rape, these men do a disproportionate amount of harm. As women become more aware of what date rape is and how it occurs, they may be able to lower the chances of it happening to them. Rape is not a private issue but a public one. Acquaintance rape cannot be considered solely a "personal" issue involving a particular man and a particular woman. It is a problem that concerns all men and all women because it deals with the basic issue of the ways in which men and women relate to each other. There is a need for colleges and universities to have rape prevention programs not only to help women protect themselves but to help men understand the issue of rape and thereby make the college campus a safer environment for everyone.

Acknowledgments

The authors wish to acknowledge the contribution of the colleges and universities that have produced their own pamphlets on date rape and form the basis for many of the ideas in this [chapter]. Among the most useful are:

Date Rape: Crossed Signals on a Saturday Night, Plymouth State College, NH
When "No!" Is Not Enough, Auburn University, AL
From Rape Awareness Comes Rape Prevention, Siena Heights College, MI
Sex and Rape, TV Style, and Resources Against Sexual Assault, University of California–Santa Cruz
Resources Against Sexual Assault, University of California–San Francisco
Date Rape Reality, Western Michigan University

The authors also wish to thank Corporal Cathy Atwell, Police community Relations Officer, University Police, University of Maryland, for her guidance in the development of this [chapter].

11

HIV PEER COUNSELING

by Joann M. Wong and Sharlene C. Pereira

As the human immuno virus (HIV) infection rates continue to increase, the concept of anonymous HIV testing sites on university campuses is rapidly gaining popularity. Many students entering college underestimate their vulnerability to becoming infected with HIV. This is due to a number of factors, including: the focus on at-risk groups versus risky behavior; the unsafe assumption that most people who are infected know they are infected and would disclose this to a sex partner; and the belief that they are in a "safe" or "clean" environment. Most are probably unaware of studies indicating that 1 in 250 Americans is infected (Surgeon General's Report, 1992). Because college students explore their sexuality and experiment with various contraception methods, as well as with alcohol or other drugs, the need for readily accessible HIV testing is high. Students often prefer an anonymous test program. They may be reluctant to use confidential testing because it involves the possibility of meeting a physician they already know and discussing personal information with a non-peer. Maintaining an anonymous HIV testing program on campus is crucial for promoting students' knowledge of their HIV status and normalizing testing among this population.

Incorporating peer counselors in the testing process is important for providing a more comfortable atmosphere for students, who often perceive peer counselors to be less threatening. Peer counseling offers the advantage of one-on-one discussion in which the counselor can devote great attention to discussing individual risk behaviors and developing appropriate strategies to reduce risk. The peer counselor's age and role similarities with the client often lead to a more informal tone during the session. As a result, it may be easier for the client to disclose intimate information and feelings. Comprehensive training qualifies peer counselors to deal with sensitive issues in a confidential and professional manner.

By providing a nonjudgmental and supportive environment, an anonymous HIV testing program attempts to lower psychological barriers for high-risk students to getting tested. Students may be more strongly influenced to change their behavior via peer influence (role modeling) as opposed to suggestions from an authority figure such as a parent or health professional. A testing program with peer counselors accommodates the specific needs and concerns of students wanting to be tested anonymously. It also encourages testing among all students as a means of reducing risky behavior and promoting sexual well-being and responsibility.

The Counselor's Role and Responsibilities

The role of an HIV test peer counselor is to educate clients and assist them in processing sensitive and personal issues related to risk assessment in an informal, safe, objective, caring, and professional environment. The peer counselor's responsibilities are:

- To educate clients about HIV and the HIV antibody test

- To serve as an expert in HIV education and riskassessment counseling

- To provide a nonjudgmental and supportive yet professional environment

- To help students assess their level of risk

- To empower and challenge students to lower their risk by exploring options and perceived barriers to risk reduction

- To provide support and referrals that facilitate entry into an early intervention program, for those students who test positive

College students vary in their general knowledge about HIV and AIDS (Acquired Immune Deficiency Syndrome). Therefore, it is very important that the HIV test peer counselor spend time to assess each client's current level of understanding and to discuss HIV transmission, prevention, and testing. The counselor should attempt to clarify any misconceptions the client may have about HIV or related issues. The following quiz addresses questions commonly raised regarding HIV and AIDS.

Test Your HIV Knowledge
TRUE or FALSE?

1. Once you've had unprotected sex with someone, it doesn't make much sense to start using condoms as a precaution against HIV or other sexually transmitted diseases.

2. Condoms can still be used properly by someone who is intoxicated since it takes a considerable amount of alcohol for someone to put on a condom incorrectly.

3. Most people can tell someone is infected with HIV if they look carefully at a person's physical appearance.

4. Early intervention—an aggressive immediate health program for an HIV/STD person—can have a beneficial impact on that person's disease progression.

5. HIV causes its adverse effect by attacking red and white blood cells in the body.

6. If I'm the one giving oral sex to someone, I am not really at risk for getting infected with HIV.

7. Deep kissing with someone puts me at some risk of getting infected with HIV.

8. Since I don't use needles, I'm not gay, and I *know* my friends, I don't really have to worry about getting infected with HIV.

9. HIV antibodies can take up to six months to develop after someone has been infected with the AIDS virus.

10. It doesn't matter if two people have unprotected intercourse if both are already infected with HIV.

11. Lubricants significantly increase condom effectiveness.

ANSWERS

1. False. Even if you've had unprotected sex with an infected person many times, it's possible that you are still negative. HIV infection doesn't occur with every incident of unprotected sex. Until you and your partner have both been tested and are sure of your HIV status, it is therefore crucial to use condoms, even if you "slipped up" or "forgot" several times.

2. False. Studies reflect that alcohol use can greatly decrease one's effectiveness in using condoms correctly. Under the influence, one is more likely to tear the condom, put it on incorrectly, or take it off incorrectly. Students under the influence suffer impaired judgment and often lose

their ability to judge whether they are in a safe situation. Regardless of tolerance level, people who mix drugs or alcohol with sex are still taking a risk.

3. False. Many people live five to twelve years after they've become infected before coming down with the symptoms of "wasting syndrome" or an opportunistic infection (Karposi's sarcoma, pelvic inflammatory disease, or pneumocystis pneumonia). HIV-positive people look healthy and vibrant like everyone else up until the point when their bodies begin developing serious infections.

4. True. Early intervention—including prophylactic treatment with drugs (such as AZT or DDI, among others) or alternative holistic treatments—may delay a seropositive person's onset of the disease. Other new treatments are available that can prolong and improve the life of some individuals with HIV-related illnesses.

5. False. HIV enters and replicates itself in T cells, a subgroup of the two classes of white blood cells. (The other class comprises the B cells.) HIV can infect but not replicate in other cells such as macrophages. According to the Centers for Disease Control, an AIDS diagnosis should be given when a person has a count of 200 or fewer T_4 cells.

6. False. Giving oral sex is risky because it involves the exchange of fluids that are known to transmit HIV. These fluids (in order of most to least infectious) are: blood, semen, vaginal secretions, and pre-cum (the small amount of fluid emitted from the penis prior to ejaculation). The person giving oral sex to an infected person can contract HIV when one of these fluids enters his or her bloodstream through a cut or sore in the mouth (not from swallowing!).

7. False. There is no risk of contracting HIV through any form of mouth-to-mouth kissing. Saliva does not transmit HIV. It is contact with blood that should be avoided.

8. False. HIV doesn't care what risk group a person belongs to. Rather, it is the person's *behavior* that creates the risk for getting infected.

9. True. The "window period" for producing antibodies lasts up to six months. After six months, virtually all people will have developed HIV antibodies if they are infected. The HIV antibody test detects HIV antibodies, *not* the virus itself. Detection of antibodies is the preferred screening method because antibodies are present throughout the bloodstream. On the other hand, the virus may be more concentrated in a smaller number of cells. Thus, detection of the virus is more difficult.

10. False. It *does* matter if two HIV-infected people engage in unprotected intercourse because it is possible to reinfect each other with more HIV. Reinfection increases the concentration of HIV in the person's body. This can lead to a faster breakdown of the immune system, thus making the individual more vulnerable to getting sick sooner.

11. True. Due to natural variations in the body's physiology, neither men nor women can always provide an adequate amount of natural lubrication. Lubricants that are water-based, such as K-Y Jelly (*not* oil-based such as whipping cream, massage oil, Crisco, etc.) can make sex safer by decreasing the friction between the condom and the anus or vagina. Lubricants often contain the spermicide nonoxynol-9, which has been shown to kill HIV on contact in a laboratory. However, since nonoxynol-9 is a detergent, some people may develop symptoms of skin

irritation. Individuals who have such a reaction should stop using nonoxynol-9.

Getting in Touch with Internal Attitudes

Good HIV peer counselors do more than disseminate knowledge. They work through the client's feelings and attitudes as well. As a peer counselor, you should be prepared to listen and explore serious topics, feelings, and fears that your clients may introduce. You are in a unique position: you may be the *first* person your client has ever confided in about homosexuality, disclosure of a rape or sexual abuse, virginity, or masturbation. It is crucial that you remain open and empathic in such circumstances.

By familiarizing yourself with the special psychosocial and educational needs of different client population groups, you can become more effective at personalizing the counseling session and relating to your clients. For example, with a female bisexual client, you may want to spend more time addressing the risks related to female sexual partners and talking about condoms and dental dams for protection. Counselors who learn more about the specific needs and interests of different types of clients are more successful in relating to them. In addition, you can present new knowledge or strategies in a way your clients can respect and understand. This increases the likelihood that they will integrate new information and skills that lead to reducing risk behaviors.

Good peer counselors are nonjudgmental, empathic, and open in their style. Before the first counseling session, it is important for you to get in touch with your own feelings about the issues related to this type of counseling. A well-planned and professionally supported training program is essential for such personal preparation. If you know how you feel about certain issues, you can more easily be conscientious about remaining nonjudgmental in your tone or direction during sessions. Achieving this awareness of your own attitudes and feelings prepares you to discuss and explore ideas with clients more freely, even if you have a strong opposing opinion with respect to your clients. The following exercises incorporate topics that you should reflect on during your training (to imagine yourself addressing in a counseling scenario).

Ethnicity
Be aware and acknowledge that people's values and attitudes about homosexuality, sexual behavior, and contraception may be tied to their upbringing and cultural identity.

Check the statements you agree with.

☐ I would feel more effective counseling someone of my own race and/or religion about HIV and AIDS issues.

☐ It could be harder to counsel Asian-Americans than African-Americans because Asians will probably be more closed and conservative in their views.

☐ I am not really in tune with the feelings and attitudes of the rising number of gay Latino young men (13 to 25 years old) regarding their homosexuality, their attitudes toward safer sex, etc. Their behavior is confusing to me.

Multiple Partners
Realize that people may disclose that they have numerous partners or have elected to exchange sex for money or drugs.

Check the statements you agree with.

☐ There's nothing worse than having to talk to someone who sleeps around every weekend with a different person.

☐ I just don't see why my peers still go to clubs for sex despite their knowledge of the risks involved.

Homophobia/Sexual Orientation

Be prepared to discuss all varieties of sexual orientation, behavior, and practices. Be ready to listen to prejudices and strong opinions with respect to people's sexual identity. On your part, try to be open and neutral in tone.

Check the statements you agree with.

☐ I don't think I could relate to a lesbian regardless of when she came out.

☐ I would feel uncomfortable discussing a bisexual's background because it's a foreign lifestyle to me.

☐ It would be frustrating and difficult for me to discuss HIV and AIDS issues and safer sex with someone who is obviously homophobic.

☐ The thought of having to interact with gay men and talk about the specifics of their sex life makes me nervous.

☐ Lesbians don't have to worry about getting infected. Nothing they do is really risky.

Experience/Age

A perceived gap in age or experience may hinder good peer counseling.

Check the statements you agree with.

☐ I think it'd be pretty difficult and uncomfortable to counsel someone who is more than five years older than I am, because there will be an age gap. They are probably a lot more sexually experienced.

☐ Deep down, I feel like I wouldn't be a good counselor for someone who uses intravenous drugs, because I've never used them or known anyone who has, either.

Gender

The client's gender may affect your comfort level in discussing sexual health issues (behavior, sexually transmitted disease, sexual assault) and encouraging condom use or other safer sex measures.

Check the statements you agree with.

☐ Men aren't concerned enough and don't understand the true issues involved in rape.

☐ It's hard to talk to women about sexual behaviors because they get embarrassed easily, or everything offends them. Women are private people and don't want to share their experiences.

☐ Men are sex fiends and difficult to negotiate with.

☐ Women should ask me to use protection if they are concerned about getting HIV or an STD [sexually transmitted disease].

The statements you just checked or considered checking indicate topics that may be difficult for you to discuss or counsel about objectively. You may want to get in touch more fully with such issues to identify the scope of your feelings and become aware of areas that may elicit biased counseling.

THE PRE-TEST COUNSELING SESSION

Getting an HIV antibody test can be a scary experience. Testing forces people to confront many issues they may have avoided or not thought about before. Consequently, peer counselors are very important in establishing an environment that is confidential, safe, objective, and caring for the people getting tested.

Establish Rapport and Set the Stage

After greeting the client, the counselor sets the tone of the pre-test session by giving the person an overview of what will happen during the session. Because getting tested can be a stressful, confusing, and anxiety-producing experience for many people, it is critical for counselors to emphasize that all discussion is entirely confidential. Counselors should encourage clients to ask questions and speak out if they feel uncomfortable or nervous during any part of the session.

Following the brief overview of the session, counselors should assist in exploring those risky behaviors that led up to the event(s) in which clients feel they were possibly infected. During this interaction, counselors assess their clients':

- Reason for coming in to get tested

- Knowledge about HIV transmission

- Knowledge about safer sex

- Attitude toward safer sex

- Actual sexual behaviors/practices

- Strategies used before that were effective or ineffective in practicing safer sex with a partner

The question "What brought you in to get tested?" is effective for opening up a discussion in order to assess people's risk of HIV infection. If they appear apprehensive or hesitant to discuss why they want to get tested, it may be helpful to reemphasize the confidentiality and anonymity of the testing process. If clients give a broad statement, such as "I came in to get tested for peace of mind" or "I thought it was a good idea," you face a choice. You can either ask an open question to elicit a more personal response or continue the session by giving out the accompanying form, the HIV Pre-test Counseling Questionnaire. You can use this form to guide the discussion about more specific issues related to risk of HIV infection.

Throughout the session, you must respect your client's comfort level in discussing sensitive issues related to the risk of HIV infection. You can help people feel at ease by keeping in mind basic attending skills:

Verbal	Nonverbal
Affirming sentences	Eye contact
Concerned/interested tone	Relaxed body posture
Paraphrasing	Head nodding
Open questions	Concerned facial expression
Using client's own words or phrases	

Assess Risk

Throughout the session, integrate your counseling skills to maintain a comfortable, objective, and nonthreatening environment for clients. Creating such an environment is important in encouraging people to assess their own risk of HIV infection as well as guiding them to develop strategies that minimize future risky behaviors. Risk assessment encompasses a broad continuum of behaviors, as shown in the next table.

	CONTINUUM OF RISKY BEHAVIORS		
High Risk	**Moderate Risk**	**Low Risk**	**No Risk**
←			→
Unprotected anal intercourse	Anal intercourse with condom, with ejaculation	Anal sex with condom, no ejaculation	Masturbation
Unprotected vaginal intercourse	Vaginal intercourse with condom	Vaginal sex with condom, no ejaculation	Massage
Unprotected fellatio with ejaculation	Unprotected fellatio, no ejaculation	Fellatio with condom	Kissing
Unprotected cunnilingus	Cunnilingus with dental dam		Abstinence
Sharing dirty needles	Cleaning needle works with bleach	Using clean needles, not sharing needles	
Needle use under the influence			

The following examples illustrate situations that may expose people to HIV infection.

1. A 23-year-old female works in a lab that conducts research on drugs to treat people infected with HIV. Since she handles needles and vials of blood infected with HIV, she is concerned about knowing her current HIV status.

2. A 32-year-old graduate student comes in to get tested. He is concerned about a blood transfusion he received years ago (in 1986) during an operation and wants to know his HIV status.

3. A 28-year-old graduate student was sexually active and practiced unprotected sex as an undergraduate. He never really thought about being at risk until hearing from one of his former partners, who just tested positive.

4. A 19-year-old female is currently seeing someone. She and her partner use condoms fairly consistently, though on a couple of occasions condoms weren't readily accessible when they had intercourse. She is concerned about her status.

When assessing someone's risk for HIV infection, it is important to identify all areas for possible exposure to HIV. In the first example, it would be helpful for you to get a sense of whether the woman was also sexually active or sharing needles for drug use. If she is at risk only because of her work in the lab, then you should proceed to discuss more specific risk factors related to her contact with HIV-infected fluids (e.g., does she wear gloves when handling the fluids? Has she ever pierced her skin with a needle containing HIV-infected blood?)

In the second example, you should reassure the client that beginning in 1985, all blood used in the United States for transfusions has been rigorously screened for HIV antibodies. The risk for HIV infection from a blood transfusion after 1985 is very low: only 1 in 225,000 units of blood that is screened for HIV antibodies is expected to be infected (Dodd, 1992). It would be important to identify any other activities this client has engaged in that would put him at risk for HIV infection (e.g., unprotected intercourse, sharing needles).

In examples 3 and 4, it would also be critical for you to identify the specific risk behaviors these individuals engaged in: type of intercourse, whether the partner ejaculated, etc. Using the preceding "Continuum of Risky Behaviors," work with these clients to assess their risk for HIV infection.

Identify the Client's Attitude for
Effective Strategy Development

Following an assessment of specific risk behavior, explore your client's attitudes toward safer sex and perceived barriers to risk reduction. Such exploration enables you to work with clients to develop appropriate and realistic strategies to reduce risk behavior.

Open-ended questions are effective in assessing people's attitudes toward practicing safer sex or needle use.

EXAMPLE

A third-year gay male student comes in to get tested. He worries that he is infected because he had unprotected anal intercourse with his partner, who refused to use a condom.

Counselor: *How did it make you feel when your partner didn't want to use a condom?*

Client: *I felt frustrated and angry. I don't mind using them but N hates using condoms—they ruin the moment. When I do ask him to use one, he avoids the question, we start kissing, one thing leads to another, and the next thing I know, we've just had anal sex.*

In this example, the counselor can get some sense of the client's attitude toward practicing safer sex. This example also illustrates that people often may not feel confident enough with their communication skills to negotiate with a partner about using protection. Consequently, you will want to focus on exploring strategies with clients about alternative ways to handle similar situations.

As a peer counselor, you are *not* meant to provide answers. Rather, your role is to encourage people to process and explore options they may not have considered with regard to protecting themselves and negotiating with a partner. You also play a critical role in helping people develop effective skills that they feel comfortable using to communicate about safer sex. Examples of questions that you may incorporate into the discussion include: "If you could recreate the scenario you just described, what would be different?" and "In your own words, how do you ask your partner to use a condom?"

It is helpful to introduce hypothetical situations and, if appropriate, to rehearse such situations in a nonthreatening environment so your client can practice negotiating with a resistant partner. It may also be effective to reverse roles: the client plays the resistant partner and you play the client's normal role. This process helps people better understand the mind-set of a resistant partner. At the same time, clients can benefit from hearing alternative responses that they can incorporate in future negotiations with partners. They can learn and modify new phrases and responses that can help them feel more confident in asserting their position.

To make sure that people understand, you need to use your clients' language or slang words. When you use medical terms, people may not ask for clarification if they are embarrassed or feel inadequate. The goal is to guide clients to a point where they feel more confident in developing assertive communication to use with a partner.

The next scenario addresses issues related to high-risk behavior.

EXAMPLE

A sophomore woman comes in to get tested. At a dorm party a year ago, she drank too much and ended up in a dorm-mate's room. She didn't really know the guy or his sexual history but ended up having vaginal intercourse with him. Since the incident, she hasn't had intercourse with anyone, and things with the guy have been awkward.

Two months ago, she got extremely sick with flu-like symptoms that lingered for several weeks. The lymph nodes under her arms got really swollen. In the past month, she's been getting an unusual rash.

This scenario illustrates that people may falsely associate long-term flu-like symptoms and swollen glands with HIV infection. Since college students endure a great deal of stress, it is also possible that their immune systems may become suppressed, making them more susceptible to getting sick or developing an unusual rash. You may want to mention that such symptoms may be the result of the body's reaction to extreme stress rather than to HIV infection.

This scenario also portrays a common yet ignored risk behavior by students: sex under the influence. It is important to help clients explore the thought process that led up to engaging in unprotected intercourse under the influence of alcohol or drugs. Questions that you may ask clients include:

> "Has this experience affected your view of sex and alcohol?" (If yes, then ask: "In what way?")

> "If you found yourself in a similar situation, what might you do differently?"

Drinking or doing drugs jeopardizes people's ability to protect themselves readily if they choose to engage in behaviors that put them at risk for contracting HIV. People who are high or drunk are not likely to want to protect themselves or be able to use protection correctly.

If clients frequently engage in unprotected intercourse while under the influence, it is important to help them explore their feelings and to develop a risk-reduction plan. Planning ahead helps people protect themselves when sexually active in an environment where alcohol or drugs are present. Examples of potential strategies to discuss are:

- Not drinking at all

- Deciding not to have sex unless a condom or dental dam is available

- Carrying condoms and lubricants routinely (via a key chain, purse, etc.)

- Deciding to stop having sex under the influence, at least for a trial period

- Going to parties with friends who have previously agreed to make sure they have a safe route home (i.e., making a contract with a friend)

- Leaving the party/situation

- Limiting the number of drinks

If a client's alcohol or drug use seems to be a problem, appears necessary for sex and enjoyment, or has an addictive character, referral for treatment may be appropriate.

After involving your client in discussing hypothetical situations, engaging in interactive role-plays, and reviewing strategies to decrease chances of HIV infection, you should bring closure to this risk assessment. This entails summarizing what was discussed, reinforcing the developed strategies, and answering any additional questions. Then you should spend a few minutes assessing how your client perceives the waiting period for results. Good questions to ask include:

"During the waiting period, are there friends or family members you can talk to if you need to?"

"How have you handled other stressful situations in the past?"

"Have you thought about what you'd do if you have a positive result [if you are infected]?"

If your client seems overanxious while discussing the waiting period, you may want to explore this topic until the person seems less anxious. Keep a reference sheet of on-campus counseling services to give to all clients in case they need resources during the waiting period.

To help enhance communication and problem-solving skills, you should identify the client's:

- Perceived barriers in communicating and negotiating with a partner

- Attitude toward using protection when sexually active or using needles

- Internal issues regarding practicing safer sex (e.g., doesn't feel comfortable buying condoms, doesn't like using them)

This next list summarizes additional issues that counselors should address to help people develop strategies to reduce risky behaviors:

- Partner's history of sexual activity and use of drugs and needles

- Partner's status regarding being tested for HIV or other sexually transmitted diseases

- Trust issues in the relationship

Incorporate Educational Component
Empowering people with correct information helps them make more informed choices regarding their degree of risky behavior. Education is also a step toward reducing misconceptions surrounding HIV. A good initial assessment of people's HIV knowledge is the first step in effective HIV education. With this information, counselors can begin educating clients at an appropriate level and pace. As issues arise, HIV education can be incorporated into the discussion. An interactive approach decreases

the possibility that clients will feel "lectured at." It also sets the stage for learning in a relaxed and supportive environment.

Common educational tools, such as visual aids and demonstrations, significantly increase clients' receptivity to information and can greatly enhance counselors' educational efforts. Brochures and handouts can easily be referred to during the session; when clients take them home, they reinforce new material such as safer sex guidelines.

While presenting information to clients, it is important to underscore that many questions about HIV transmission are still unanswered. A good example of this is reflected in a recent study indicating that cleaning needle works with a 10 percent bleach solution was much less effective in reducing HIV infection than previously thought (Shapshak et al., 1993). Now it is recommended that people use 100 percent bleach for cleaning needles. Counselors should encourage clients to be proactive and to seek updated information on HIV and AIDS.

Based on standardized protocol, you should touch on the main educational subjects. How much you cover each topic depends on each client's experience. These topics include:

Confidential vs. anonymous testing
Routes of HIV transmission
The HIV antibody test (ELISA, Western Blot)
Risk behavior vs. risk group
Sex under the influence of alcohol or other drugs
Safer sex with latex barriers (condoms, dental dams, plastic wrap)
Discussing HIV status with potential partners
HIV early intervention programs

If you forget to go over one of these topics for any reason, you should bring it up in the post-test session. You can do so after you give the test result and check on your client's commitment to stay negative and/or to implement behavior changes.

Your role is to discover what your client already knows about HIV and AIDS and expand on this, or to find out what the person doesn't know and then fill in the blanks. Good ways to start include questions such as:

"When did you first learn about HIV/AIDS?"
"What do you know about HIV transmission and AIDS?"
"Give me an idea of how familiar you are with HIV information."

Open-ended introductory questions encourage people to talk, which gives you a better sense of which educational topics to address. For instance, does the client need to know more about lubricants, STDs, or the relative risks of unprotected anal, vaginal, and oral sex? Basic peer counseling techniques such as paraphrasing and open questions help you avoid a monologue. Another good question for finding the limits of the person's understanding of HIV and related issues is:

"Do you feel you could educate a friend or younger sibling about HIV and AIDS?"

During the pre-test counseling session, you can discuss and demonstrate correct and effective use of latex barriers. This may be especially helpful for someone who has never used condoms or dental dams, who feels inhibited or uncomfortable about using latex barriers, or who has trouble eroticizing condom or dental dam use. You may choose to give your clients an information sheet that outlines the steps for effective and proper condom use. Handouts alone are not enough, however. If people are mature and responsible enough to be engaging in sexual activity, they also need to be mature and responsible enough to discuss and practice condom use.

Other important educational aids to have readily accessible in the counseling room include a dildo, condoms, and female condoms or dental dams. From time to time, you will meet students who have never seen or used a condom. In this case, a demonstration is especially important and life-saving. Furthermore, many students are not familiar with dental dams or the female condom. You should be comfortable demonstrating how to use these forms of protective latex. You should also mention other important information about latex barriers, such as the fact that condoms, unlike birth control pills, can protect against most STDs when used consistently and properly.

You can dispel uncomfortable feelings by saying, "I'd like to talk a little about how to use a condom effectively." While you demonstrate (using a dildo), your client can refer to the handout. If the counseling program does not have a dildo, you may want to bring in a banana or cucumber. Or you can use your fingers to demonstrate proper condom use. The most effective way to teach this is first to demonstrate and then to observe the client handling the condom. You should provide feedback as appropriate. Another effective measure is to ask if the client has ever experienced breaks or other problems with condoms. You and your client can then troubleshoot the particular problem. For instance, what can be done about a condom slipping off during withdrawal, or breaking during use?

Continuity Between Sessions

Because the program includes two counseling sessions—a pre- and a post-test meeting—it is important to ensure that you do both. This preserves the anonymity and privacy of the sessions and maintains your client's comfort level. By being familiar with your client and her or his background, you can reemphasize those issues you discussed previously (e.g., risk behaviors). In the second session, you can also cover any topics you did not address in the pre-test session. To accommodate this, you need to tell your clients during the pre-test session that, except in the case of an emergency, they will most likely see you again for the post-test session.

In the event that another counselor does have to substitute for you, that counselor should read the client's pre-test questionnaire to learn about the person's risk behaviors and to find out whether that person has had unprotected sex within the past six months. This prepares the counselor to advise the client to get retested in the future. First, though, the substitute counselor needs to relieve any apprehensions or anxieties the client may have about seeing a different counselor. The substitute should also feel free to explore the person's particular situation briefly so as to better integrate the test result.

ISSUES RELATED TO ANONYMITY

Several considerations arise in creating an anonymous format for testing and counseling peers on a college campus.

Counseling Someone You Know

When students call in to make appointments, they are told the full name of the counselor they will be meeting. At this point, to maintain anonymity, students who know their counselor may request a different one. However, some callers don't recognize a counselor's name; only upon meeting do they realize they know each other. Here's an example.

Counselor: *Hi.*

Student: *Oh, hi. Hey, I didn't know you did this.*

Counselor: *Yeah, I counsel every Wednesday morning. Since we know each other, you should feel free to reschedule with another counselor in order to maintain your anonymity in getting tested. We have a policy in which counselors don't counsel people we know, because we do ask pretty personal questions that may make things awkward between the counselor and client outside this environment. Your coming in today will stay completely confidential, of course. How do you feel about rescheduling?*

Student: *Sure, I'd rather do that.*

As this example indicates, counselors really should not counsel people they know. Anonymity for the client is violated. In addition, if counselors proceed with counseling someone they know, issues may come up during the session that put both people in an uncomfortable position. Clients may not be completely open and honest with a counselor they know, thus preventing the counselor from seeing the complete picture and discussing the situation fully. Even if the counseling were to go smoothly between two people who knew one another, they may later find themselves in an uncomfortable situation outside the session concerning information discussed during counseling.

Example 1

A client had sex with a good friend of the counselor's. The counselor didn't know about it. The counselor has internal conflict over whether or not he can speak to the good friend about it.

Example 2

A client is seeing the counselor's best friend. During the session, the client reveals he cheated on his partner with another person.

These examples illustrate that peer counselors may hear things that jeopardize their relationships with clients and mutual friends. The relationships may experience new pressures and conflicts that could easily have been avoided if those counselors had not counseled people they knew.

Sometimes clients may be your classmates. Both you and the client may recognize each other but have completely different circles of friends. In such situations, you should gauge your own comfort level about counseling such people and ask them whether they are comfortable going ahead with the session.

Another possibility is a student who insists on having you as a counselor because you are a friend. It is important for you to validate your friend's concern and request, but then explain that this situation is against the program's policy. It could place both parties in a difficult situation (1) upon disclosure of the test results or (2) because of certain issues that may arise during the counseling session. You should advocate that the friend reschedule with another counselor.

The accompanying table summarizes situations that may arise and provides guidelines on how to handle the session.

SITUATION	ACTION
Good friend wants you as an HIV peer counselor because you are a friend.	Don't counsel. Have client reschedule with another counselor.
Client is someone you know well.	Don't counsel. Have client reschedule with another counselor.
Client is someone with whom you have a class	Acknowledge familiarity, ask whether client wants to continue session or obtain another counselor.
Client is a stranger.	Counsel.

Encountering a Client Elsewhere
Two people are seated next to each other in a class.

Counselor: [Thinks] Hmm . . . he looks really familiar. Hey, that's the guy I counseled last month!

Client: [Thinks] Oh, no! I'm sitting next to the counselor I had when I got tested. God, I hope he doesn't say anything to me!

The reality is, regardless of how large a college campus is, a chance exists that people will randomly bump into each other. It can sometimes be uncomfortable if you bump into students you have counseled. In such situations, the rule of thumb is: *Don't mention anything about the individual getting tested unless that individual does so* FIRST.

If you bump into someone between the two sessions, it is best to leave it up to the client to broach the topic of the test. If the person brings up the test and talks in depth about her or his concerns and anxieties over waiting for the results, you should listen, acknowledge the feelings, and then refer the person to appropriate resources. These might be a counseling hotline or a friend. It is not appropriate to act as a counselor outside of sessions.

Other policies that might be incorporated into the program include the following. Clients asking counselors out on dates during the counseling session is not appropriate; counselors asking clients out on dates during the counseling session is not appropriate; exchanging phone numbers is also not appropriate.

Bringing a Friend to the Session

Counseling sessions are designed to maintain confidentiality with clients. Due to the nature of the topics dealt with during a session, it is best to counsel the individual alone. As sensitive issues are discussed during the pre-test session, allowing the client's friend to sit in may inhibit the client from being completely open and honest about choices and behaviors that created the risk for HIV infection. Most clients are fine with sitting through a pre-test session alone. It is more common for people to ask if a friend can come along to get the results.

In some states, however, the law mandates that HIV antibody test results be given only to the person who took the test. After the results are given and if the counselor feels comfortable including someone else, the client may then have a friend sit in on the session. When a positive result is given, the client may want the friend to come in for support in handling the shock of the news and the processing. Before asking the friend to come in, the counselor should make sure personal issues are already covered.

Having an Intern Sit In

Training for HIV test peer counselors includes sitting in and observing actual counseling sessions. To ensure the client's anonymity, the trainee or intern should sit out of sight in another room while the client arrives. The counselor then asks the client about any objections to having an intern observe the session. You should emphasize that this is completely optional and reassure the client that the intern will be a silent observer who focuses on your performance. Also, it is important to stress that the client's decision will not affect the nature of the counseling session.

If the client consents, the counselor should give the intern's full name. If the client still feels fine having that intern come in, the counselor leaves to get the intern. The intern should come in, say hello, and then sit in an unobtrusive position and silently watch the ensuing interaction.

If the client feels uncomfortable about having the intern sit in, the counselor should go tell the intern to reschedule observing for another session.

EMERGENCY SITUATIONS

The testing process raises strong emotions in people, and emergencies sometimes occur during counseling. Here's one example.

Counselor: *So how do you think the next two weeks will be for you as you wait for the results?*

Client: *I'm really scared. I don't have anyone to talk to about this. With everything I've done, I'm sure I'm infected. I can't imagine living if I'm positive. I might as well be dead.*

In rare situations, for the client's overall well-being and safety, counselors may need to violate anonymity and confidentiality. All peer counseling programs should have a system already in place for counselors to turn to in emergency situations. Since college campuses differ as to their resources for crisis intervention, it is important for students involved with an HIV antibody test peer counseling program to work with the institution to establish policies and procedures for handling emergencies.

In the foregoing scenario, the student implies not wanting to live. The counselor should listen to the student and explore in more depth precisely what the client means. Questions may include: "What do you think you would do if the results came back positive?" If the response implies or expresses suicidal ideas, the counselor may choose to seek back-up support.

Counselors can refer to the following checklist (San Mateo County, 1991) when confronted with a potential crisis.

Signs of Potential Risk
Here are some of the signs that your client may be approaching an emergency or crisis.

- Disclosure of inability to cope
- Despondency, feelings of helplessness, and/or suicidal ideation
- Extreme anger or rage and/or homicidal ideation
- Social isolation (no support system and/or inability to request assistance)

Assessment of Risk
If you recognize the foregoing signs or have any other concerns about clients, you need to assess the risk that they may hurt themselves or others. Look for the following factors.

- Presence of and specificity of plans regarding suicidal ideation

- Presence of and specificity of plans regarding homicidal ideation

- History of past behaviors related to homicidal and/or suicidal gestures. *Example:* "Have you ever tried or thought about committing suicide before?")

- Recent losses or other traumatic events in the person's life

Treatment Interventions
If you find any of the foregoing signs or assessment factors, consider these interventions.

- Identify, explore, and validate the client's ability to cope with past crises. Reinforce positive self-image. *Examples:* "Have you had difficult things happen to you before? What happened? How did you handle that situation?" and "Have you ever tried or thought about committing suicide before?"

- Assist client with concrete problem-solving techniques. *Example:* "Where will you go after you leave this session? Is there a friend you can go and see?"

- Encourage expression of feelings during the counseling session. *Example:* "I know this is scary. This is a safe place to talk about some of the feelings you're having. Can you tell me more about the thoughts and feelings you're having right now?"

THE POST-TEST COUNSELING SESSION

Coming back for a test result can be a more frightening and anxiety-producing event than the pre-test experience. Be sensitive to your clients' fears and anxiety.

Giving a Negative Result

Here is one scenario.

> *The counselor arrives to set up a room for a post-test session. Just as he finishes putting out some brochures and condoms, his client arrives ten minutes early. She appears nervous and jittery.*

Client: *Hi. I know I'm early. I had a hard time sleeping last night and ended up waking up early today. But I'm glad you're here—is it okay that we start a little earlier?*

Counselor: *Sure, come on in.* [They both sit down, and the post-test session begins.] *So, you mentioned having a hard time sleeping last night. Did you have trouble sleeping at other times since you came in to get tested?*

Client: *Yeah. I'm just really nervous about my results. I didn't really start feeling nervous till these last couple of days. Can you just tell me if I'm positive or not?*

Counselor: *It does get to be more nerve-wracking as you get closer to the day you come in for your results. But now you're here, so if you give me your card with the code number, we can make sure it matches with the number on this lab slip.* [They look at the code number to make sure it matches with the code on the lab slip with the test results.]
> *Your test result is negative. Do you have any questions before we talk about what these results mean?*

After greeting the client and addressing any immediate questions or concerns, you must verify the code number to ensure a correct test result is given. If your client has forgotten the slip that has the code number, she or he needs to bring it in before you can give the test results. Someone who loses the slip should be issued a new code slip and have blood drawn again. This is done to guarantee that the client is given the correct result.

After verifying the code and conveying the test results, proceed to assess your client's need for a later test (since HIV antibodies take up to six months to show up in a person who has been infected). If a person's last exposure to possible HIV infection occurred over six months before the pre-test date, then the results accurately reflect the person's HIV status. However, if the last exposure to possible HIV infection occurred *within* six months of the pre-test date, then you should encourage the client to return for another test.

Make sure your client understands that engaging in risky behaviors means having to wait at least six months from the time of the last risky behavior before getting tested for an accurate result. To determine the level of risk over the past six months, you should ask specific questions. The following examples would warrant recommendations for a retest.

Unprotected intercourse (anal, vaginal, oral) with a partner of unknown HIV status

Unprotected intercourse with an intravenous drug user

Injected drug use (shared needles)

Blood-to-blood contact with a person of unknown HIV status

During the post-test session, it is also important to explore what the test results mean for the client ("What do these test results mean to you?"). You also need to discuss future strategies to maintain an HIV-free status ('On a scale from 1 to 10—where 1 indicates no desire to practice safer sex, and 10 indicates consistent use of appropriate protection, communicating with your partner, etc.—where would you place yourself?). This gives you a chance to assess the person's commitment to stay negative. If the commitment is low, you and your client should discuss issues related to commitment. In addition, you can address any issues that went uncovered during the pre-test session and answer any questions.

Usually, a negative test result elicits a very relieved and joyful reaction from the client. However, sometimes you may encounter someone who appears very apathetic, even upset by a negative test result. In such situations, it is critical for you to explore why the person is reacting this way ("How do you feel about your test result?"). The person may feel guilty for not being infected: "After doing all the things I've done, I can't believe I'm not infected." Allow the client to express anxiety, spend time exploring feelings, and then provide referrals for additional support from campus and community psychological services.

Since the client is in session a total of two times, you should not expect to change or stop the person from behaving in ways that put him or her at risk for HIV infection. After all, your role is not to change the way your clients behave; this would not be a realistic goal. Rather, you help people identify areas in which they are putting themselves at risk and process alternative strategies to prevent HIV infection. You should treat the post-test session with a negative test result as an opportunity to engage the client in open dialogue about feelings, attitudes, and plans. Ideally, the client plans to integrate risk-reduction behaviors that minimize the chance of HIV infection.

Giving a Positive Test Result

Perhaps one of the most difficult tasks for an HIV antibody test peer counselor is telling a person who has tested positive. There is no easy way to tell someone who is infected with HIV. However, you can provide support in many ways: by offering encouragement, compassion, and referrals for the person.

The anonymous HIV antibody test program at our university is still relatively young, so we lack the necessary depth of experience to address all issues that may arise during post-test sessions for a positive test result. However, some basic elements exist that an HIV antibody anonymous testing program should have in place to prepare peer counselors for giving a positive test result to clients. These components include:

- Additional training. Prior to the post-test session, you should consult with appropriate supervisory staff about specific issues that may arise during the session. (Supervisory staff may include a clinical psychologist and a physician and/or health promotion director at your campus's health center.)

- Option for substituting counselors. If the pre-test counselor is relatively new to the program and is not comfortable delivering a positive test result, then a more senior peer counselor may be called to conduct the post-test session. Prior to the session, the pre-test counselor briefs the senior (substitute) counselor on the client's situation. The senior counselor then consults with appropriate supervisory staff.

As in any post-test session, you should check the client's code slip to verify that the code matches the code on the lab slip. Following verification of the code number, ask, "Do you have any questions before we discuss your test results?" It is important to follow the client's lead as to when to disclose the test result. When appropriate, you should state in a direct, neutral tone: "Your test result is positive." Before proceeding, wait for the person's response. If your client has brought a friend, this is the appropriate time to ask the client about having the friend join the session.

Instead of discussing risk behaviors during a post-test session with a positive test result, you should proceed to assess the client's reaction to the test result by exploring with the person:

- What the test results mean

- What the next steps will be

- What medical/psychological resources are available

We suggest the following guidelines for giving a positive test result.

I. Integration of Test Result
   A. Cognitive Integration
      1. Explore your client's understanding of medical meaning of test result.
      2. Clarify misconceptions and answer questions in a simple, direct manner.
   B. Emotional Integration
      1. Validate and normalize feelings ("I know this is scary.")
      2. Allow your client to lead the session. Provide a safe, caring environment for free expression.

II. Medical Follow-up
   A. Have ready a list of campus health services, and discuss options.
   B. Explain other options for medical care and support services at county programs, which may maintain anonymity. If appropriate (if your client asks about a Health Maintenance Organization or other health care facility), explain that most physicians and health care plans offer confidential care and services.
   C. Reassure your client that decisions do not need to be made immediately, and that support will be available when needed.

III. Hope, Advocacy, and Empowerment
   A. Consistently reflect realistically hopeful statements without discounting the person's concerns.

B. Focus on promising research efforts (promising new drugs).
C. Focus on "quality of life" issues.
D. Encourage utilization of recommended referral services.
E. Encourage your client's active participation in addressing health needs/concerns.

Make sure your client understands the meaning of the test result, and work with the person about how to cope with this HIV-positive status.

In some cases, the post-test counseling session may not cover all the components mentioned in the foregoing outline. Some clients are in a state of shock and thus not able to process such information during the session. In such situations, you should offer the option to schedule a return appointment, either with you (to maintain anonymity) or with a campus health center's medical/psychological professional on a confidential (but not anonymous) basis.

SUMMARY

To be helpful and resourceful as an HIV antibody test peer counselor, it is important to keep in mind that getting tested for HIV antibodies may be one of the most frightening, intense, and anxiety-provoking events in a person's life. Given the depth of personal issues a counselor addresses with a client, it is critical for you to create a safe, objective, and caring environment. Peer counseling does more than foster a nonintimidating atmosphere to get tested. That environment is also an opportunity for developing and reinforcing clients' strategies and skills (through education, hypothetical situations, and role plays) to reduce future occurrences of unsafe and risky behaviors.

OUTLINE OF COUNSELING SESSIONS

A. Pre-Test Counseling Session

Components	Counseling Issues
Introduction	Establish credibility and confidentiality/anonymity of testing program.
Testing Procedures	Review the testing procedure and process.
Risk Assessment	Allow client to express own assessment ("What brings you here to take the test?").
Knowledge/Attitude Toward Safer Sex	Assess for denial, intellectualizing, feeling removed, patronizing attitude.
Communication	Maintain a nonjudgmental and open style. Be sensitive to client's anxiety, stress level. Barriers: language, psychological.
Exploring strategies	Process issues with client. Role-play relevant hypothetical situations.
Support Network	Give referrals as appropriate.

B. Post-Test Counseling Session (Negative Result)

Components	Counseling Issues
Verification of Code Slip	If client brought code slip, verify that its code number matches the one on the test result. Then proceed to next component.
	If client forgot to bring along the code slip, reschedule appointment.
	If client lost the code slip, arrange for redrawing blood and reschedule a post-test session.
Revelation of Test Results	Structure the session based on client's reaction.
Integration of Test Results	Explore client's understanding of test result and any emotional reaction(s).
	Explore client's commitment to maintain HIV negative status
Assessment of Need for Retest	Discuss whether client's last risk exposure was within the six-month window period. If so, discuss importance of a retest.

C. Post-Test Counseling Session (Positive Result)

Components	Counseling Issues
Verification of Code Slip	If client brought code slip, verify that its code number matches the one on the test result. Then proceed to next component. If client forgot to bring along the code slip, reschedule appointment. If client lost the code slip, arrange for redrawing blood and reschedule a post-test session.
Revelation of Test Results	Structure the session based on client's reaction.
Integration of Test Results	Check that client understands the medical meaning of the result. Validate and process feelings. Be open and empathetic as the person expresses emotions.
Referrals for Future Care	Discuss available options for emotional support and medical care, including alternative treatment. Give referrals to physicians and community HIV support groups, as appropriate.

HIV Antibody Pre-Test Counseling Questionnaire

Demographic Data
Age: _____ Gender: _____
Undergraduate: (1) (2) (3) (4+)
Graduate/Postdoc: (   )
Partner: (   )
Nonstudent: (   )

Ethnic Background:
(   ) African-American
(   ) Asian/Pacific Islander
(   ) Hispanic/Latino
(   ) Native American/Alaskan
(   ) White
(   ) Other: _____

Information
Have you been treated for a sexually transmitted
disease in the last 12 months? (Y) (N)

How many HIV antibody tests have you had?
(0) (1) (2) (3) (4) (5+)

Date of last negative result: _____
Date of first positive result: _____

Women only:
Do you think you may be pregnant? (Y) (N)
Do you breastfeed? (Y) (N)

Behavior
Check **ALL** the items that apply to you.

No (Never)
Yes (More than 6 mos. ago) [>6]
Yes (Within past 6 months) [<6]

	NO	YES >6	YES <6
Sex under the influence of alcohol/other drugs	( )	( )	( )

	NO	YES >6	YES <6
Oral sex with a condom or latex barrier			
Gave	( )	( )	( )
Received	( )	( )	( )
Oral sex without a condom or latex barrier			
Gave	( )	( )	( )
Received	( )	( )	( )
Anal sex with a condom			
Insertive	( )	( )	( )
Receptive	( )	( )	( )
Anal sex without a condom			
Insertive	( )	( )	( )
Receptive	( )	( )	( )
Vaginal sex with a condom			
Insertive	( )	( )	( )
Receptive	( )	( )	( )
Vaginal sex without a condom			
Insertive	( )	( )	( )
Receptive	( )	( )	( )
Shared needles	( )	( )	( )
Transfusion with uncertain blood supply	( )	( )	( )
Sexual contact with partner of opposite sex	( )	( )	( )
Sexual contact with partner of same sex	( )	( )	( )

Comments or questions: _____

_____

_____

FOR OFFICE USE ONLY:

Code number: _____

Pre-test date: _____ Post-test date: _____

Result: _____

Pre-test counselor: _____

Post-test counselor: _____

Test Election: (1) Anonymous (2) Confidential
                (3) Not tested here

APPENDICES

A Peer Counseling Training Program:
Rationale, Curriculum, and Evaluation

by David Dorosin, Vincent D'Andrea,
and Richard Jacks

This appendix is based on the presentation by Drs. David Dorosin, Vincent D'Andrea, and Richard Jacks at the 1977 meeting of the American College Health Association. It discusses the rationale for establishing a college peer counseling center, the way one particular training program was developed, and the data used to evaluate that program's effectiveness.

Some years ago, a number of student groups came to us, interested in peer counselor training. This opportunity immediately raised three questions: (1) How much staff time—a scarce resource—should we expend in this activity? That is, would it be a "wise investment" of professional time, and by what criteria should we decide? (2) Since ethnic minority groups, contraception counseling groups, drug counseling groups, and even university staff were interested in such training, what might constitute a core curriculum that would be applicable to such a variety of interested groups? (3) How could we evaluate the quality and impact of the training?

This book shares the answers we arrived at: why we felt this program would be a good investment of professional time, the content of our curriculum, and our methods for evaluating our program.

RATIONALE

Even before the inception of the program, the idea of students helping students had been important to us. For example, we had spent time selecting and orienting residential staff, facilitating interactions between professionals from the counseling service staff and residential staffs, and collaborating in the establishment of a student-run drug crisis center in the late 1960s (Wolf et al., 1968).

The first organization to become interested in peer counseling at Stanford was a group of students called "The Bridge," who were concerned about the drug problem on campus and attempted to offer alternatives to drug use. This group set up a crisis intervention, information, and counseling center that devoted itself to the welfare of other students.

Another strong theme of The Bridge has been affiliation—coming together as a group for a common purpose. Through such affiliation comes mutual support, heightened individual confidence, sharing of information, and collective action.

A third theme has been the gaining of a better and clearer sense of self through participation in counselor training. One of the results most commonly reported by counselors has been that they feel a clearer sense of self and a heightening of self-esteem. Through practicing openness and self-disclosure, through the ongoing support of the group, and through fulfilling a valued role in the group, many have found the experience of being a peer counselor an important one in going from youth to adulthood.

A fourth theme within The Bridge is providing meaningful adult roles for young people, something that our society seldom does. A meaningful role is one that involves responsibility for others: the adult is expected to assume such responsibility, whereas the youth generally is not. For those who are interested in careers as teachers, counselors, psychologists, or doctors, or in other professions that involve responsibility for another person, the peer counseling experience offers a chance to fulfill an adult role.

A fifth theme of The Bridge is providing greater social and interpersonal skills. For some, the peer counselor training is "intimacy training" that might be important in their own personal lives. For others, it teaches social skills that might be useful at work. Through training and interaction, peer counselors have achieved a better understanding of individual psychology, group process, and ways of facilitating communication and interaction.

A sixth and last theme in The Bridge is learning adaptive and coping intrapersonal skills. These coping skills, as formulated by White (1974), involve cognitive, intrapsychic mechanisms and behaviors for dealing with both environmental situations and emotional and maturational states. The peer counselors learn these skills from others—by observing, by identifying, by learning precepts, by training, by following examples, and by coaching. Most people learn such skills as a part of everyday life, but in peer counselor training we feel there is a heightening of this "normal" process.

THE TRAINING COURSE: PROCESS OF CHOICE AND CONTENT

As more student groups expressed interest in peer counseling, we began to review our training program more systematically with two major questions in mind: What kind of training program would provide the best content and potential for evaluation? What program might have a sufficiently broad appeal so that we would not have to redesign the training program for each group?

A committee of students and staff—mostly staff—was organized. This committee reviewed the rationale for and the mechanism of the peer counselor training. Tapes were reviewed, literature was read, and people were interviewed. The committee then drew three major conclusions: (1) There is a broad interest in peer counseling among students, both in using peer helpers and in becoming peer helpers. (2) The microcounseling technique of Ivey (1974) seems most suitable as a basic model for training peer counselors. (3) Basic skill training should be required for every student who wishes to be a peer counselor; specialized training should also be required for those wishing to be a part of a special-interest peer counseling group (e.g., Health Service, or Career Counseling and Placement Center).

Our course in basic skills is based on the microcounseling technique: students learn skills and videotape themselves during role plays to get immediate feedback. The basic course consists of six two-hour sessions that each focus on a specific skill:

1. Basic attending skills
2. Open invitation to talk
3. Paraphrasing
4. Reflection of feelings
5. Summarizing
6. Integration of all skills

Each session begins with a videotaped mini-lecture and demonstrations of the specific skill to be learned that day. The students then practice and view each other's role plays. They then discuss their experiences, paying attention to what is effective or ineffective in peer counseling (Ivey & Gluckstern, 1974).

EVALUATION

We have attempted to evaluate three separate aspects of this program: the attitudes of the trainers and trainees about the training, the effectiveness of the training, and the quality of the actual counseling done by people who took the training.

Attitudes of trainers and trainees about the training. Evaluation forms filled out by trainers and trainees at the end of each session have been consistently positive. The trainees report growing feelings of competence, personal growth in relationships with peers, and increased ability to apply the new skills to real-life situations.

There was some criticism of the original lecture tapes—criticism focusing on a lack of diversity. We subsequently modified the videotapes, using more people, using both negative and positive models in the role plays, and increasing the variety of topics. Feedback on the new videotapes has been much more positive.

Effectiveness of the training. Three training groups were selected in the spring of 1975 for this more formal evaluation: six males from the Gay People's Union, eight females from the married-student housing area on the campus, and eight Chicano students from the university. We first had each trainee do a seven-minute videotaped interview of a "standard client." At the end of the training program, we videotaped the same trainees interviewing the same clients. The videotapes were then presented to a group of raters consisting partly of professionals on the training staff. No trainer evaluated people whom he or she had actually trained. The trainees were evaluated on each of the various skills taught in the program.

The results of these evaluations are shown in the accompanying diagrams. The post-training videotapes showed a higher frequency of open questions, paraphrases, reflections of feeling, and summarizations; and they showed a lower frequency of topic jumps and closed questions. There was also a significant increase in the overall quality between the pre-training and post-training evaluations.

Quality of counseling by trainees. A second evaluation study was undertaken in the Career Planning and Placement Center on the Stanford campus. In this study, students coming to the center were randomly assigned to either peer or professional counselors. Prior to the counseling session, students were asked to complete a questionnaire that addressed the following areas: previous experience with the center, attitudes and opinions regarding the relative value of peer versus professional counseling along five dimensions, and a checklist indicating

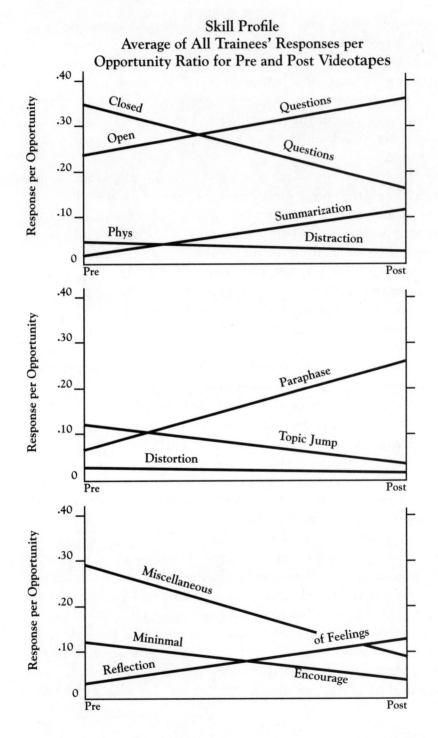

Skill Profile
Average of All Trainees' Responses per
Opportunity Ratio for Pre and Post Videotapes

their preferences for types of services available (peer or professional) by types of problems and issues presented.

Following the session, students completed two questionnaires. The first asked them to rate counselor behavior and activity along specific and nonspecific dimensions. The second replicated the pre-interview questions.

The results showed that students tended to rate peer counselors more highly after their session. This was especially so for assessments of general counseling skills displayed by the peer counselors. Professional counselors were rated more highly along dimensions having to do with greater and more specific information displayed, but there was little change from the initial ratings along counseling dimensions. After meeting with peer counselors, students tended to rate them more highly. This generalized to perceptions of peer counselor competence in non-career counseling areas (e.g., personal, crisis, problem-solving).

CONCLUSIONS

1. There is broad student interest in peer counselor training.

2. University and college counseling centers should encourage interested students to develop peer counseling services to supplement the existing professional counseling service.

3. A peer counseling service should be operated and evaluated with the same care as a professional clinical service.

APPENDIX B

SUGGESTED PEER COUNSELING CURRICULUM

by Vincent D'Andrea and Peter Salovey

A good peer counselor training program relies primarily on experiential learning through role-playing and other exercises, supplemented with didactically presented material and group discussion. We recommend that listening and counseling skills be presented slowly, one step at a time. Subsequent sessions can be used to integrate skills. Videotape training is invaluable.

We have found it most appropriate to schedule two class sessions each week. The first is a two-hour session in which we introduce the "skill of the week," present and discuss good and bad role-play models, and (if time allows) give students a chance to practice the skill. In the second session, students meet in groups of four or five with an experienced counselor for 90 minutes. This combines more intensive practicing with critical feedback from the counselor/trainer.

The material in this book actually is best presented in two ten-week courses. We call the first course "Introduction to Peer Counseling and Basic Attending Skills," for which we recommend the following syllabus.

Week 1 Introduction, nonverbal attending skills
     2 Open questions
     3 Paraphrasing

4   Working with feelings
5   Summarizing
6   Integrating all skills learned so far, loose ends, etc.
7   Decision making and problem solving
8   Crisis counseling (including sexual assault counseling)
9   Depression
10   Suicide

For the second ten-week course, "Advanced Peer Counseling," we recommend the following curriculum.

Week 1   Review of listening skills
2   Overview of counseling skills, differences between counseling and therapy, role and responsibility of peer counselors
3   Contracts
4   Confronting
5   Interpreting
6   Counseling gays, lesbians, and bisexuals
7   Ethnic perspectives
Weeks 8–10   Ethics in peer counseling and special topics appropriate to the counseling center at which students will be counseling. (For example, advanced suicide or rape crisis counseling skills for hotline volunteers, HIV information for test-program peer counselors, contraceptive information for birth-control counselors, vocational guidance information for career counselors, information about campus resources for residential advisors.)

We use this curriculum for training peer counselors to work in a general college campus drop-in and telephone counseling service. Your particular program may require you to modify this training sequence. Obviously, you should tailor the training that your peer counselors receive to the goals of your program. Determine what kinds of activities peer counselors in your program will be engaged in and then design your program accordingly. For instance, counselors in a strictly academic advising role probably only need one ten-week training course that covers the five basic listening skills plus information about careers and programs. Suicide, crisis, and depression do not need to be presented at all. Generally, if suicide and crisis are not concerns of your counseling program, you can replace weeks 8 through 10 in the introductory course with the material from weeks 8 through 10 in the advanced class.

APPENDIX C

A SURVEY OF CAMPUS PEER COUNSELING ACTIVITIES*

by Peter Salovey and Vincent D'Andrea

[Since about 1970] there has been a growing acceptance of peer counseling, particularly on college campuses. [We] refer to campus peer counseling as the use of active listening and problem-solving skills together with knowledge about human growth and mental health by students in order to help, advise, and counsel other students. . . . The basic premise underlying peer counseling is that students are often capable of solving many of their own problems of daily living if given the chance. The role of the peer counselor, then, is not to solve another person's problems for him/her, nor to give bald advice, interpret, or diagnose. Rather, the peer counselor assists clients in finding their own solutions by clarifying thoughts and feelings and by exploring various options and alternatives.

The use of paraprofessionals in counseling roles has a reasonably systematic research history in the psychological literature (Durlak, 1979). Generally, minimally trained nonprofessional counselors are rated by clients as no less effective than their professional counterparts. However, there has been little

*Reprinted by permission from the *Journal of American College Health, 22* (1984), 262–265. Originally presented as part of a symposium on peer counseling chaired by Vincent J. D'Anddrea at the annual meeting of he American College Health Association, St. Louis, MO, on May 26, 1983.

research on the actual implementation of nonprofessional (i.e., peer) counseling programs, although there have been some interesting descriptions (e.g., Giddan & Austin, 1982). Thus, the purpose of this study was to document peer counseling activities at colleges and universities in the United States and Canada. Particular attention was paid to the roles ascribed to peer counselors, the typical problems with which they are confronted, the training that they receive, and the institutional constraints (e.g., financial, and the availability of professional liaisons) under which they must work.

METHOD

A three-page questionnaire and explanatory cover letter were mailed to the Director of Counseling Services at 200 colleges and universities randomly selected from the mailing list of the Association of University and College Counseling Center Directors.* Within one month, 156 completed questionnaires had been received back in postage-paid envelopes, a 78 percent return rate. Many counseling organizations also included additional descriptive materials with their surveys. Of the 156 counseling directors who responded, 122 (78 percent) indicated active peer counseling programs on their campuses. These 122 questionnaires were then retained for more thorough analyses.

RESULTS AND DISCUSSION

Peer Counselor Roles

Table 1 indicates the various settings in which peer counseling occurs on college and university campuses. Twenty-eight different counseling roles were identified, with residence hall counseling, academic tutoring, and academic problem solving the most common. More psychologically oriented peer counseling programs were found on only about one-third of the campuses surveyed. Student counseling organizations popular in the past

*We would like to thank Dr.Robert L. Arnstein, Chief Psychiatrist of the Division of Mental Hygiene, University Health Services at Yale University, for providing this mailing list and for his encouragement.

decade, such as drug and alcohol abuse centers, seem rather infrequent today.

Table 1
Peer counselor roles
(in order of frequency of mention)

Role	N	Percent
Residence hall counseling/Advising	96	79
Academic tutoring	76	62
Academic problem solving	68	56
Services for minority students	58	48
Services for women	47	39
Career guidance services	43	35
Suicide and crisis intervention	42	34
General psychological counseling	41	34
Contraception/Abortion counseling	31	25
Gay/Lesbian counseling	26	21
Rape/Battered women counseling	21	17
Freshman orientation	15	12
Draft registration counseling	12	10
Alcohol/Drug counseling	8	7
Health/Wellness counseling	8	7
Support group facilitating	5	4
Financial aid counseling	5	4
Peer ministry/Religious counseling	4	3
Disabled student counseling	4	3
Admissions counseling	3	2
Legal counseling	3	2
Exit interviewing	2	2
Herpes/AIDS/VD counseling	2	2
Veterans benefits advising	2	2
Commuter student assistance	1	1
Eating disorders counseling	1	1
Student ambulance/EMT	1	1
Life-long learning counseling (returning students)	1	1

Problems Encountered

Table 2 lists the problems most frequently brought to peer counselors. Academic difficulties were most often mentioned, with problematic friendships and romances also quite common.

More serious or sensitive problems areas like suicide or sexual dysfunction were typically not presented to peer counselors, although the presentation of depression was relatively common.

Table 2
Types of problems brought to peer counselors
(from most to least frequent)

Problem	M	S.D.
Academic difficulties	2.22	1.56
Friendship relationships	2.82	1.76
Romantic relationships	3.56	1.62
Career/Future anxieties	3.75	2.20
Depression	4.42	2.39
Parental difficulties	5.08	1.84
Monetary problems	5.60	2.37
Sexual problems	6.57	1.77
Suicide	8.29	1.98

Other problems mentioned but not scaled:

Alcohol and drug abuse	Independence issues
Roommate difficulties	Anxiety/Stress
Eating disorders	Study skills
Religious conflicts	Loneliness
Competency/Self-esteem difficulties	Car-pooling
Role conflicts	Time management

NOTE: Problems were scaled such that M = 1 for most frequently encountered problems and M = 10 for the least frequently encountered problems.

Quantity of Peer Counselors and Clients

As described in Table 3, the number of peer counselors at any one campus ranged from 2 to 450, with an average of about 107. This result reveals a surprisingly large community of peer counselors on many campuses. If these figures are representative, this survey alone reflects about 12,000 peer counselors. On the average campus, approximately one-fourth of the student body makes use of a peer counselor in a typical academic year, and there are nearly 3 peer counselors for every 100 students. Again, the range of utilization is quite high—at some campuses, nearly every student must deal with peer counselors in various bureaucratic settings (e.g., when a student decides to declare a major), whereas on other campuses, peer counselors are seen only on an emergency/as needed basis.

Table 3 Use of peer counselors on campuses			
	M	S.D.	Range
At any one time, how many peer counselors are there on your campus?	107.2	284.2	2 to 450
What percentage of the student body makes use of peer counseling services in an academic year?	25.8	25.5	1 to 100%
Number of counselors per 100 students	2.8	3.1	.1 to 18

Peer Counselor Training

The training of peer counselors is summarized in Tables 4, 5, and 6. The primary conclusion reached in this area was on the lack of agreement about the appropriateness of any one particular training model, training procedure, or use of training personnel. As indicated in Table 4, only 36 percent of peer counselors receive substantial training prior to becoming counselors. Such training, when it exists, is done either by professionals from the student health or counseling service or by professionals from the specific organization at which the student will work (e.g., career guidance specialists train students who will work in a career planning peer counseling center).

No one training model was typically endorsed. Over half of the respondents indicated that either an eclectic "model" or no particular model at all guide their training programs. For the remaining respondents, Ivey's *Microcounseling Techniques and Basic Attending Skills* seemed to be the most pop

Table 4
Peer counselor training programs

Type	N	Percent
Brief workshops (< 10 hours)	45	37
Long class (> 10 hours)	44	37
Inservice training	13	11
No training	1	1
Unclassified	19	15
Total	122	100

Table 5
Who trains peer counselors?

Trainer	N	Percent
Professional counseling center staff	53	43
Professional staff from specific setting	39	32
Professional hired for this purpose	7	6
Housing/Residential education staff	7	6
Other students	4	3
Unclassifiable	12	10
Total	122	100

Table 6
Training models used

Model	N	Percent
No particular model	57	46
Micro-counseling/Basic attending skills (Ivey; Carkuff)	18	15
Client centered (Rogers)	10	8
Eclectic/Mixture	8	7
The skilled helper (Egan)	7	6
Crisis intervention (Huff; Delworth & Rudow)	6	5
Student development (Perry)	5	4
Students helping students (Ender, et al.)	3	2
Cognitive-behavioral (Mahoney & Thoresen; Meichenbaum; Beck)	3	2
Interpersonal process recall (Kagan)	2	2
Human relations/Interpersonal skills (Pfieffer & Jones)	2	2
Psychosocial human development (Erikson; Chickering)	1	1
Total	122	100

ularly used, followed closely by Rogerian training programs and systems based on the work of Egan. It is clear that carefully designed studies are needed to evaluate the relative effectiveness of these various training models. Perhaps such studies would lead to greater consensus regarding the appropriateness of any one of these approaches.

Institutional Constraints: Funding

As indicated in Table 7, where funding information is available, it is clear that few peer counseling programs are very well endowed. Many programs try to survive on minimal or no funding whatsoever. Only 14 programs were funded above $10,000 annually, perhaps the minimum needed to train, staff, and publicize an average sized, comprehensive peer counseling service. The sources of these monies, depicted in Table 8, range from a variety of public funds, particularly Federal Work Study, to typical university sources such as the Dean of Students' Office or the professional counseling and health service. Only two programs generated their own incomes, one through an annual crafts fair and the other by charging a small fee for services.

SUMMARY AND IMPLICATIONS

The results of this survey indicate the following about campus peer counseling:

1. Peer counseling is widespread on college and university campuses. The large majority of campuses utilize peer counselors in some capacity.

2. Peer counselors are employed in a large variety of roles on campuses but are most commonly found in residence halls and academic assistance centers.

3. Academic problems and relationship problems are the most common client concerns brought to peer counselors.

4. Over 100 peer counselors work on the average campus at any given time.

Table 7
Annual budget

Dollars annually	N	Precent
0	17	14
1-1,000	12	10
1,001-5,000	9	7
5,001-10,000	8	7
10,001-15,000	4	3
15,001-20,000	1	1
>20,000	9	7
Don't know	62	51
Total	122	100

Table 8
Primary source of funding

Source	N	Percent
Federal grant/Work study	16	13
Dean of student affairs	15	12
Student government/Student fees	14	11
State government	13	11
Dean of housing	13	11
Health service/Counseling service	12	10
Charity (United Way, etc.)	2	2
Self-generated	2	2
County government	1	1
Other	14	11
No response	20	16
Total	122	100

NOTE: A program may actually have more than one source of funding.

5. Over 25 percent of the student body on the average campus uses peer counseling services in a typical academic year.

6. Peer counselor training programs vary widely. Many students do not receive adequate training prior to becoming counselors.

7. No particular training model is uniformly endorsed by a plurality of campuses. More research needs to be carried out to identify the benefits and effectiveness of a variety of possible training options.

8. Many peer counseling programs are poorly funded; most counseling center directors are unaware of the funding situation of their programs.

9. The relatively high incidence of "don't know," "unclassifiable," and blank responses to various questions on the survey indicates a lack of systematic record-keeping at many peer counseling centers. All centers, no matter what their size, should collect accurate data regarding clients served, counselors trained, and monetary considerations.

APPENDIX D

A SUICIDE HOTLINE CALL*

Don: *Hello. Counseling Center.*

Pete: *Hi.*

Don: *Hello, who's this?*

Pete: *My name is Pete.*

Don: *Hi, Pete. I'm Don.*

Pete: *Hi. My name's Pete, and I think I'm going to kill myself.*

Don: *What's going on, Pete?*

Pete: *What's going on is that I've just got a lot of shit going on in my life, and I'm going to kill myself. I've got a gun right here.*

Don: *Uh huh.*

Pete: *And I called you. You're supposed to be able to do something about it, right?*

Don: *Yeah. The first thing I'd like to do about it, Pete, is to talk to you—try to find out a little more about what's going on.*

---

*This appendix is the transcript of a telephone role-play from a training course at The Bridge (Stanford University).

Pete: *I don't want to talk—I want some help!*

Don:*Uh, sometimes it . . .*

Pete: *I've been talking all my life, and it hasn't done me any good. I need some help!*

Don: *I'm here to help you, Pete, and I really want to do that. Sometimes it does help if you can let somebody know exactly what's going on. I'll try to see if, together, we can work out a plan or something that can improve things for you.*

Pete: *What's going on is that I've got this gun here, and it's a .22, and it's loaded, and I got my finger on the trigger. That's what's going on.*

Don: *Okay. Could I ask where you are, Pete?*

Pete: *I'm sitting in my apartment.*

Don: *Are you alone, or is anyone else . . .*

Pete: *Yeah, I live alone.*

Don: *You live alone.*

Pete: *Downtown, in a crummy little apartment.*

Don: *What's the address, Pete?*

Pete: *Don't . . . .. Never mind what the address is. Hey! Are you tracing this?*

Don: *No, I'm not, Pete.*

Pete: *How do I know you are not tracing this call? If I think you're tracing, I'm going to hang up on you.*

Don: *Yeah, well, what I can tell you, Pete, is that I am not tracing it, and more generally, I can tell you that I am really going to be honest with you in this call. That's one of the things that I can do, to give you straight answers and straight talk. And I won't lie to you, Pete. I promise, and I am not tracing* this call. I couldn't trace the call even if I wanted to. We don't have that capability.

Pete: Okay, well, you better not be.

Don: I'd really like to know a little bit about what's going on, Pete. It would help me to think about suggestions I could make.

Pete: Yeah, well, what's going on is my life is just a mess. That's why I am sitting here with this goddamn gun.

Don: Yes. Has something happened recently, Pete, that's really brought it to a head?

Pete: Yeah. I lost my job.

Don: I see.

Pete: And my old lady just split.

Don: Uh huh. When did she leave?

Pete: About three days ago. I've been up since then. I haven't been eating. I'm so wired, I can't get to sleep.

Don: When was the last time you ate, Pete?

Pete: I don't know. I don't know. Two days ago, maybe?

Don: Uh huh. It's really got you really upset, huh?

Pete: Yeah. I'm really upset, and you know, I don't see any options. That's why I'm sitting here with this gun. I've just had it, you know?

Don: Have you ever tried suicide before?

Pete: Yeah. Yeah.

Don: When was that?

Pete: About two years ago.

Don: And what did you do then?

Pete: *Well, I applied to go to grad school, 'cause I'd been working for about six years, and I just didn't dig that at all, and so I was trying to get into school, and I applied, and I couldn't get in.*

Don: *Uh huh. And what happened?*

Pete: *I took a bunch of pills.*

Don: *Uh huh.*

Pete: *My old lady came home and found me.*

Don: *I see. How did you feel after that whole episode about trying to kill yourself and not doing it?*

Pete: *I felt pretty stupid, I guess. Stupid and embarrassed. I mean, like, you know, that's why I've got a gun now. I mean, the pills, you know, like they obviously don't work very well. There's a long time span. Somebody can find you. With this gun, though, you know, like any minute it could be all over. Like, while you're talking to me right now, I could blow my brains out.*

Don: *Yeah. That's really true.*

Pete: *I just want to make sure you know that.*

Don: *Yeah, I do. I do know that. And, I know that it's up to you—that you can make that decision. And I want you to know that I really hope that you'll talk to me and that you won't pull that trigger.*

Pete: *Well, I don't have anybody else to talk to. That's why I have to rely on you.*

Don: *Sometimes we have to start somewhere, and I'm glad that you called. And I'm glad that you're talking to me, and I really want to try to help you to think about other things that you can do.*

Pete: *Like what?*

Don: *Well, I'm wondering if there is anyone else that you've thought about talking to? Anyone else that you're in contact with?*

Pete: *Well, my parents live back East. I moved out here, you know, from Massachusetts, went to college, and then I got a job. And so, I guess—I don't know, I don't have many friends. I guess I'm sort of isolated. You know, like I was sitting here and thinking, wow, who could I call that I could really tell this to, and there wasn't anybody.*

Don: *So, you really did want to tell this to somebody, huh?*

Pete: *Yeah, I don't know. I guess I feel like I do and I don't. I don't know. You know, things are just going around and around in my head. Like, I have these flashes where I just say, "The hell with it. I'm going to do it," you know? And then I back off from it a little. I don't know, it's just sort of going up and down, and up and down, and up and down.*

Don: *What are you saying to yourself in those times when you're backing off a little? What's the argument there? What kind of thoughts do you have there?*

Pete: *Well, I guess I hope maybe I can get back with my old lady. I don't know. I don't know. But she's been putting up with me for, like, four or five years, and she just final-ly got disgusted.*

Don: *Is this the first time that you two have split?*

Pete: *Well, no. When I tried the other time, a couple of years ago, she split too.*

Don: *Uh huh.*

Pete: *But I convinced her to come back. I don't know. I just—I don't know.*

Don: *What did she say this time when she left, Pete?*

Pete: *She said—see, I drink, too. I mean, that's another prob-*
lem I've got. She said she couldn't handle my getting drunk all
the time. Ah . . . she couldn't handle—she says I'm depressed
all the time, which is true. I mean, what can I say? It's true. I
am. It's true.

Don: *Yeah.*

Pete: *And, she just couldn't handle it anymore. She felt like I*
was too much of a downer for her. You know, I agree with her.
I mean, you know, maybe—I'm too much of a downer for
everybody.

Don: *So where does the relationship stand now? She left three*
days ago?

Pete: *She left, and I haven't heard from her. You know, she*
hasn't called. I guess she just got fed up. I don't know, she's
probably staying with friends or something.

Don: *You don't know where she is?*

Pete: *No. She hasn't called. I think—you now, she's throughwith*
all this.

Don: *Are there any . . . . Do you have any relatives other than*
your parents? Anybody closer?

Pete: *Relatives? No. All of my relatives live back East, pretty*
much.

Don: *How would you like things to be, in terms of . . . when you*
get back together with—what is your wife's name?

Pete: *Faye.*

Don: *Faye. When you got back together after the last time you*
attempted, what kinds of things were you . . . did you have in
mind that you wanted to see happen? What kinds of things
were you working toward?

Pete: *With her, you mean?*

Don: *With that relationship, or in general.*

Pete: *I don't know. I'd like, I'd like, you know. I don't know. I just want to feel good. You know what I mean.*

Don: *Yeah. Yeah, I do.*

Pete: *And I wasn't feeling good. I wasn't feeling good in my job, you know, like I just feel my job is just a mess! It's boring work, and I don't like the people there, and it's a real shitty place to work, and I don't have much in common with those people.*

Don: *So there wasn't really much incentive to stay there anyway, huh?*

Pete: *No. No, I sort of got myself fired, almost. That's like . . .*

Don: *Yeah, you really figured you could do better for yourself, huh?*

Pete: *I just couldn't handle the pressure anymore. Like, I just always felt there was a lot of pressure on me. Pressure being around people. Being around people is pressure for me, for one thing. That's probably why I don't have many friends.*

Don: *Yeah.*

Pete: *And I have been trying to work on that, and trying to work with my old lady. And it just doesn't work out. And that's why I am sitting here with this gun.*

Don: *How are you feeling, talking to me? What kinds of feel-ings do you have about me?*

Pete: *I don't know. I feel like I don't know if you know what I'm talking about.*

Don: *Uh huh. I think I do, at least part of it. I can't feel the feelings that you're feeling. I know that you're frustrated, and you're feeling like you don't have any options open to you. I can't feel it as intensely as you're feeling it, but I do*

*understand some of the issues. I certainly understand the thing
about wanting to have people to talk to. I'm the same way.
That's real important to me, and that's a really tough area.*

Pete: Yeah, but why is it so hard for me? I mean, I see other
people around. They don't have trouble. They make relationships. They have friends, you know? And that's just so
hard for me.

Don: Do you think that being married . . .

Pete: Okay, we're not married. We're just living together.

Don: I see.

Pete: Are you married?

Don: No, I'm not.

Pete: Okay. Well, have you ever thought about committing
suicide? I mean, how do you get off, sitting there talking to
people?

Don: Oh, I have thought about suicide, and that's maybe one of
the reasons why I thought about doing this. Not that I was
above people who would think about that, but rather, I'd had
some sense that that was a place I was at once, too, and that a
lot of the feelings are feelings that come up again. I think we all
go through that from time to time. I think the difference, Pete,
between me and you is that right now in my life I do have a
little more support, maybe—you know, some things and some
people that I can turn to. And so, when something like what's
happened to you comes along, I've got a little more strength.
And you just happen to be at a time when you got caught off
guard, you know, with nothing to fall back on. I really think
that that's the main reason we think about suicide.

Pete: Yeah, but it's been like that all my life. I mean, it's not like
my life's real hunky-dory, and then I went into a bad period

and got caught off guard. It's like, you know, it's been like this all my life. And I'm getting tired of it!

Don: *What . . .*

Pete: *You know, like, what can I do, man? What can I change? How can I get people to—how can I feel comfortable with people?*

Don: *Well, one thing you could look at is the job. You know, you could think about what it was about that last job that you didn't like, and think about maybe trying to get in an area where you are more comfortable, 'cause that can be a real way of getting in touch with people, too. You know, if you are comfortable on your job, you are more open with the people that you're meeting on your job.*

Pete: *Okay. It wasn't so much that it was a bad job. It's just that being around people made me nervous, you know? Like, somebody would come into my office to talk to me, and I'd get nervous, you know? It wasn't that a different job would put me around people, and then things would be okay. It's being around people that's the problem.*

Don: *Well, I feel like I'm beginning to know you a lot better. I don't know how you are feeling about talking to me, but it seems to me there are some things that we can work with here.*

Pete: *I don't have any answers yet from you. What I need is answers.*

Don: *Pete, are you holding the gun?*

Pete: *Yeah. I've got it in my hand.*

Don: *I'm wondering, just while you're talking to me, if you could put the gun down. Just because, if you are going to die . . .*

Pete: *How about if I put it in my mouth instead?*

Don: *Uh uh. I really don't want you to do that, Pete. My sense is that you're wanting to talk to me, and even though you're frustrated because I'm not giving you all the answers that you want, you do want some answers. You do want to work on this thing.*

Pete: *Well, what can I do? Tell me something I can do.*

Don: *Well, in terms of your discomfort with other people, there are some ways to work on that. Have you ever tried any sort of counseling? Have you ever gone to a professional who has some background in interpersonal relationships, and talked it out with them?*

Pete: *Yeah, you know, when I tried with the pills, I got hauled off to the emergency room, and I was in the County Mental Health crap for a while. But, you know, those guys are jerks. I know more than they do. I mean, you know, they just want to get you out so they can take care of rape cases, or whatever. You know? I mean, people in real emergencies.*

Don: *There are some counseling agencies in the area here that aren't part of that system—that are much smaller and more personal.*

Pete: *Yeah, well, how much do they cost?*

Don: *They are not expensive, Pete.*

Pete: *A small fortune?*

Don: *No, really, they are not expensive. There is a family service agency in town which is a small organization that has a lot of branches, and it's well known and well established. But it's a much more personal thing. The first visit is five dollars, and thereafter, they set up a sliding scale based on your ability to pay. It's not that expensive, and I'm thinking that maybe just getting started with something like that might make a big difference. It wouldn't necessarily be a long-term thing, but just to have a sense that you are doing something, you know.*

Because right now, with Faye leaving and you losing the job, both, you are really kind of at a standstill. That's the way it seems to me. There's not much going on.

Pete: Well, I sure the hell don't know where to go next or what to do next. You know how hard it is to get jobs around here?

Don: Yeah, I do.

Pete: You know, like getting a job, you know . . .

Don: Have you ever heard of New Ways to Work?

Pete: Yeah.

Don: It's a place in town, and again—

Pete: Yeah, but I've known lots of—

Don: It's not a big bureaucratic kind of thing.

Pete: Okay. I know that I can be able to get a job. I mean, I've known people who have gone down there. I mean, they've got all these high-falootin' ideas about job-sharing and stuff, but when it comes to the nitty-gritty of getting you a job, you know, they can't do it.

Don: Well, I think there are two things going on here, Pete. I think, you know, there are practical decisions that you have to make about the job. You're going to be making some decisions about where to go with your relationship with Faye. You know, I realize that we haven't really even talked about that, but you are going to have to kind of do some things in those areas. But there are also your feelings, and I really think that if we could begin working on some of these things, even before it's all worked out and resolved—before you have a job, for instance—it can feel better for you. It can feel like you are at least headed somewhere. And I think that makes a difference. Maybe you feel a little bit of that just in talking to me. I don't know. I hope so.

Pete: *Well, at least you are willing to talk to me. I mean, you know, most people, if I said I had a gun in my mouth, they'd freak out.*

Don: *Yeah, well, I'll be honest with you. That's scary for me.*

Pete: *Well, okay, I'm glad to hear that, 'cause that tells me a little bit about, you know . . .*

Don: *But, you know, I don't know . . . . There's not too much I can do about that, to tell you the truth. If you are going to shoot yourself, you are going to shoot yourself. I can't stop you. So, maybe the best thing I can do is not to try to wrestle with you about that, but try to help you with what's behind it.*

Pete: *Yeah, I guess. You know, the major thing is Faye leaving. I can go through a lot of shit, you know, with her around, but, like, she's pretty much my only social con-tact. And with her gone, that's just like somebody just kicked out the last piling underneath me.*

Don: *Yeah, that's really tough—especially just three days ago. You must still be right in the middle of all those feelings.*

Pete: *Yeah, I'm just . . . yeah, sure, I guess I'm in shock. The feelings are hard, I guess. I guess I'm not feeling a lot of feelings. I'm feeling angry.*

Don: *Uh huh. Angry at whom?*

Pete: *Angry at her. Angry at my job. Angry at myself. Just angry at the world. Angry because I've been trying so long, and it hasn't worked. I'm just—I don't know. I'm angry now, and it will probably turn into depression, which is my normal state.*

Don: *Yeah, I'm hoping that if we kind of stay with it—we talk about it a little more now and line up something, you know, that you can stay with, that if you are dealing with it and doing something about it—that you won't fall into that depression.*

Sometimes depression is hardest if you're just wallowing in it,
you know? And I know that's rough with . . .
Pete: *Wallowing! You think I'm wallowing?*

Don: *No, I don't. I don't think you're wallowing. I mean, I*
think you picked up the phone and called me. I've talked to
people that—I see people that aren't really asking for help, that
aren't looking for specific things to do, like you are. They have
just given up, and I think that really feeds the depression.
What I'd like to suggest, for one thing, is that maybe you could
come in and we could sit down and talk about it face to face.
I'd really like to meet you, and sometimes that can be a more
effective thing.

Pete: *No. I don't know about coming in, I mean. Like, this is all*
anonymous. You are not tracing the call or anything?

Don: *That's right. All I know is your first name, right now. You*
know, I just think that that would be a little more personal
thing. And, you know, we've got a lot of materials here that
we could look through, thinking about what to do. But just in
terms of just your feelings, I think it might be helpful to be able
to talk to someone face to face. Maybe if you're not sure about
the counseling, that would be a good first step.

Pete: *Well, I think I'd probably feel better talking to you than*
going into some counseling agency and saying, "Well, I just
decided to kill myself."

Don: *Yeah, yeah, that's—I know that's hard. I think that one of*
the things that's maybe a little different about this counseling
center, too, is that, you know, we're not pro-fessionals. I am
not a professional, Pete. I'm a volunteer. And I feel like I've
got some pretty good training, but I don't feel like you are a
client or, you know, somebody that's . . . that I'm any better
than you. It would be more just kind of two guys talking. And
yet, I have some experience in terms of what's in the com-

munity and also talked to some people that have been in similar posi-tions, and maybe I could be helpful. I'd really like you to

do that, if you'd be willing, and my schedule's real flexible. We could set that up almost any time.

Pete: Yeah, I don't know. You know, like I've been sitting here and talking to you, and you know, I could, you know, I could make one more try. But I don't know. It just feels . . . I feel real tired, just tired.

Don: I understand that.

Pete: Tired of feeling.

Don: How about this, Pete? How about if we at least make an agreement that you won't use that gun tonight, and that I'll give you a call in the morning. And then we'll see then how you are feeling and whether you'd like to come in then. You know, one night, Pete. It's your life.

Pete: Okay. I mean, it's what, 11:30 now, you know? And I've been . . . like, I've been up for two days and, you know, I'm pretty wired up. And there's a lot of funny things going in and out of my head, you know. I'd like to be able to get some sleep.

Don: You know, I think that would probably help a lot. You know, you've got so many things going on, Pete. You've lost a job, and Faye left, and you are upset about that. And now, on top of that, you're tired and you haven't eaten for two days.

Pete: Yeah, every time I eat, I just puke it back up.

Don: Yeah?

Pete: You know, and . . .

Don: You know, I really—this may sound funny, but you know, on one level, I really believe that you have a right to kill yourself . . .

Pete: *Damn true.*

Don: *Yeah, well, I do believe that, but I'd like to see you make that decision when you're—I'd like to see that be, you know, sort of a carefully considered decision. You know? Like, something you decide about when you're a little more together. You are upset now, and you're tired.*

Pete: *I'm never going to be together! Words, words, words! You're just giving me a lot of words!*

Don: *Well, you said you'd like to get a night's sleep to see how you'd feel after that.*

Pete: *But I feel like I've gotta make this decision tonight. I mean, it's gotta be tonight, or—like waiting a day, that—no, it's gotta be tonight.*

Don: *How are you feeling about killing yourself right now, Pete?*

Pete: *I don't know. I go up and down on it.*

Don: *Okay. What about right now?*

Pete: *Yeah, right now, I feel like, you know, I feel like . . . you're saying all these things, and that's all real nice, but I, you know, I mean, like this has been going on for a long time.*

Don: *Yeah. I think we need to start somewhere, Pete, uh, and I really believe that it doesn't have to go on like this.*

Pete: *Wait a minute. When you say "we"—if I come in and talk to you tomorrow—say like I talk to you for an hour, and that's it. So big deal, you know? Where does the "we" end up?*

Don: *Well, I feel like I have a relationship with you, Pete. I really do. I mean, you have told me a hell of a lot, you know, in a short period of time. I really feel involved. I really feel like I am in this thing, and, uh . . .*

Pete: *Well, you are. You'll probably feel pretty bad if I blow my brains out right now.*

Don: Yeah. Yeah, I will. I'll have some strong feelings about that. But I think one of the things that you can do that maybe you haven't done before—and one of the things you have already begun to do by just calling and being willing to talk to me—is, you know, to reach out to another person, to let contact with another person be part of working out the problem. You know, not just talk-ing about places in town to go. We're talking about you and me.

Pete: Yeah, but that's what's so hard! Like, if I let you into my life, you know? If I come and see you tomorrow, and say, okay, yeah, I'm going to trust this guy. What's going to happen? Are you just going to split, like everybody else? I mean, you know, that's—you know, it's real hard for me to trust people. It's really hard for me. You know, this is hard to do right here.

Don: Yeah, I understand that.

Pete: I guess I'm asking, are you going to leave me? "Say, well, nice talking to you today. I'm going home and having dinner."

Don: Well, I can tell you that I am not going to say that tomorrow. I can tell you that I really am interested in you, and I feel like we can work on this thing together over a period of time. I really feel that. And I also think that, you know, you're having the experience of reaching out a little bit to me. And opening up a little bit with me will make it a little bit easier the next time with somebody else, too. I'm not saying I'm going to solve all your problems. You know, we both know that that's bull-shit. But I think you'll be in a better place to do that again and again, and that's why when I said I know that it's hard reaching out to people, that's what I mean. You know, it's a rough thing for all of us to do, but it gets a little easier, I think, each time. You get a little more strength each time.

Pete: Yeah, I guess I just don't want to be hurt. I guess I feel like I could really get hurt.

Don: *Well, you are talking about killing yourself. I think there would be more in it for you talking to me tomorrow than dying. I really—that's my feeling.*

Pete: *I guess what I'm saying is it almost is less pain to kill myself than to go through the other pain, the pain of maybe getting hurt—hurt by somebody.*

Don: *Well, I understand that. I mean, I know what you mean. You know, in a sense that's what . . . we all make that decision or take that risk in dealing with people every day, you know? You put yourself on the line a little bit with someone. You take a little bit of risk, and I can understand that at some point you might not be willing to do that anymore, and I honestly believe that you are not at that point, Pete. I think in talking to you today, I'm hearing that you're not at that point. You are talking to me.*

Pete: *I don't know. Maybe I'm not, maybe I am. I'm just mixed up—feeling real mixed up.*

Don: *Yeah. How about this, Pete? How about if you hang up now, and we make an agreement that you won't shoot yourself in the next hour, and I'll give you a call back in an hour. You know, give you a chance to think about it a little bit, or take a shower, or do whatever you want to do. Kind of get away from it a little bit, and then I'll give you a call back, and we'll see where you're at.*

Pete: *Okay, for an hour. All right.*

Don: *You know? And, uh . . .*

Pete: *But if I start feeling real bad, I can call you back, right?*

Don: *Yeah, I'll be right here, because I know you're real upset tonight, and it seems like every hour it might change a little bit. So let's see where it is in an hour. Can you tell me what your phone number is, Pete?*

Pete: *No deal. No deal. I don't want any cops out here.*

Don: *Pete, I promise I won't send the cops.*
Pete: *What do you want to know my phone number for? I'm going to call you.*

Don: *Well, to be honest with you, that's a selfish thing. You know, if I hang up, and I don't have your number, I might not ever hear from you again, and that'd be real rough for me.*

Pete: *Yeah, but if I give you my number, I am going to lose control. I mean, I don't know what could happen. I don't know. You might send the police out here.*

Don: *Okay, Pete, I'm telling you I am not going to send the police, and I'll tell you why I am not going to send the police. I think if I send the police, that anger that you are feeling is just going to get worse.*

Pete: *That's damn straight. I'm going to take a bunch of them with me if you send any cops out here.*

Don: *Yeah, I believe that you might do that. I certainly believe that you might shoot yourself if I did that. You know, the feelings that I talked about that I have, they are really there, and I really do care about you, and I care about you staying alive, and I'm not going to do that. I also am just not going to lie to you for that rea-son. But I'm asking you to—*

Pete: *What do you want my number for? If I'm going to call you, what do you want my number for?*

Don: *I told you. I want it for my peace of mind, so that I know that I can get in touch with you. I mean, hell, you can shoot yourself the minute you hang up, you know. If you wanted to, you could do that. The reason I'm not—and I'll be honest with you about another thing, Pete. If I thought you were just about to do that, I would be thinking about trying to get somebody over there to help you, you know. Because your life is really important to me. But what I'm feeling about this conversation is that we are making a little bit of progress, and that you would be willing to back off a little bit, take an hour, and talk to me again. I believe that you'd be willing to do that.*

Pete: *What'd you say your name was again?*

Don: *I'm Don.*

Pete: *Okay. Okay. All right, I'll give you the number, but don't send anybody out here.*

Don: *I promise I won't send anyone, Pete. Okay, what's your phone number?*

Pete: *Okay. 321-5261.*

Don: *Okay, Pete.*

Pete: *Okay. Well, what am I supposed to do now?*

Don: *Well, I just thought maybe a little bit of time by yourself might be good, too. I mean, we can keep talking if you want to. I can try to get a little more specific about some things.*

Pete: *I'm getting kind of tired. Maybe I'll just try to lie down and get some rest a little. My body just feels like I've been through the mill.*

Don: *Yeah. Maybe you could go to sleep.*

Pete: *Yeah, I think I'll do that.*

Don: *Pete, I'm really glad that you called me, and in a way I feel good about talking to you.*

Pete: *You feel good about talking to me?*

Don: *I mean, I know it's a lot of rough stuff that you're going through, but I really feel good about your being willing to open up about it with me, and I feel like maybe we can work on it. And you know, maybe some good can come out of this.*

Pete: *I hope so! 'Cause it's sure time for things to turn around. They have been going the wrong way for a long time.*

Don: *Yeah. Okay, well, let's hang up now, and I'll give you a call back in an hour.*

Pete: *Okay, what time is that going to be? What time is it? I've even lost track of time.*

Don: *It will be quarter to one.*

Pete: *Okay. And if, okay, if I don't—if you ring for a minute—I might be in the other room sleeping, so it may take me a couple of minutes to get to the phone.*

Don: *Okay. I'd just as soon—you know, on the one hand, I'd like you to get some sleep, but as you say, things are going up and down tonight. I'll check with you that one time, and if you are asleep, then we don't have to talk. You can go right back. Okay?*

Pete: *Okay.*

Don: *But I would like to talk to you again tonight.*

Pete: *Okay. Good-bye, Don.*

Don: *Talk to you soon. Bye.*

MYTHS ABOUT GAY, LESBIAN, AND BISEXUAL PEOPLE

by Nadja Gould

Myth
Gay men are effeminate (limp wrists, high voices), and lesbians are masculine or "butch" (short hair, ride motorcycles).

Fact
These descriptions may apply to some gay people, but they are not true for the vast majority. Gay men and lesbians come in all shapes and sizes, and it is impossible to tell them apart from their straight counterparts. A frequent reaction to someone coming out is "I never would have guessed."

On the other hand, one of the things gay people often like about being gay is that it gives them more freedom to express and acquire positive traits usually associated with the other sex, in addition to ones traditionally ascribed to their own sex. For women, this means that they can be independent, strong, analytical, mechanical, "successful." For men, it means they can be supportive, in touch with their emotions, creative, spontaneous, sensitive.

Myth
Bisexuals are really semi-closeted gays and lesbians who are just too scared to come out.

Fact
For some, bisexuality is a transitional phase; for others, it may be a genuine lifetime identity. Often a person does not know which until midlife. Thus, your task as a peer counselor may be to explore the particular meanings and manifestations that bisexuality has for your particular client.

Myth
Women become lesbians because they can't get a man, have had bad experiences with men, or just haven't found the right man yet.

Fact
The current consensus among researchers is that a person's potential for experiencing love and sexual attraction is set at a relatively early age and cannot be changed by subsequent conditioning. Thus, a woman's attraction for other women appears in spite of other experiences she might have. On the other hand, it is not uncommon for women to feel that, although they may have had enjoyable and close love relationships with men, they find relationships with women richer and more satisfying. Some women use the term "woman-identified woman" to express their personal and political stance.

Myth
In gay couples, one person usually plays the male role, and one the female role.

Fact
While this is sometimes true for both gay men and lesbians, most gay people seek equality in relationships and enjoy freedom from conventional sex roles.

Myth
Gay teachers seduce children and therefore should not be hired in any school system.

Fact
Gay people are no more interested in having sex with children than straight people are. Nearly all the sexual assaults by teachers on children are perpetrated by straight men.

Myth
Having gay teachers might cause a child to become gay.

Fact
Most gay people are aware of gay feelings long before encountering other gay people. Children of gay parents show the same spectrum of sexual preference as other children. A lonely gay youngster struggling to come out may, on the other hand, be comforted and encouraged by knowing that a teacher or some other important adult is gay.

Myth
People are either straight or gay.

Fact
Studies have shown that the vast majority of people have had close emotional and/or sexual experiences with same-sex partners. Furthermore, a person's sexual orientation can change during his or her lifetime. Many people become aware of gay or bisexual feelings later in their lives, often after marriage and children.

Myth
Gay people are doomed to be unhappy.

Fact
Recent studies show that gay people are not more or less happy than straight people, but that as children and adolescents, they may have a difficult and painful time coming to terms with their differences because of the way others misunderstand and treat them.

Myth
Homosexuality is a disease.

Fact
In 1973, the American Psychiatric Association voted to remove homosexuality from its list of pathological conditions. No responsible, well educated doctor, therapist, or teacher adheres to this outmoded and discredited theory.

Myth
Homosexuality can be cured.

Fact
This myth is related to the disease theory of homosexuality and therefore is not valid. Nonetheless, when they are young and/or struggling with their identity, gay people may attempt to make their gay feelings go away by trying to fall in love with someone of the opposite sex. They may seek help through certain religious institutions or through therapy. These attempts are notably unsuccessful. Therapy that seeks to help people become more comfortable with and accepting of their true feelings tends to be much more successful.

Starting an Anonymous Peer Counseling Program for HIV Antibody Testing

by Joann M. Wong and Sharlene C. Pereira

Starting an HIV anonymous antibody test program requires a considerable amount of effort on the part of even the most interested and motivated students. Obstacles to developing such a program may include gaining institutional support and securing adequate funds to implement the program successfully. Yearly expenses include lab fees, condoms and dental dams, brochures, advertising, educational aids, and training fees. It may be possible to use small student-organization grants or other available monies to cover some expenses.

To begin, you must get support for your program from your campus health center. Then you need the approval of various university policy committees. As a group of students organized to initiate a program, you should be prepared to address concerns regarding whether it is appropriate for students to give other students such significant medical information, and specifically how your program will operate.

Direct support from campus health center staff and administration may help you gain approval at the university level. Health center representatives may attend meetings or participate in other activities to advocate for such a program and to lend medical credibility.

Institutional support from the campus health center is also essential for several other reasons. It links the peer counselors to professional staff who are essential to your program's administration and who can supervise the active counselors and those in training. Your program will depend on various professionals, such as lab technicians (who are necessary to draw the blood and perform the antibody tests) and physicians (to act as consultants and provide information regarding the latest trends in treatment and prevention). A health education director or specialist is important for addressing questions involving HIV prevention and specific medical information. A psychologist is crucial for supervising students by addressing concerns about counseling dynamics. A physician also serves an important function by acting as a consultant and being available should a counselor need medical information to respond to a client's concern.

In addition, professional staff can co-lead weekly clinical supervisory meetings that refine counseling skills, improve effectiveness as health educators, and provide an ongoing opportunity to consult with them regarding specific issues. Professional staff also provide counselors with emotional and psychological support on an individual basis. This can make a tremendous difference when a counselor has a particularly difficult session or needs to inform a client of a positive test result. Professional staff are vital to linking the program and its members to other related university functions and structures.

The professionals who become involved will spend approximately six to ten hours per month in program-related activities. During the program's startup months, their time commitment is often even greater.

TRAINING PEER COUNSELORS

Currently, trainings are held for new counselors two times per year. Each training period takes place over the course of two quarters. The training schedule is as follows.

Quarter 1

Interested students:

- Fill out an application
- Take an introductory class in peer counseling
- Attend an intensive two-day training led by a state-certified HIV/AIDS educator. (This requirement may be waived if the student has extensive background in peer counseling.) This training is funded by the campus health center.

Quarter 2

Counselors-in-training:

- Attend an organizational meeting to learn the specific procedures and policies of the established program
- Attend two two-hour sessions to refine their counseling skills through role-plays under professional supervision
- Sit in or "intern" as silent observers at two pre-test sessions
- Get tested for HIV themselves and share their experiences at a supervisory meeting

During the role-play sessions of the Quarter 2 training, the professional staff observe as counselors-in-training practice leading pre-test sessions. (The physician's participation is optional.) Then staff members critique and offer advice based on their experience.

The following quarter, new counselors can begin to counsel, provided that they attend the mandatory weekly one-hour clinical supervisory session. In our program, we ask counselors to choose a weekly time block (of one to three hours) for their sessions. New counselors who are unable to counsel due to class conflicts may take the quarter off and return to the program when their schedules permit. On occasion, special continuing-education meetings cover particular topics of interest (e.g., sexual assault, updates on medical treatment for AIDS patients).

HISTORY OF THE PROGRAM AT STANFORD UNIVERSITY

The impetus to have peer conduct HIV test counseling arose from the belief that more students would voluntarily be tested if they could meet with a nonjudgmental peer rather than a potentially intimidating physician. Challenged by the university's Health Promotion Program (HPP) director and coordinator of the introductory AIDS class, one student sought out various other students' reactions to getting tested for HIV. Many told him of feeling apprehensive about revealing their identity, their fear of doctors' condescending attitudes, and their perceived difficulty in discussing sexual behavior with a health professional. Convinced that setting up an anonymous test site would increase students' perceived barriers to getting tested for HIV, a group of students collaborated with the HPP director in setting up a pilot program at the campus health center.

Assessment has come primarily from two sources. At the end of the post-test session, each client received an anonymous evaluation questionnaire. All participating counselors and staff have also provided feedback. To date, the anonymous HIV antibody test program has been well received. Students have expressed appreciation for the counselors' knowledge, objectivity, and professionalism. Other feedback includes students' concern about the lack of available appointments and the two-week waiting period for test results.

REFERENCES AND RECOMMENDED READINGS

CRISIS COUNSELING

Aguilera, D. C. (1990). *Crisis intervention: Theory and methodology*, Sixth edition. St. Louis, MO: Mosby.

Caplan, G. (1964). *Principles of preventive psychiatry*. New York: Basic Books.

Delworth, U., & Rudow, T. (1972). *Crisis center hotline: A guidebook to beginning and operating*. Springfield, IL: Charles C. Thomas.

Directory of national helplines: A guide to toll-free public telephone service numbers. Ann Arbor, MI: Pierian Press (1994).

Hoff, L. A. (1978). *People in Crisis*. Reading, MA: Addison-Wesley.

Hyman, S. E., & Tesar, G. E. (1994). *Manual of psychiatric emergencies*. Boston: Little, Brown.

Kennedy, E. C. (1981). *Crisis counseling: An essential guide for nonprofessional counselors*. New York: Continuum Books.

Lester, D., & Brockopp, G. (1973). *Crisis intervention and counseling by telephone*. Springfield, IL: Charles C. Thomas.

Roberts, A. R. (Ed.) (1990). *Crisis intervention handbook: Assessment, treatment, and research*. Belmont, CA: Wadsworth.

Slaikeu, K. A. (1984). *Crisis intervention: A handbook for practice and research*. Boston: Allyn & Bacon.

CROSS-CULTURAL COUNSELING

American Psychological Association (1993, Jan.). Guidelines for providers of psychological services to ethnic, linguistic, and culturally diverse populations. *American Psychologist, 48*(1), 45–48.

Aranda, M. P. (1990). Culture-friendly services for Latino elders. Special Issue: Counseling and therapy for elders. *Generations, 14* (1), 55–57.

Atkinson, D. R., & Gim, R. H. (1989). Asian/Pacific American cultural identity and attitudes toward mental health services. *Journal of Counseling Psychology, 36*(2), 209–121.

Atkinson, D. R., Maruyama, M., & Matsui, S. (1978). Effects of counselor race and counseling approach on Asian/Pacific Americans' perceptions of counselor credibility and utility. *Journal of Counseling Psychology, 25*(1), 76–83.

Atkinson, D. R., & Matsushita, Y. J. (1991). Japanese-American acculturation, counseling style, counselor ethnicity, and perceived counselor credibility. *Journal of Counseling Psychology*, 38(4), 473–478.

Atkinson, D. R., Morten, G., & Sue, D. W. (1989). *Counseling American minorities*. Dubuque, IO: W. C. Brown.

Bamford, K. W. (1991). Bilingual issues in mental health assessment and treatment. *Hispanic Journal of Behavioral Sciences, 13* (4), 377–390.

Berg, J. H., et al. (1988). Effects of racial similarity and interviewer intimacy in a peer counseling analogue. *Journal of Counseling Psychology, 35* (4), 377–384.

Bernal, M. E., et al. (1990). The development of ethnic identity in Mexican-American children. *Hispanic Journal of Behavioral Sciences, 12*(1), 3–24.

Bonilla, L., et al. (1990). A comparison of Latino, Black, and non-Hispanic White attitudes toward homosexuality. *Hispanic Journal of Behavioral Sciences, 12*(4), 437–452.

Brown, P. (1990). Black social workers in private practice: Challenges and dilemmas. *Journal of Independent Social Work, 5*(1), 53–67.

Buck, M. R. (1977). Peer counseling from a Black perspective. *Journal of Black Psychology, 3* (2), 107–113.

Carpenter, R. A., et al. (1985). Peer-managed self-control program for prevention of alcohol abuse in American Indian high school students: A pilot evaluation study. *International Journal of Addictions, 20*(2), 299–310.

Chang, S. C. (1991). *Asian American history*. Boston, MA: Twayne Publishers.

Cheung, F., & Snowden, L. (1990). Community mental health and ethnic minority populations. *Community Mental Health Journal, 26*(3), 277–291.

The Crisis (1981, Oct.). Suicide taking its toll on Blacks (p. 401).

D'Andrea, M., & Daniels, J. (1991). Four stages of multicultural counseling training in counselor education. Special Issue: Multiculturalism as a fourth force in counseling. *Journal of Counseling & Development, 70*(1), 29–36.

Domino, G., et al. (1987). The relation of acculturation and values in Mexican Americans. Special Issue: Acculturation research. *Hispanic Journal of Behavioral Sciences, 9*(2), 131–150.

Draguns, J. G. (1976). Counseling across cultures: Common themes and distinct approaches. In P. Pedersen, W. J. Lonner, & J. D. Draguns (Eds.), *Counseling across cultures*. Honolulu: University Press of Hawaii.

Fabrega, H. (1990). Hispanic mental health research: A case for cultural psychiatry. *Hispanic Journal of Behavioral Sciences, 12*(4), 339–365.

Faulkner, C. W. (1981). Racism: What should you do? *The Observer*, December 3–9, C-6.

French, L. (1989). Native American alcoholism: A transcultural counselling perspective. Special Issue: Counselling women and ethnic minorities. *Counselling Psychology Quarterly, 2*(2), 153–166.

Gim, R. H., Atkinson, D. R., & Whiteley, S. (1990). Asian/Pacific American acculturation, severity of concerns, and willingness to see a counselor. *Journal of Counseling Psychology, 37*(3), 281–285.

Hendin, H. (1969). *Black suicide*. New York: Basic Books.

Hess, R., & Street, E. (1991). The effect of acculturation on the relationship of counselor ethnicity and client ratings. *Journal of Counseling Psychology, 38*(1), 71–75.

Ho, M. K. (1992). *Minority children and adolescents in therapy*. Newbury Park, CA: Sage Publications.

Horner, D., & Vandersluis, K. (1981). Cross-cultural counseling. In G. Althen (Ed.), *Learning across cultures* (pp. 30–50). Washington: National Association of Foreign Student Affairs.

Hu, H. C. (1975). The Chinese concepts of face. In D. G. Haring (Ed.), *Personal character and cultural milieu* (p. 452). Syracuse, NY: Syracuse University Press.

Institute of International Education (1993). *Open doors 1992/93*. Report on international educational exchange.New York: Institute of International Education (809 United Nations Plaza, New York, NY 10017-3580).

Jones, N. S. (1990). Black/white issues in psychotherapy: A framework for clinical practice. *Journal of Social Behavior & Personality, 5*(5), 305–322.

Juarez, R. (1985). Core issues in psychotherapy with the Hispanic child. *Psychotherapy, 22*, 441–448

Kahn, M. W., & Fua, C. (1985). Counselor training as a therapy for alcohol abuse among Aboriginal people. *American Journal of Community Psychology, 13*(5), 613–616.

Kitayama, S., & Markus, H. (Eds.) (1994). *Emotion and culture*. Washington, DC: American Psychological Association.

LaFromboise, T. D., et al. (1988). Cultural and cognitive considerations in the prevention of American Indian adolescent suicide. Special Issue: Mental health research and service issues for minority youth. *Journal of Adolescence, 11*(2), 139–153.

Locke, D. C., et al. (1987). Effects of peer-counseling training on psychological maturity of Black students. Special issue: Blacks in U.S. higher education. *Journal of College Student Personnel, 28*(6), 525–532.

Lubin, B., et al. (1986). Comparison of Mexican and Mexican American college students on the Spanish (American) version of the Depression Adjective Check List. *Hispanic Journal of Behavioral Sciences, 8*(2), 173–177.

Mack, D. E. (1989). Peer counseling: Increasing Mexican-American and Black student contact with a university counseling center. *Journal of College Student Development, 30*(2), 187–188.

Marin, G., et al. (1989). A comparison of three interviewing approaches for studying sensitive topics with Hispanics. *Hispanic Journal of Behavioral Sciences, 11*(4), 330–340.

Martinez, A., Huang, K., Johnson, S., & Edwards, S. (1989). Ethnic and international students. In P. A. Greyson & K. Cauley, *College psychotherapy*. New York: Guilford Press.

Mason, J. C., et al. (1982). Paraprofessional training of Indian and Alaskan native mental health workers. *White Cloud Journal, 2*(4), 3–8.

Mena, F. J., et al. (1987). Acculturative stress and specific coping strategies among immigrant and later generation college students. *Hispanic Journal of Behavioral Sciences, 9*(2), 207–225.

Menchaca, M. (1989). Chicano-Mexican cultural assimilation and Anglo-Saxon cultural dominance. *Hispanic Journal of Behavioral Sciences, 11*(3), 203–231.

Miller, K. L. (1989). Training peer counselors to work on a multicultural campus. *Journal of College Student Development, 30*(6), 561–562.

Morales, A. (1971). Distinguishing psychodynamic factors from cultural factors in the treatment of Spanish-speaking patients. In N. N. Wagner & M. J. Haug (Eds.), *Chicanos: Social and psychological prospectus* (pp. 279–280). Saint Louis: C. V. Mosby Company.

Moore, W., Jr., & Wagstaff, L. (1974). *Black education in white colleges*. San Francisco: Jossey-Bass.

National Asian Pacific American Legal Consortium (1993). *Audit of violence against Asian Pacific Americans*. Washington, DC: NAPALC (1629 K Street, NW, Suite 1010, Washington, DC 20006).

Native Hawaiian Study Commission (1988). *The native Hawaiian people* (vol. 2, chapter 8). Part of a report submitted to the Committee on Energy and Natural Resources of the U.S. Senate and the Committee on Interior and Insular Affairs of the U.S. House of Representatives.

Ohnuma, K. (1990, Dec. 7). Asian blackbelt fends off 6 attackers in Seattle. *Asian Week*, p. 3.

Ong, P., & Azores, T. (1991). *Asian Pacific Americans in Los Angeles: A demographic profile*. Public policy project. Los Angeles: Asian American Studies Center, University of California.

Parrillo, V. N. (1980). *Strangers to these shores: Race and ethnic relations in the United States*. Boston: Houghton Mifflin.

Pedersen, P. (1987). The frequent assumptions of cultural bias in counseling. *Journal of Multicultural Counseling & Development, 15*(1), 16–24.

Pedersen, P., Lonner, W. J., & Draguns, J. D. (1976). *Counseling across cultures*. Honolulu: University Press of Hawaii.

Pedersen, P., & Pedersen, A. (1989). The cultural grid: A complicated and dynamic approach to multicultural counseling. Special Issue: Counselling women and ethnic minorities. *Counselling Psychology Quarterly, 2*(2), 133–141.

Peng, S. (1988, Apr.). *Attainment status of Asian/Pacific Americans in higher education*. Paper presented at a conference of the National Association for Asian and Pacific American Education, in Denver, CO.

Ponterotto, J. G., et al. (1986). Afro-american students' attitudes toward counseling as a function of racial identity. *Journal of Multicultural Counseling and Development, 14*(2), 50–59.

Pye, L. (1968). *The spirit of Chinese politics: A study of authority crisis in political development.* Cambridge, MA: MIT Press.

Ramirez, M. (1991). *Psychotherapy and counseling with minorities: A cognitive approach to individual and cultural differences.* New York: Pergamon Press.

Rodriguez, R. (1974-1975). Going home again: The new American scholarship boy. *The American Scholar, 44*(1).

Rueschenberg, E., et al. (1989). Mexican American family functioning and acculturation: A family systems perspective. *Hispanic Journal of Behavioral Sciences, 11*(3), 232–244.

Ruiz, R. A., & Padilla, A. M. (1977, March). Counseling Latinos. *Personnel and Guidance Journal*, pp. 401–408.

Sanchez, E., & Mohl, P. (1992). Psychotherapy with Mexican-American patients. *American Journal of Psychiatry, 149*, 626–630.

Smith, E. M. (1989). Black racial identity development: Issues & concerns. *Counseling Psychologist, 17*(2), 277–288.

Speight, S. L., et al. (1991). A redefinition of multicultural counseling. Special Issue: Multiculturalism as a fourth force in counseling. *Journal of Counseling and Development, 70*(1), 29–36.

Suan, L. V., & Tyler, J. (1990). Mental health values and preference for mental health resources of Japanese-American and Caucasian-American students. *Professional Psychology: Research and Practice, 21*(4), 291–296.

Sue, D. W., & Sue, D. (1990). *Counseling the culturally different: Theory and practice.* New York: Wiley.

Sue, D. W., et al. (1992). Multicultural counseling competencies and standards: A call to the profession. *Journal of Counseling and Development, 70*(4), 477–486.

Sue, S., Fujino, D., Hu, L., Takeuchi, D., & Zane, N. (1991). Community mental health services for ethnic minority groups: A test of the cultural responsiveness hypothesis. *Journal of Consulting and Clinical Psychology, 59*(4), 533–540.

Sue, S., & Okazaki, S. (1990). Asian-American educational achievements: A phenomenon in search of an explanation. *American Psychologist, 45*(8), 913–920.

Takaki, R. (1989). *Strangers from a different shore.* New York: Penguin Books.

Time (1987, August 31). The new whiz kids (pp. 42–51).

Toupin, E. A. (1980). Counseling Asians: Psychotherapy in the context of racism and Asian-American history. *American Journal of Orthopsychiatry, 50*(1), 76–86.

Trippi, J., & Cheatham, H. E. (1991). Counseling effects on African-American college student graduation. *Journal of College Student*

Development, 32 (4), 342–349.

U.S. Bureau of the Census (1990). *Census of population: General population characteristics, United States summary.* Washington, DC: U.S. Government Printing Office.

U.S. Department of Education, National Center for Education Statistics (1993). *Digest of education statistics.* Washington, DC: U.S. Government Printing Office.

U.S. Department of Education, National Center for Education Statistics (1994). *The condition of education.* Washington, DC: U.S. Government Printing Office.

Vohra, S., et al. (1991). A cross-cultural training format for peer counselors. *Journal of College Student Development, 32*(1), 82–84.

Yau, T. Y., Sue, D., & Hayden, D. (1992). Counseling style preference of international students. *Journal of Counseling Psychology, 39*(1), 100–104.

Young, T. J. (1989). Treatment of multicultural counseling in correctional psychology textbooks. *Psychological Reports, 65* (2), 521–522.

Zuniga, M. E. (1988). Assessment issues with Chicanas: Practical implications. *Psychotherapy, 25*, 288–293.

ETHICS

Abelson, R., & Nielson, K. (1967). History of ethics. In P. Edwards (Ed.), *The encyclopedia of philosophy*, Vol. 3. New York: Macmillan.

Alves, J. T. (1959). *Confidentiality in social work.* Washington, DC: The Catholic University of America Press.

American Psychological Association (1989). *Ethical principles of psychologists.* Washington, DC: APA Press.

Beyerstein, D. (1993). The functions and limitations of professional codes of ethics. In E. R. Winkler & J. R. Coombs (Eds.), *Applied ethics: A reader.* Cambridge: Blackwell Press.

Brabek, M. M. (Ed.) (1989). *Who cares: Theory, research, and educational implications of the ethic of care.* New York: Praeger.

Brown, R. D. (1985). Creating an ethical community. In H. J. Canon & R. D. Brown (Eds.), *Applied ethics in student services.* San Francisco: Jossey-Bass.

Canon, J. H., & Brown, R. D. (1985). How to think about professional ethics. In H. J. Canon & R. D. Brown (Eds.), *Applied ethics in student services.* San Francisco: Jossey-Bass.

Chenault, J. (1969). Help-giving and morality. *Personnel and Guidance Journal, 48:* 89–96.

Collins, P. H. (1989). The social construction of black feminist thought. *Signs: Journal of Women in Culture and Society, 14*(4), 745–773.

Delworth, U., & Seeman, S. (1984). The ethics of care: Implications of Gilligan for the student services profession. *Journal of College*

Student Personnel (Nov.), 489–492.

Fuqua, D. R., & Newman, J. L. (1989). Research issues in the study of professional ethics. *Counselor Education and Supervision, 29*, 84–93.

Gilligan, C. (1982). *In a different voice: Psychological theory and women's development.* Cambridge, MA: Harvard University Press.

Gilligan, C. (1986). Reply by Carol Gilligan. In L. K. Kerber, C. G. Greeno, E. E. Maccoby, Z. Luria, C. B. Stack, & C. Gilligan, On In a different voice: An interdisciplinary forum. *Signs: Journal of Women in Culture and Society, 11*(2), 304–333.

Gilligan, C. V., Ward, J. V., Taylor, J. M., & Bardig, B. (1988). *Mapping the moral domain: A contribution of women's thinking to psychological theory and education.* Cambridge, MA: Harvard University Press.

Huston, K. (1984). Ethical decisions in treating battered women. *Professional Psychology: Research and Practice, 6*, 822–832.

Iasenza, S. (1989). Some challenges of integrating sexual orientations into counselor training and research. Special Issue: Gay, Lesbian, and Bisexual Issues in Counseling. *Journal of Counseling and Development, 68*(1), 73–76.

Johnston, K. (1985). Two moral orientations—two problem-solving strategies: Adolescents' solutions to dilemmas in fables (Ed.D. dissertation). Cambridge, MA: Harvard University Graduate School of Education.

June, L. N., Curry, B. P., Gear, C. L. (1990). An 11-year analysis of black students' experience of problems and use of services: Implications for counseling professionals. *Journal of Counseling Psychology, 37*(2), 178–184.

Kitchener, K. S. (1985). Ethical principles and ethical decisions in student affairs. In H. J. Canon & R. D. Brown (Eds.), *Applied ethics in student services.* San Francisco: Jossey-Bass.

Kochman, T. (1981). *Black and white: Styles in conflict.* Chicago: University of Chicago Press.

Kohlberg, L. (1969). Stage and sequence: The cognitive developmental approach to socialization. In D. Goslin (Ed.), *The handbook of socialization theory and research.* Chicago: Rand McNally.

Larrabee, M. J. (Ed.) (1993). *An ethic of care: Feminist and interdisciplinary perspectives.* New York: Routledge.

Luria, Z. (1986). A methodological critique. In L. K. Kerber, C. G. Greeno, E. E. Maccoby, Z. Luria, C. B. Stack, & C. Gilligan, On In a different voice: An interdisciplinary forum. *Signs: Journal of Women in Culture and Society, 11*(2), 304–333.

Lyons, N. (1983). Two perspectives: On self, relationships, and morality. *Harvard Education Review, 53*(2), 125–146.

May, L., & Sharratt, S. C. (1994). *Applied ethics: A multicultural approach.* Englewood Cliffs, NJ: Prentice-Hall.

Muehlman, T., Pickens, B., & Robinson, F. (1985). Informing clients about the limits to confidentiality, risks, and their rights: Is self-disclosure limited? *Professional Psychology: Research and Practice*, 3: 385–397.

Pollitt, K. (1992). Are women morally superior to men? *The Nation*, 255(22): 799–807. (Letters of criticism, with rebuttal, appear in *The Nation*, 25(9), 290, 319–320.)

Tennyson, W. W., & Strom, S. A. (1986). Beyond professional standards: Developing responsibleness. *Journal of Counseling and Development, 64:* 298–302.

Waithe, M. E. (1989). Twenty-three hundred years of women philosophers: Toward a gender undifferentiated moral theory. In M. M. Brabek (Ed.), *Who cares: Theory, research, and educational implications of the ethic of care*. New York: Praeger.

Wicker, A. W. (1985). Getting out of our conceptual ruts: Strategies for expanding conceptual frameworks. *American Psychologist, 40:* 1094–1101.

Winston, R. B., & Dagley, J. C. (1985). Ethical standards statements: Uses and limitations. In H. J. Canon & R. D. Brown (Eds.), *Applied ethics in student services*. San Francisco: Jossey-Bass.

GAY, LESBIAN, AND BISEXUAL ISSUES

Bell, A. P., Weinberg, M. S., & Hammersmith, S. K. (1981). *Sexual preference: Its development in men and women*. Bloomington, IN: Indiana University Press/Alfred C. Kinsey Institute for Sex Research.

Blumenfeld, W. J., & Raymond, D. (1988). *Looking at gay and lesbian life*. Boston: Beacon Press.

Buhrke, R. A., & Douce, L. A. (1991). Training issues for counseling psychologists in working with lesbians and gay men. *Counseling Psychologist, 19* (2), 216–234.

Coleman, E. (1987). Assessment of sexual orientation. In E. Coleman(Ed.), *Psychotherapy with homosexual men and women*. New York: Haworth Press.

de Monteflores, C. (1986). Notes on the management of difference. In T. S. Stein & C. J. Cohen (Eds.), *Psychotherapy with lesbians and gay men*. New York: Plenum.

Gonsiorek, J. (Ed.). (1985). *A guide to psychotherapy with gay and lesbian clients*. New York: Harrington Park Press.

Hencken, J. D. (1984). Sexual-orientation self-disclosure. Unpublished doctoral dissertation. University of Michigan, Department of Psychology.

Herdt, G. (1989). Gay and lesbian youth: Emergent identities and cultural scenes at home and abroad. In G. Herdt (Ed.), *Gay and lesbian youth*. New York: Harrington Park Press.

Hetrick, E. S., & Martin, A. D. (1987). Developmental issues and their resolution for gay and lesbian adolescents. In E. Coleman (Ed.), *Psychotherapy with homosexual men and women.* New York: Haworth Press.

Iasenze, S. (1989). Some challenges of integrating sexual orientations into counselor training and research. Special Issue: Gay, lesbian, and bisexual issues in counseling. *Journal of Counseling and Development, 68*(1), 73–76.

Nichols, S. E. (1986). Psychotherapy and AIDS. In T. S. Stein & C. J. Cohen (Eds.), *Psychotherapy with lesbians and gay men.* New York: Plenum.

Shively, M., & DeCecco, J. (1977). Components of sexual identity. *Journal of Homosexuality, 3:* 41–48.

Sophie, J. (1987). Internalized homophobia and lesbian identity. In E. Coleman (Ed.), *Psychotherapy with homosexual men and women.* New York: Haworth Press.

Troiden, R. R. (1989). The formation of homosexual identities. In G. Herdt (Ed.), *Gay and lesbian youth.* New York: Harrington Park Press.

Wertheimer, D. M. (1990). Treatment and service interventions for lesbian and gay male crime victims. Special Issue: Violence against lesbians and gay men: Issues for research, practice, and policy. *Journal of Interpersonal Violence, 5*(3), 384–400.

Wolf, T. J. (1987). Group counseling for bisexual men. *Journal for Specialists in Group Work, 12*(4), 162–165.

HIV ISSUES

Baiss, A. (1989). A peer counselling program for persons testing HIV antibody positive. *Canadian Journal of Counselling, 23*(1), 127–132.

Bracho de Carpio, A., et al. (1990). Hispanic families learning and teaching about AIDS: A participatory approach at the community level. Special Issue: Hispanics and AIDS. *Hispanic Journal of Behavioral Sciences, 12*(2), 165–176.

Brown, V. B. (1990). The AIDS crisis: Intervention and prevention. *New Directions for Student Services,* Spr (49), 67–74.

Cantania, J., Coates, T., Stall, R., Turner, H., Peterson, J., Hearst, N., Dolcini, M., Hudes, E., Gagnon, J., Wiley, J., & Groves, R. (1992, November 13). Prevalence of AIDS-related risk factors and condom use in the United States. *Science, 258:* 1101–1106.

Cantania, J., Kegeles, S., & Coates, T. (1990, Spring). Towards an understanding of risk behavior: An AIDS risk reduction model (ARRM). *Health Education Quarterly, 17*(1), 53–72.

de Vroome, E., Sandfort, T., & Tielman, R. (1992, July). *Overestimating the risk of orogenital sex may increase unsafe anogenital sex.* Paper presented at the International Conference on AIDS, Amsterdam, The Netherlands.

Dodd, R. (1992). American Red Cross. (Editorial.) *New England Journal of Medicine, 327:* 419–420.

Factors influencing behavior and behavior change. (1991, October). Final report of the Theorists' Workshop, Washington, DC.

Gambe, R., et al. (1989). Group work with gay men with AIDS. *Social Casework, 70*(3), 172–179.

Herek, G. M. (1984). Beyond "homophobia": A social psychological perspective on attitudes toward lesbians and gay men. *Journal of Homosexuality, 10:* 1–21.

Kalibala, S., et al. (1989). AIDS and community-based care in Uganda: The AIDS support organization TASO. *AIDS Care, 1*(2), 173–175.

Kaminsky, S., et al. (1990). Life enhancement counseling with HIV-infected Hispanic gay males. Special Issue: Hispanics and AIDS. *Hispanic Journal of Behavioral Sciences, 12*(2), 165–176.

Krieger, I. (1988). An approach to coping with anxiety about AIDS. *Social Work, 33*(3), 263–264.

Marin, B. V., et al. (1990). Differences between Hispanics and non-Hispanics in willingness to provide AIDS prevention advice. Special Issue: Hispanics and AIDS. *Hispanic Journal of Behavioral Sciences, 12*(2), 153–164.

McEwan, R. T., McCallum, A., Bhopal, R. S., & Madhok, R. (1992). Sex and the risk of HIV infection: The role of alcohol. *British Journal of Addiction, 87:* 577–584.

Morales, E. S. (1990). HIV infection and Hispanic gay and bisexual men. Special Issue: Hispanics and AIDS. *Hispanic Journal of Behavioral Sciences, 12*(2), 212–222.

O'Leary, A., Goodhart, F., Jemmott, L. S., & Boccher-Latimore, D. (1991). Predictors of safer sex on the college campus: A social cognitive theory analysis. *Journal of American College Health, 40:* 254–263.

Safer sex guidelines: A resource for researchers and educators. (1987). Brochure. Toronto, Ontario: Canadian AIDS Society.

San Mateo County (1991). *HIV counseling: Sharing the news.* Trainee's manual, version 2.2. San Mateo County, CA: Office of AIDS.

Shapshak, P., McCoy, C. B., et al. (1993). Letter to the editor. *Journal of AIDS, 6:* 218–219.

Surgeon General's report to the American public on HIV infection and AIDS (1992, Dec.). Washington, DC: Center for Disease Control and Prevention, National Institutes of Health, and Health Resources and Services Administration.

Wallack, J. J., et al. (1991). An AIDS bibliography for the general psychiatrist. *Psychosomatics, 32*(3), 243–254.

RESIDENT ASSISTANTS

Boswinkel, J. P. (1986). The college resident assistant (RA) and the fine art of referral for psychotherapy. *Journal of College Student Psychotherapy, 1*(1), 53–62.

Frisz, R. H., et al. (1987). Student user evaluations of peer advisor services. *Journal of College Student Personnel, 28*(3), 241–245.

Fuehrer, A., et al. (1988). Individual and situational factors as predictors of burnout among resident assistants. *Journal of College Student Development, 29*(3), 244–249.

Hetherington, C., et al. (1989a). Resident assistant burnout: Factors of job and gender. *Journal of College Student Development, 30*(3), 266–269.

Hetherington, C., et al. (1989b). Resident assistants: Training to define personal boundaries. *Journal of College Student Development, 30*(3), 274–275.

Russel, J. H., et al. (1987). Evaluation of a program of peer helping for first-year students. *Journal of College Student Personnel, 28*(4), 330–336.

Schinke, S. P., et al. (1979). Crisis-intervention training with para-professionals. *Journal of Community Psychology, 7*(4), 343–347.

Schuh, J. H. (1981). *Increasing the educational role of residence halls.* San Francisco: Jossey-Bass.

Shipton, W. C., & Schuh, J. H. (1982). Counseling problems encountered by resident assistants: A longitudinal study. *Journal of College Student Personnel, 23:* 246–252.

Winston, R. B., Jr., & Buckner, J. D. (1984). The effects of peer helper training and timing of training on reported stress of resident assistants. *Journal of College Student Personnel, 25*(5), 430–436.

Wolf, M., Dorosin, D., & D'Andrea, V. (1968). *How to be there when you're there: A guide to handling student problems in the residences.* Counseling and Psychological Services, Stanford University.

Sexual Assault

Bart, P. B., & O'Brien, P. H. (1985). *Stopping rape: Successful survival strategies.* Elmsford, NY: Maxwell House.

Benedict, H. (1985). *Recovery: How to survive sexual assault: For women, men, teenagers, and their friends and families.* Garden City, NY: Doubleday.

Ehrhart, J. K., & Sandler, B. R. (1985). *Campus gang rape: Party games?* Washington, DC: Association of American Colleges/Project on the Status and Education of Women.

Estrich, S. (1991). *Real rape.* Cambridge, MA: Harvard University Press.

McDermott, J. (1979). *Rape Victimization in 26 American Cities.* Washington, DC: U.S. Department of Justice. As cited in P. B. Bart & P. H. O'Brien (1985), *Stopping Rape* (p. 131). New York: Pergamon Press.

Pritchard, C. (1985). *Avoiding rape on and off campus.* Wenonah, NJ: Sate College Publishing.

Sweet, E. (1985, Oct.). *Date rape: The story of an epidemic and those who deny it.* Ms., 56.

Suicide

Avery, D., & Winokur, G. (1978). Suicide, attempted suicides and relapse rates and depression. *Archives of General Psychiatry, 38:* 749.

Beck, A. T., Resnick, H. L. P., & Lettieri, D. J. (1986). *The prediction of suicide*. Philadelphia: Charles Press.

Bruyn, H. B., & Seiden, R. H. (1965). Student suicide. *Journal of the American College Health Association, 14:* 69–77.

Characteristics of 26,000 suicide prevention center patients. *Bulletin of Suicidology, 6:* 24–34.

Devries, A. G. (1966). A potential suicide personality inventory. *Psychological Reports, 18:* 731–738.

Drye, R., Goulding, R., & Goulding, M. (1973). No-suicidedecisions: Patient monitoring of suicidal risk. *American Journal of Psychiatry, 130: 2.*

Evans, J. & Boyd, M. (n.d.). *Suicidal crisis*. Riverside, CA: Helpline Volunteer Center.

Friedman, P. (Ed.) (1967). *On suicide: With particular reference to suicide among young students*. New York: International Universities Press.

Friedrich, M. C., et al. (1985). An interdisciplinary supervised student program focused on depression and suicide awareness. Paper presented at the annual meeting of the National Association of Social Workers (New Orleans, LA, January 31–February 3, 1985).

Goodwin, D. W. (1973). Alcohol in suicide and homicide. *Quarterly Journal of Studies on Alcohol, 33:* 33–64.

Hatton, C. L., & Volente, S. M. (1984). *Suicide, assessment, and intervention*. Norwalk, CT: Appleton-Century-Crofts.

Hawron, K., et al. (1978). Attempted suicide and suicide among Oxford University students. *British Journal of Psychiatry, 132:* 506–509.

Herring, R. (1990). Suicide in the middle school: Who said kids will not? *Elementary School Guidance and Counseling, 25*(2), 129–137.

Hollinger, P. (1978). Adolescent suicide: An epidemiological study of recent trends. *American Journal of Psychiatry, 135:* 754–757.

Knight, J. (1968). Suicide among students. In H. L. P.Resnik (Ed.), *Suicidal behaviors*. Boston: Little, Brown.

LaFromboise, T. D., et al. (1988). Cultural and cognitive considerations in the prevention of American Indian adolescent suicide. Special Issue: Mental health research and service issues for minority youth. *Journal of Adolescence, 11* (2), 139–153.

Lipschitz, A. (1990). *College suicide: A monograph*. New York: American Suicide Foundation.

Martin, D., et al. (1987). A peer counselor crisis intervention training program to help prevent adolescent suicide. *Techniques, 3*(3), 214–218.

Mauk, G. W., et al. (1991). Peer survivors of adolescent suicide: Perspectives on grieving and postvention. Special Issue: Death and adolescent bereavement. *Journal of Adolescent Research, 6*(1), 113–131.

McIntire, M. S. & Angle, C. R. (1980). *Suicide Attempts in Children and Youth*. New York: Harper & Row, pp. 1–13.

Mishara, B., et al. (1976). The frequency of suicide attempts. *American Journal of Psychiatry, 136:* 516–520.

Motto, J. (1979). The psychopathology of suicide: A clinical model approach. *American Journal of Psychiatry, 136:* 516–520.

Rosenkrautz, A. (1978). A note on adolescent suicide. *Adolescence, 13:* 208–214.

Shneidman, E. S. (1985). *Definition of suicide.* New York: Wiley.

Seiden, R. (19). Campus tragedy. *Journal of Abnormal Psychology, 71*(66): 389.

Slaby, A. E., & Garfinkel, L. F. (1994). *No one saw my pain: Why teens kill themselves.* New York: Norton.

U.S. Department of Health and Human Services, National Center for Health Statistics (1991). *Health United States 1990.* Washington: U.S. Government Printing Office.

Whitaker, L. C., & Slimak, R. E. (Eds.) (1990). College student suicide. Special issue. *Journal of College Psychotherapy, 4:* 3–4.

Wold, L. (1971). *Suicide among youth.* Washington, DC: U.S. Public Health Service.

THEORY AND TRAINING

Beck, A. T. (1976). *Cognitive therapy and the emotional disorders.* New York: International Universities Press.

Berg, J. H., et al. (1988). Effects of racial similarity and interviewer intimacy in a peer counseling analogue. *Journal of Counseling Psychology, 35*(4), 377–384.

Berne, E. (1964). *Games people play: The psychology of human relationships.* New York: Random House.

Bowen, N. H., et al. (1985). Women helping women: A peer counseling service. *Women & Therapy, 4*(2), 43–51.

Bratter, B., et al. (3990). The maturing of peer counseling. Special Issue: Counseling and therapy for elders. *Generations, 14*(1), 49–52.

Brown, W. F. (1976). Effectiveness of paraprofessionals: The evidence. *Personnel and Guidance Journal, 53*(4), 257–263.

Buck, C. B., & Pineda, C. (1985). A peer counseling training module for campus outreach and support services. Paper presented at the annual meeting of the California Association for Counseling and Development, San Diego, CA.

Burns, D. D. (1980). *Feeling good: The new mood therapy.* New York: Morrow.

Caplan, G., & Killilea, M. (Eds.) (1976). *Support systems and mutual help.* New York: Grune & Stratton.

Carkhuff, R. R. (1969). *Helping and human relations,* Vol. 1. New York: Holt, Rinehart & Winston.

Carr, R. A. (1981). *Theory and practice of peer counseling/Le co-conseil theorie et pratique.* Ottawa: Canadian Commission of Employment and Immigration.

Carr, R. A. (1984). Theory and practice of peer counseling. *Educational & Vocational Guidance, 42,* 1–10.

Carroll, M. R., & King, V. G. (1985). The peer helping phenomenon: A quiet revolution. *Counseling & Human Development, 17*(9), 1–8.

Cooper-White, P. (1990). Peer vs. clinical counseling: Is there a place for both in the battered women's movement? *Response to the Victimization of Women & Children, 13*(3), 2–6.

Cormier, W. H., & Cormier, S. (1991). *Interviewing strategies for helpers: Fundamental skills and cognitive behavioral interventions*. Pacific Grove, CA: Brooks/Cole.

Danish, S. J., & Brock, G. W. (1974). The current status of paraprofessional training. *Personnel and Guidance Journal, 53*(4), 299–303.

Delworth, U. (1974). The paraprofessionals are coming! *Personnel and Guidance Journal, 53*(4).

de Rosenroll, D. (1989). A practitioner's guide to peer counselling research issues and dilemmas. *Canadian Journal of Counselling, 23*(1), 75–91.

de Rosenroll, D. A., et al. (1990). A centralized approach to training peer counselors: Three years of progress. *School Counselor, 37*(4), 256–260.

DiPaulo, J (1980). Training of American Indian mental health professionals. *White Cloud Journal, 2*, 8–13.

Dorosin, D., D'Andrea, V., & Jacks, R. (1977). A peer counselor training program: Rationale, curriculum and evaluation. *Journal of American College Health, 25*(4), 259–262.

Durlak, J. A. (1979). Comparative effectiveness of paraprofessional and professional helpers. *Psychological Bulletin, 86*, 80–92.

Egan, G. (1982). *The skilled helper*, Second edition. Monterey, CA: Brooks/Cole.

Egan, G. (1985). *Exercises in helping skills: A training manual to accompany the skilled helper*. Monterey, CA: Brooks/Cole.

German, S. C. (1979). Selecting undergraduate paraprofessionals on college campuses: A review. *Journal of College Student Personnel, 20*(1), 28–34.

Giddan, N. S., & Austin, M. J. (Eds.) (1982). *Peer counseling and self-help groups on campus*. Springfield, IL: Charles C. Thomas.

Gordon, V. N. (1992). *Handbook of academic advising*. Westport, CT: Greenwood Press.

Goulding, R., & Goulding, M. (1978). *The power is in the patient: A TA/Gestalt approach to psychotherapy*. San Francisco: T.A. Press.

Gruver, G. G. (1971). College students as therapeutic agents. *Psychological Bulletin, 76*, 111–128.

Hailey, R. T. (1989). The impact of peer supervision on the counseling effectiveness of beginning counselor trainees. *Dissertation Abstracts International, 49*(8-A), 2112.

Harman, . M., & Baron, A. (1982). A student-focused model for the development of counseling services. *Personnel and Guidance Journal, 50*, 290–293.

Hill, L. (1990). Facing life transitions: A peer counseling program. *Journal of College Student Development, 31*(6), 572–573.

Hinrichsen, J. J., & Zwibelman, B. B. (1979). Longitudinal evaluation of service demand at a university peer counseling center. *Journal of Counseling Psychology, 26*(2), 159–163.

Homme, L. (1970). *Use of contingency contracting in the classroom.* Champaign, IL: Research Press.

Ivey, A. E. (1974). *Microcounseling: Innovations in interviewing training.* Springfield, IL: Charles C. Thomas.

Ivey, A. E., & Gluckstern, N. (1976). *Basic influencing skills.* North Amherst, MA: Microtraining Associates.

Ivey, A. E. (1978). *Microcounseling: Innovations in interviewing, counseling, psychotherapy, and psychoeducation.* Springfield, IL: Charles C. Thomas.

Ivey, A. E., & Downing, S. (1980). *Counseling and psychotherapy: Skills, theories, practice.* Englewood, NJ: Prentice-Hall. [See especially chapter 11, sections 8–11.]

Ivey, A. E., & Gluckstern, N. (1974). *Basic attending skills: An introduction to microcounseling and helping.* Amherst, MA: Microcounseling Associates.

Ivey, A. E., & Matthews, W. J. (1984). A meta-model for structuring the clinical interview. *Journal of Counseling and Development, 63:* 237–243.

Jacks, R., Bottjer, F., & D'Andrea, V. (1978). Student perceptions of the relative competence of peer and professional counselors in a career counseling setting. Unpublished manuscript. Counseling and Psychological Services, Stanford University.

Kagan, N. (1972). *Influencing human interaction.* East Lansing, MI: Michigan State University, College of Education and Human Medicine.

Kazdin, A. E. (1994). *Behavior modification in applied settings.* Pacific Grove, CA: Brooks/Cole.

Kingsland, L. J., et al. (1986). Peer programs in post-secondary institutions in Canada. Canadian *Journal of Counselling, 20*(2), 114–121.

Krumboltz, J. D., Scherba, D. S., Hamel, D. A., & Mitchell, L. K. (1982). Effects of training in rational decision making on the quality of simulated career decisions. *Journal of Counseling Psychology, 29:* 618–625.

Lawson, D. (1989). Peer helping programs in the colleges and universities of Quebec and Ontario. *Canadian Journal of Counselling, 23*(1), 41–64.

Lenihan, G., et al. (1990). Using student paraprofessionals in the treatment of eating disorders. *Journal of Counseling & Development, 68*(3), 332–335.

Luft, J., & Inghan, H. (1963). The Johari window: A graphic model of awareness. In J. Luft (Ed.), *Interpersonal relationships in group processes: An introduction to group dynamics.* Palo Alto, CA: National Press Books.

Lyons, J. W. (1983). Foreword in D'Andrea & Salovey (1983), *Peer counseling: Skills and perspectives.* Palo Alto, CA: Science & Behavior Books.

Mahoney, M. J., & Thoresen, C. W. (1974). *Self-control: Power to the person*. Monterey, CA: Brooks-Cole.

Meilman, P. W. (1986). Meeting the mental health needs of medical students: The effects of a peer support program. *Journal of College Student Personnel, 27*(4), 373–374.

McMullin, R. E. (1986). *Handbook of cognitive therapy techniques*. New York: Norton.

Miller, K. L. (1989). Training peer counselors to work on a multicultural campus. *Journal of College Student Development, 30*(6), 561–562.

Morey, R. E., et al. (1989). Peer counseling: Students served, problems discussed, overall satisfaction, and perceived helpfulness. *School Counselor, 37*(2), 137–143.

Morrill, C. M., et al. (1987). Peer helpers: Overview and caution. *International Journal of Adolescence & Youth, 1*(1), 33–37.

Okun, B. (1976). *Effective helping: Interviewing and counseling techniques*. Belmont, CA: Wadsworth/Duxbury.

Okun, B. (1990). *Seeking connections in psychotherapy*. San Francisco, CA: Jossey-Bass.

Paritzky, R. S. (1981). Training peer counselors: The art of referral. *Journal of College Student Personnel, 22*(6), 528–532.

Pedersen, P. (1987). The frequent assumptions of cultural bias in counseling. *Journal of Multicultural Counseling & Development, 15*(1), 16–24.

Rioch, M., et al. (1963). NIMH pilot study in training and mental health counselors. *American Journal of Orthopsychiatry, 33*, 678–690.

Robinson, S. E., et al. (1991). Peer counselors in a high school setting: Evaluation of training and impact on students. *School Counselor, 39*(1), 35–40.

Russel, J. H., et al. (1990). Evaluation of peer-advisor effectiveness. *Journal of College Student Development, 31*(5), 388–394.

Sala, I. T. (1986). Role-playing: A useful tool in the training of peer counselors and other mental health paraprofessionals. *Techniques, 2*(1), 67–75.

Salovey, P., & D'Andrea, V. (1984). A survey of campus peer counseling activities. *Journal of American College Health Association, 32*, 262–265.

Schinke, S. P., et al. (1979). Crisis-intervention training with paraprofessionals. *Journal of Community Psychology, 7*(4), 343–347.

Silver, E. J., et al. (1992). Effects of a peer counseling training intervention on psychological functioning of adolescents. *Journal of Adolescent Research, 7*(1), 110–128.

Smith, R. A. (1971). A strategy for health manpower. *Journal of American Medical Association, 10* (217): 1362–66.

Tinsley, H. E. A., et al. (1984). Relation between expectancies for a helping relationship and tendency to seek help from a campus help provider. *Journal of Counseling Psychology, 31*(2), 149–160.

Varenhorst, B. B. (1983). *Real Friends: Becoming the Friend You'd Like To Have*. San Francisco: Harper & Row.

Vijayalakshmi, S., et al. (1985). Effect of human relations training on the students' ability to function as peer counselors. *Journal of Indian Academy of Applied Psychology, 11*(1), 31–38.

White, R. W. (1974). Strategies of adaptation: An attempt at systematic description. In G. Coelho, D. Hamburg, and R. Adams (Eds.), *Coping and adaptation.* New York: Basic Books.

Wolberg, L. (1967). *The technique of psychotherapy,* 2nd ed. New York: Grune & Stratton.

INDEX

Other books from Science & Behavior

Passage To Intimacy by Lori H. Gordon, Ph.D.   **12.95 QPB**
Based on the key concepts and skills from Lori Gordon's Heralded PAIRS (Practical Application of Intimate Relationship Skills) program, *Passage to Intimacy* emphasizes concrete, substantive techniques that make a difference in the quality of a couple's life together. Gordon identifies three hopes and three fears that determine the path to intimacy for each of us, offers a framework for guidance through the illustrative Relationship Road Map and provides the PAIRS tool kit for solving problems.

New Peoplemaking by Virginia Satir   **19.95 QPB**
Revised and expanded seminal work on families, with over a million copies sold in 12 languages. It expresses her most evolved thoughts on self-worth, communication, family systems, and the ways people relate to each other.

Satir Step-by Step   **16.95 QPB**
A Guide to Creating Change in Families, by Michele Baldwin & Virginia Satir
Annotated transcripts of Satir doing family therapy—showing what she is thinking and how she selects a particular phrase or intervention—and then an account of her theoretical foundations and methods.

Conjoint Family Therapy by Virginia Satir   **17.95 QPB**
Third edition of this universally recognized classic in family therapy. In the introduction Satir writes, "I offer this book as a conceptual frame around which to organize your data and your impressions, rather than something to be memorized . . . a suggested path."

Meditations of Virginia Satir   **10.95 QPB**
Peace Within, Peace Between, Peace Among, by Anne Banman & John Banmen
A compilation of Virginia's meditations and essays that illuminate and guide readers on the complex interplay of mind, body, emotions, and spirit. Presented in a series of short, highly readable meditations for use individually or with groups.

The Satir Model   **23.95 hardcover**
Family Therapy and Beyond, by Virginia Satir, John Banmen,
  Maria Gomori & Jane Gerber
The most definitive book on the theoretical aspects of Satir's approach to therapy. Comprehensive organization of her concepts, therapeutic applications, and innovative interventions. Winner of the AAMFT 1984 award for Satir research.

Family Reconstruction   **19.95 QPB**
The Living Theater Model, by Sharon Wegscheider-Cruse, Kathy Higby,
  Ted Klonyz & Ann Rainey
Family Reconstruction is an active and dramatic therapy tool created by Virginia Satir to help people reclaim freedom of choice and self-worth. The living theater model of family reconstruction seeks to reframe current thinking in order to promote a bigger picture of reality, to increase self-worth, to break the power of compulsive behavior in order to provide freedom of choice, and to develop safe and useful relationship skills.

Grandparenting by Sharon Wegscheider-Cruse   **14.95 QPB**
Inspired by the transformation that occurred in her life after the birth of her first grandchild, Wegscheider-Cruse shares her experiences as a loving grandmother and a family therapist of 25 years. Playfully illustrated and easy to read, *Grandparenting* explores the joys and difficult issues associated with grandparenting today, including over 50 activities designed to enrich the bond between grandparent and grandchild. This is a perfect book for any grandparent, foster grandparent, aunt, uncle, neighbor, or friend who plays a grand "role" in a child's life.

ORDER FORM

Tear out and mail this form to:

Science & Behavior Books, Inc.
2225 Grant Road, Suite #3
Los Altos, CA 94024

Please Send Me:

___ copies of *Peer Counseling*	$29.95	$ _____
___ copies of *Passage To Intimacy*	$12.95	$ _____
___ copies of *New Peoplemaking*	$19.95	$ _____
___ copies of *Satir Step by Step*	$16.95	$ _____
___ copies of *Conjoint Family Therapy*	$17.95	$ _____
___ copies of *Meditatons of Virginia Satir*	$10.95	$ _____
___ copies of *The Satir Model*	$23.95	$ _____
___ copies of *Family Reconstruction*	$19.95	$ _____
___ copies of *Grandparenting*	$14.95	$ _____
Tax (add 7.75% for CA residents)		$ _____
Freight & Handling ($3 first book, $1 each add'l)		$ _____
Total Amount Enclosed		$ _____

☐ *Please send me a free catalog.*

Name: _____

Address: _____

City:_____ State: _____ Zip: _____

Phone: (   ) _____

Charge to my credit card: Visa: ☐   MasterCard ☐

CC#: _____

Expiration Date: _____

Signature: _____

Phone (800) 547-9982 or Fax (415) 965-8998

WITHDRAWN